PRATT F

Published 1996 by

HERITAGE BOOKS, INC.
1540E Pointer Ridge Place
Bowie, Maryland 20716
1-800-398-7709

ISBN 0-7884-0512-8

A Complete Catalog Listing Hundreds of Titles
On History, Genealogy, and Americana
Available Free Upon Request

PRATT FAMILIES OF VIRGINIA
and
ASSOCIATED FAMILIES

Primarily The Descendants
of
Oliver Pratt
1784-1832

ALSO BY W. N. HURLEY, JR.

The Blood of Irish Kings

Circuit Rider

Montgomery Village, A New Town

Willie Neal and Josephine, A Legacy of Love

Just Ramblin' Along

The Ancestry of William Neal Hurley, III

Neikirk-Newkirk-Nikirk, Volumes 1 & 2

Hurley Families in America, Volumes 1 & 2

John William Hines 1600, And His Descendants

Maddox, A Southern Maryland Family

Lowder Families in America

Dedicated to the memory of my dear mother

Josephine Davis Pratt Hurley

September 3, 1895 - February 7, 1988

CONTENTS

INTRODUCTION

The surname, Pratt, is said to be of French origin. When the use of surnames first became popular, many were assigned or used based on the occupation of the owner, where he lived, or some other significant reason. Pratt, in both French and English, is said to mean, "*one who lives on or near a meadow.*" The Latin word pratum, which is probably the root of the name, means meadow, or bottom. It has also been said that the name was applied to cunning or astute persons.

One early member of the family was Sieure de Preaux, who is said to have accompanied Duke Robert of Normandy during the First Crusade in 1096-1098. The family established in England at the time of the Norman Conquest, where they are found thereafter. One John de Prates married Marjorie de Brones in the year 1200. A William de Pratellis accompanied King Richard, the Lion Heart, on the Third Crusade from 1182-1192.

Coats of Arms

The Arms of Pratt appear in Burke's *General Armory*, which carries eleven listings for family members. The Arms of the Marquess of Camden are listed marshalled with Pratt and Jeffreys, and those of Reverend Joseph Pratt of Cabra Castle in County Cavan, confirmed by Betham, Ulster, are marshalled for Pratt and Coach. The other nine listings are for various Pratts, and each listed Arms is somewhat similar.

It should first be noted that, under ancient rules of heraldry, the successive sons of a family could assume the Arms of their father, but only by placing a mark of cadence upon the shield, or by differencing; that is, reversing colors, or some other basic change, while retaining the primary identity. In modern usage, according to a recent letter from the Lancaster Herald at the College of Arms in London, those practices are no longer particularly encouraged.

The basic Arms can be followed in each of those listed in Burke, and for our purposes of demonstration, we will here describe the Arms listed for Joseph Pratt, Esquire, County Meath, temp. Charles II, entered Ulster Office 1680, his wife Lydia, daughter of Abraham Clement of Killenacrate, County Cavan.

The blazon reads: *Argent, on a chevron sable between three pellets, each charged with a martlet of the field, as many mascles as the last. Crest - a falcon proper belled and jessed or.*

The first color listed is that of the basic color of the shield; in this case it is silver (*argent*). The next part of the description covers any division of the shield, in this case *on a chevron*, which means that there is an inverted "V" (like the chevron worn on his sleeve by a private in the army), running across the middle of the shield. The next word given is *sable*, which means that the chevron is black.

The description goes on to state that the chevron is *between three pellets*. A pellet is simply a round black dot, and when an odd number is designated, as in three, two of them appear side by side in the upper portion of the shield, above the chevron; the third in the lower portion, centered below the chevron. The pellets are said to be *charged with a martlet of the field*. A martlet is a small bird, similar to a dove, and it is always shown in side view, facing to the left as the viewer sees it. Each of the three pellets has such a bird shown upon it (*charged*), and they are the color of the field (that is, the shield), or silver.

We now return to the peculiar sentence structure, and read, *....on a chevron.......as many mascles as the last*. A mascle is a diamond shaped symbol and, in this case, there are three of them (*as many as the last* - the pellets and martlets). These diamond emblems are placed one in the point of the chevron, and one down each arm. They are silver outlined, with a black central diamond.

Each of these charges on the shield have a specific meaning. There are a series of nine distinct charges signifying successive sons of a family. One of them is the martlet, which indicates the fourth son. The mascles on the chevron signify a son born outside the marriage, but nonetheless recognized by his father.

Generally, there would be a helmet placed atop the shield, with a mantle flowing down the sides in the colors silver and black. Atop the helmet is the torse, a cloth winding using the silver and black colors alternately. Over the torse rises the crest, in this case a hunting falcon in natural color (*proper*). It has a bell around its neck, and jesses (straps) on its legs, and they are gold (*or*).

Pratts of America

The Pratt families, and their descendants, with whom we will here deal, primarily originated in the southwest counties of Virginia before the Revolutionary War. They were found in the areas which later became the counties of Washington, Smyth, Wythe, Tazewell and Russell. During the same period, and later, other members of the family are found in Tennessee, North Carolina and Kentucky, who are perhaps related to the base family with whom we are here dealing. Their descendants are many, and have scattered all over America, as have so many other families of similar origins.

The serious researcher into the Pratt families, and their numerous branches, would be well advised to obtain a copy of *The Pratt Directory,* 1995 revised edition, compiled by Jane Pratt Lovelace, published by Ancestor House, 417 West McNair Street, Chandler, Arizona 85224. It is a monumental work, hard-cover, running to one thousand and fifty-five pages, including a number of fine old photographs.

Another book in my small library, worthy of mention, is titled *Abraham, The Father of us All - A Pratt Family History.* Produced by Kenneth Charles Pratt in 1968 at Oxford, Connecticut, it follows the lineage of Thomas Pratt of Watertown, Massachusetts.

The relatively small lineage that we will research here is but one of a very large general family in America. Perhaps most of the early Pratt immigrants settled in the New England colonies, with a much smaller number appearing in Virginia, as will be discussed in the text. As stated earlier, the Pratt families with whom I am most concerned were found chiefly in Smyth County, in southwest Virginia. Some of the research over the past twenty years or so has carried me further afield, primarily into eastern Tennessee, and there is little doubt that we are dealing with members of the same large family. To better understand these relationships, it is first important to know how and why they migrated as they did.

Migratory Patterns

Most of the colonial movements took place up and down the east coast in some manner. In my local library, in their map section,

I found a copy of the map made in 1751 by Joshua Fry and Peter Jefferson. It was titled: *A Map of the Most Inhabited part of Virginia containing the whole Province of Maryland with Part of Pennsilvania, New Jersey and North Carolina.* The map is quite detailed, with the location and names of numerous streams, towns, bridges, ferries, schools and churches, ordinaries, trails and trading paths. It designates major geographic features, counties, mountains, and so on.

Among the principal features of the map is the location of what was known as the *Great Philadelphia Wagon Road,* which ran from Philadelphia across the southern part of the colony of Pennsylvania to about present-day Hagerstown, Maryland. It then turned south through the valley of Virginia and on as far as Charleston, South Carolina. At about the present-day location of the town of Fincastle, near Roanoke, Virginia, the Wilderness Road led west through the Cumberland Gap into Kentucky and the Ohio country. That does not show on the 1751 map, since the Gap was not discovered by Colonel James Patton until his expedition into western Virginia in 1748.

Another main artery came down the east coast from Philadelphia, through New Castle, Delaware, and on to a ferry crossing of the Potomac at Alexandria. From there, it continued south as far as Petersburg, Virginia, where it joined the Trading Path leading to the Catawba and Cherokee Indian Nations in western Carolina. Our ancestors travelled these trails, and while they were often seeking to go further west, the Appalachians formed an impenetrable barrier, and many of them settled in the hills and mountains along the eastern slopes of the Blue Ridge.

They usually travelled in groups of more than one family, with several wagons, oxen, children, and all that they possessed. As a result, familiar family names are found grouped together in most of the areas in which we find our own family.

In our discussion, we will refer to county names as they presently exist. However, it is important to recognize that the area under study has passed through many county boundaries. For example, Smyth County was not formed until 1832, and then from parts of Washington and Wythe Counties. They had, in turn, been formed from part of old Montgomery County; Washington in 1776, and Wythe in 1789. Montgomery was erected from old Botetourt in 1776, and it had been formed from part of Spotsylvania County in 1734. And so, as can be seen, the researcher into family history must first be aware of this sequence of county development, so that each jurisdiction can be searched for family records.

Geographically, Smyth County, Virginia, is divided into three great and fertile valleys, running generally from northeast to southwest across the county. They are locally known as Rich Valley, the westmost of the three; Middle Valley; and Rye Valley in the southeast. Each of these valleys is traversed by a fork of the Holston River. The North Fork of the Holston originates from one spring across the county line in neighboring Bland County, and from a second spring in Tazewell County. It then runs the length of Rich Valley, and on through the length of neighboring Washington County and a small corner of Scott County. The river crosses into Tennessee at the corner of Sullivan and Hawkins Counties, near the city of Kingsport. South of the city, the North Fork is joined by the combined Middle and South Forks, and the Holston continues onward across Hawkins County, and to the southwest, finally converging with the great Tennessee River, and its waters ultimately make their way to the Mississippi, and south to New Orleans.

The Middle Fork of the Holston begins its journey near the border of Smyth and Wythe Counties, and flows through the Middle Valley, and then across Washington County, where it joins the South Fork near the city of Abingdon. The South Fork starts at the great springs near Sugar Grove and flows through Rye Valley, and across Washington County, to its junction with the Middle Fork near Abingdon. The combined portions of the river then flow on into Sullivan County, Tennessee, east of Bristol. From there, it flows westward across Sullivan County until it joins the North Fork south of Kingsport.

To the west of the Holston, in the valley of Russell County, is found the Clinch River, which flows to the southwest through Russell and Scott Counties, Virginia, to enter Hancock, Tennessee, on a course generally parallel to the Holston. It also runs onward to join the Tennessee, and finally the mighty Mississippi.

This river system, running through the fertile valleys of southwest Virginia, together with the great buffalo trails of the period, provided the transportation arteries for the early pioneers between Virginia and Tennessee, and they moved freely and frequently along them. Before 1747, Stephen Holston came alone into the wilderness of what is now Smyth County, and camped near the spring at the headwaters of the Middle Fork of the Holston, where he acquired title to one thousand, three hundred acres of the valley land. He was drawn to the river and what might lay ahead, so he sold his corn right, and travelled by canoe down the Holston, the Tennessee, the Ohio, and the Mississippi to Natchez. He returned first to his original home in Culpeper County, Virginia, and finally settled on the Holston in eastern Tennessee. He was the first of many to make such a journey, and his name was given to the river system he explored. Before his arrival, the river was called the Indian River; the French called it the Cherokee; the Indians knew it as Hogoheegee.

For a thorough and enlightening history of the region, the reader is referred to *Smyth County History and Traditions*, by Goodridge Wilson, originally published in 1932; reprinted in 1976 by Commonwealth Press of Radford, Virginia.

In 1745, Colonel James Patton of Augusta County, Virginia, received a grant of one hundred and twenty thousand acres of land west of the mountains. He and his son-in-law, Colonel John Buchanan, who was Deputy Surveyor of Augusta, began immediately to explore and map the area, laying claim along the James River and the New River. In 1746, Buchanan entered claims in present-day Smyth and Washington Counties, along the Middle and South Forks of the Holston. In his journals, which survive, Buchanan mentions in 1746 meeting one Charles Sinclair, who was reportedly an Englishman who had been living alone for some time in the solitude of the deep woods. He had Buchanan lay out a tract of one thousand acres in his name along the South Fork, which is known to this day as Sinclair's Bottom.

The earliest settlers encountered many problems with the Cherokee Nation, and the British government closed the area to settlement until the signing of the Treaty of Fort Stanwix in 1768. During the interim, of course, a number of brave souls entered the region, laying claim to choice tracts of land, and holding them against the Indians and other adventurers.

After the region was officially opened, settlers came from eastern Virginia, Maryland, Pennsylvania, and other colonies, and some direct from Ireland, England and Scotland. Among these early arrivals were members of the Campbell family, some of whom would later marry members of the Pratt family. This illustrious family will be discussed in one of the chapters of our study.

Dr. Joseph Williams of Emory and Henry University, whose wife is a Pratt descendant, noted that, in the 1810 census of Washington County, Virginia, Henry Pratt was listed next to the household of Joseph Cole, which led him to believe that Henry came from New England and New York with the Coles, Bishops, Wheelers and others about 1780, when they settled in Sinclair's Bottom, south of the present town of Chilhowie. Dr. Williams, who is deceased, also suggested that Henry Pratt may have been related to the Wheelers, since Oliver is also a common name in that family.

Industry in Smyth County

In Rich Valley, Smyth County, there is a small, quiet community which is still identified by a road sign as being the village of Chatham Hill. It is located along the North Fork of the Holston River, and was reportedly one of the earliest, busiest centers of business activity in the area. In *Smith County History and Traditions*, Goodridge Wilson includes a letter written by Doctor T. C. Sexton in 1932. Chatham Hill is well-described there as being the oldest post office and trading center for the region. He states that a few years before the war (apparently the Civil War), Chatham Hill boasted an iron forge, a large grist mill, carding machine, saw mill, boat yard, wagon shop, blacksmith shop, cabinet maker, two large general stores, and one saloon. Dr. Sexton mentions that the boat-building was by Pratt and Ferguson.

Visits by the author to Chatham Hill as late as 1986 do not even suggest the type of activity described. There is still a small Methodist church and a handful of other buildings, together with some stone foundations. There is a small iron bridge across the Holston, which is quite still and shallow. Goodridge Wilson says in his book that the first mill in Rich Valley was that of Thomas Tate, which was designated at the head of batteaux navigation by the

Virginia Board of Public Works, and the river was made navigable to this point at state expense.

Each year, flatboats loaded with beeswax, homespun, maple sugar and other farm products, as well as pig iron, plaster and salt were floated down the river to market on the spring flood. They went regularly to Kingsport and Knoxville, Tennessee, and even as far as New Orleans, by floating down the Holston to the Tennessee and the Ohio Rivers, and finally joining the Mississippi. The boats were launched as far upstream as Chatham Hill, where a boatyard was operated by William Henry Pratt and others into the nineteenth century. These flatboats were made of local poplar, peeled and split with an axe and wedge, and the heavy timbers dressed and fitted. The boats were seldom under sixty feet long, and often as much as ninety feet long by sixteen feet wide. The boatmen would guide these large boats down the rapids of the swollen river, and having delivered their goods, sold the boats for timber, and made the long walk back home along the river bank.

It is apparent, then, that there was a considerable amount of commerce up and down the Holston River between Virginia and Tennessee, and thus migration could easily have occurred within the region. It is not surprising to find Pratt family members in both areas, and to assume that a relationship exists between them, as will be reported in the text of the study.

*To be ignorant of what occurred before you were born
is to remain always a child.
For what is the worth of human life unless it is
woven into the lives of our ancestors?*

- Cicero

CHAPTER 1

The First Arrivals

Members of the Pratt family were among the earliest arrivals in America, and they came in considerable numbers. In Philby's major work, *Passenger and Immigration Lists Index*, there are about one hundred and ten listed individuals with the Pratt surname from as early as 1607, when John Pratt came to Virginia, up through the late 1800s. There are at least a dozen listed before 1700 to Virginia, and several more to Jamaica, Barbadoes, Maryland and Delaware; any of whom could easily have moved into Virginia. Many more Pratts settled in New England, although my studies have not extended to that area.

Simply to demonstrate some of the early immigration, we have listed a few here, particularly in the early years:

Planters of the Commonwealth, by Charles Edward Banks, shows some sixty persons at Plymouth, aboard the ship *Anne*, William Pierce, Master, July 10, 1623. Among them is Joshua Pratt.

The Winthrop Fleet of 1630, also by Banks, reports the fleet with the *Arbella* as flagship, and ten other ships, including *Mayflower*, to Salem, Massachusetts, between May and July, 1630, with seven hundred persons aboard, including Abraham Pratt and wife, Jane, settled at Roxbury. He was a surgeon with the English army in Holland. He and his wife were lost at sea off the coast of Spain in 1644.

Early Virginia Immigrants, by George Cabell Greer, lists five Pratt immigrants to Virginia and the parties who transported them; probably as indentured servants:

Jonathan Pratt, 1637; William Farrar, Henrico Co.
Andrew Pratt, 1637; Elizabeth Parker, Henrico Co.
John Pratt, 1651; William Taylor, Northumberland Co.
Mary Pratt, 1653; William Dittye, Charles City Co.
Thomas Pratt, 1655; Thomas Ballard, Gloucester Co.

1

Immigrants to America, by Joack and Marion Kaminkow lists John Pratt from Borkin Parish, Essex County, England, schoolmaster, for four years service in Maryland at the age of 18 years. Agent Christopher Veale of Shoreditch, in Middlesex. March 21, 1719.

Bristol and America lists Lawrence Pratt between 1663 and 1679 on the ship *Constant Martha* to Virginia.

List of Emigrants to America, 1600-1700, by John Camden Hotten, includes a number of references:

Isabel Pratt, February 16, 1623, living on the neck of land near James City, Virginia; and again, February 4, 1624 in the Muster of Inhabitants of the Neck of Land near James City; and that she arrived on the *Jonathan*.

Thomas Pratt, age 17 years, from Gravesend, London, on board the *America*, William Barker, Master, to Virginia on June 23, 1635.

Richard Pratt, age 18, from Gravesend, London, on board the *Expedition*, Peter Blackler, Master, for Barbadoes, on November 20, 1635.

The Original List of Persons of Quality, by Hotten, lists a grant of land by patent for 150 acres to Richard Pratt as a settler in the Corporacion of Charles Cittie, Territory of Great Weyonoke, Virginia, in 1626.

Emigrants from England to America, by Michael Ghirelli lists Edward Pratt, age 15, bound to Nathaniel Redman for five years in Jamaica, dated April 9, 1686.

From my research, it appears that most early immigrants to America were bond servants, whose passage was paid by others. In many cases, immigrants were sent to the colonies by the courts for a broad range of petty offenses. In either case, the immigrant was bound out for service for a specified number of years, usually from four to seven, and after that, became a free man. Their indentures could be sold and traded, and they were bound to serve whatever master owned those rights. In many respects, their position was but little better than that of the slaves, with the exception, of course, that they would one day be free. They could be punished for any infraction of the rules, and their indentures extended as part of that punishment. Upon being set free, however, they generally received two sets of clothes, enough corn for a year, the tools of their trade, and fifty acres of land. Many of these bonded men were sent first to the large plantations on Jamaica, Barbadoes and the Indies, and upon completion of their servitude, made they way to the mainland colonies, where land was said to be available.

The Pratts have made a name for themselves in a number of instances. In 1831, Enoch Pratt came from Massachusetts to the city of Baltimore, and created a mercantile business that made him very wealthy. Before his death, without children, he had established and funded the *Enoch Pratt Free Library* of Baltimore, and contributed substantial sums of money to the *Maryland School for the Deaf* in Frederick, Maryland. His home in downtown Baltimore is today part of the museum and headquarters of the Maryland Historical Society.

Thomas George Pratt was Governor of the State of Maryland in the late 1800s. Charles Pratt (1830-1891) was associated with John D. Rockefeller and was one of the wealthiest men in America, and a benefactor of the *Pratt Institute* in Brooklyn, and the University of Rochester, as well as Amherst College.

The Pratts have figured prominently in the development of the Church of Jesus Christ of Latter Day Saints. Orson Pratt is credited with having arranged the Book of Mormon into chapters and verses. His brother Parley Pratt appears in much of the history of the church as well. The brothers, Joseph and William Pratt, made the trip west into Utah with the original band of the Mormon party, first under Joseph Smith and, after his death, with Brigham Young.

It appears that "our" set of Pratts may well tie in with the New England families. We have seen excerpts from *The Pratt Family of North Carolina and Alabama, 1966*, by Margaret U. Lofquist, found at the DAR library in Washington. These are reports of the probable descendants of one Richard Pratt, born c.1764, perhaps in Maryland, and married to Rebecca in 1789 in Rockingham County, North Carolina. One of the comments in the papers states, in part: *"William Pratt, who lived in Rockingham County at the time of the Revolution, was said to have been a brother or possibly a cousin of Richard Pratt. Several years ago contact was made with descendants of William living in the county and one of these recalled that her father has told her that the Pratts had come from*

3

Massachusetts to Baltimore, Maryland; and thence to southern Virginia, and finally to Rockingham County."

At the National Archives, I found pension files from the Revolutionary War for Jonathan Pratt and Stephen Pratt of Virginia; and Thomas Pratt and Zebulon Pratt of North Carolina.

The first Federal Census of 1790 for Virginia, and several other states, was reportedly lost when the British burned the Capital in the War of 1812. Available records at the Archives have been compiled from miscellaneous lists of taxables made at different periods just prior to 1790. In what is now utilized as the reconstructed census of 1790, only three Pratt families appear in the state of Virginia, although in 1810, there are twenty-eight families with the Pratt surname. The three in 1790 were:

Thomas Pratt in Amherst County in 1783; four white persons in the household.

Thomas Pratt in Amherst County in 1785; five white persons in the household (probably the same individual).

William Pratt in Richmond County in 1785; five white persons in the household.

The Archives contains a *List of Virginia Taxpayers, 1782-1785*, which includes:

Bable Pratt, Accomack County
Scarburgh Pratt, Accomack County
Comfort Pratt, Accomack County
John Pratt, Bedford County
John Pratt, Louisa County
John Pratt, Montgomery County
Jonothan Pratt, Culpeper County
Joseph Pratt (2), Culpeper County
Thomas Pratt, Culpeper County
William Pratt, Culpeper County
Zephaniah Pratt, Culpeper County

Also at the Archives, *Virginians in the Revolution* includes thirteen listed Pratts:

Babel Pratt; 9th Regt, Continental Line

Benjamin Pratt; Sgt, War Dept records

David Pratt; 5th Regt, Continental Line

James Pratt; 7th Regt, Continental Line

John Pratt; corporal, 2nd Va Brigade, Continental Line

John Pratt; Captain Adam Clements Co., Virginia Militia

John Pratt; corporal, 3rd and 4th Regts, Continental Line

Jonathan Pratt; Orange Co, Va, 73 years of age in 1833 on Militia Pension Lists.

Shubael Pratt; Surgeon, Va Regt, March 12, 1778 to June 12, 1779. Also written Sheubel, Shubal.

Stephen Pratt; Wayne Co, Kentucky, at age 70 in 1833 on the Militia Pension Lists.

Thomas Pratt; Revolutionary records, Virginia Archives

William Pratt; 9th and 15th Regts, Continental Line

Zorobabel Pratt; Infantry, War Dept records

CHAPTER 2

Henry Pratt
Pre 1765- ?

Henry Pratt appears in the census of 1810 for Washington County, Virginia, with a wife, two sons and five daughters. None of the other family members are named, nor are definitive ages stated, which did not occur in the census reports until 1850. In the same census, there are three other male Pratts listed, each in their own household, each born between 1784 and 1794, and each with a female of the same age range, and no children.

We have made the assumption that Henry was the father of each of these boys, in addition to the un-named two boys and five girls still in his household at the time of the census. The 1830 census of Monroe County, Tennessee, contains the household of Henry Pratt, with the following free whites listed only by sex and age range: two males under 5 years; one male 5 to 10 years; one male 20 to 30 years; one male, 50 to 60 years. Two females under 5 years; one female 5 to 10 years; one female 20 to 30 years. This would appear to be the household of Henry Pratt, Jr. and his wife, Nancy Carter Pratt, with their young children. The eldest male in the household is perhaps Henry Pratt, Sr., living with his son.

Minutes of the Court of Pleas and Quarter Sessions for Greene County, Tennessee, for October 26, 1819 (page 468) provide that Henry Pratt, Sr. is to receive the sum of forty dollars for one year. Strangely, the court ordered that ten dollars of the total be paid at the time of the order, and that the remainder be paid quarterly *"provided the said Pratt shall be alive at the time that said quarters allowances may become due and payable."* The reference to Henry Pratt, Sr. implies the existence of Henry Pratt, Jr.

Minutes of the Court of Greene County in 1820-1822, while referring to a road boundary, mention *"Henry Pratt's old place near Greenville."* Henry Pratt, Jr. was not married until 1820, so it is rather unlikely that the reference would have been to his home property; the Court must have been referring to the elder Henry.

Further, in the 1880 census of Washington County, Missouri, Alexander R. Pratt (1832), who will be discussed further, stated that both his parents were born in Virginia.

In 1832, the Land Lottery of Georgia made available for distribution and settlement that part of the Cherokee Nation which was in Georgia. In addition to those persons who had lived in the area for not less than three years, veterans of the Revolution were given extra draws in the lottery. Henry Pratt received 40 acres in lot 30, 17th District, First Section of then Cherokee County. We assume from this record that Henry Pratt, Sr. was a veteran, since he did not appear to satisfy residency requirements. He apparently did not settle on the land, and probably sold it, as did many veterans. Henry Pratt, Sr., and his unknown wife appear to have been the parents of at least nine children, probably born in Virginia:

1. Bernard, born between 1784 and 1794, and found in the 1810 census of Washington County, Virginia, with a wife of the same age range.
2. Fielden, born between 1784 and 1794, and also found in the 1810 census in his own household, with a female of the same age range. There is a reported marriage of Fielden Pratt to Jane Boyd on August 11, 1807 in Washington County, Virginia. Additionally, in the *Tennessee Mortality Schedules for 1850, 1860 and 1880 Combined*, found at the Rogersville Library, in Hawkins County, Tennessee, there is a listing reporting the death of Fielding Pratt, age 67, born in Virginia, died in June, 1850 in Wilson County, Tennessee. The report states that he was a farmer, and that death was the result of drowning. This would suggest that Fielding was born c.1784.
3. Oliver, born c.1784/94, our direct ancestor, of whom more in Chapter 5.
4. Henry, Jr., born c.1800, and of whom more in Chapter 3
5. A son, born between 1794 and 1810
6. A daughter, born between 1794 and 1810
7. A daughter, born between 1794 and 1800
8. A daughter, born between 1794 and 1800
9. Cynthia Ann, born between 1800 and 1810, of whom more in Chapter 4

CHAPTER 3

Henry Pratt, Jr.
1800-1843/50

Early in 1992, I received extensive notes on members of the Pratt family from Floyd Thomas Pratt (1948). He was then living in St. Charles, Missouri, and operating *Pratt Investigations*, specializing in family history, missing persons, and background searches. One would assume from his occupation that Tom should be a rather reliable source, and his data was so well presented that I am willing to accept it as being as close to the facts as we are likely to get.

In any case, Tom presents evidence to conclude that this Henry Pratt, Jr., is a son of Henry Pratt, who appeared in the 1810 census of Washington County, Virginia, with a wife, two sons, and five daughters in his household at that time. We have reported on the family of Henry Pratt (Sr.) in the chapter immediately preceding this section of our study.

The 1830 census of Monroe County, Tennessee, includes the household of Henry Pratt (there listed without the Jr.). In the household, there are two males under five years; one male 5 to 10 years; one male 20 to 30 years (Henry, Jr.); and one male 50 to 60 years (perhaps his father, Henry, Sr.) There are also two females under 5 years; one female 5 to 10 years; and one female 20 to 30 years (his wife, Nancy Carter Pratt).

The 1840 census of Washington County, Missouri, Richwoods Township, includes the household of Henry Pratt, with one male under 5 years; one male 5 to 10 years; and one male 40 to 50 years (Henry, Jr.). Also one female under 5 years; two females 5 to 10 years; one female 15 to 20 years; and one female 40 to 50 years (Nancy Carter Pratt).

There is a deed in Book K, page 384, dated July 2, 1838 in Monroe County, Tennessee, in which one John Dyer conveys a two acre parcel of land to the Trustees of the Methodist Episcopal Church at Ebenezer Meeting House and Camp Grounds. The trustees include Henry Pratt, as well as Lewis Carter, who is related to Nancy Carter, wife of Henry, Jr. This indicates that Henry Pratt, Jr., moved his family from Monroe County, Tennessee to Washington County, Missouri, between the 1838 deed, and the 1840 census taking.

If Tom is correct, and from all the evidence it appears that he is, then this Henry Pratt, Jr. was a brother of Oliver Pratt, born c.1784, who is the direct lineal ancestor of this author.

Henry Pratt, Jr. was born between 1800 and 1803, probably in old Washington County, Virginia, and died between 1843 and 1850 in Crawford County, Missouri. He was married October 3, 1820 in Greene County, Tennessee to Nancy Carter, born about the same time period, and died November 17, 1875 in Washington County, Missouri. Her father was Jesse Carter, born c.1774 at Arnettsville, Monongalia County, Virginia (later in West Virginia), and died in August, 1849 in McMinn County, Tennessee. Jesse was married January 9, 1798 in Greene County to Susannah Harmon, born c.1775 and died September 4, 1865 in McMinn County, Tennessee.

After Henry's death, Nancy Carter Pratt married secondly March 21, 1852 in Crawford County, Missouri, Absalom Blanton, born 1802, widower of Cynthia Ann Pratt (1800/10), sister of Henry. That couple had children, and there were marriages between the children and grandchildren of both of Nancy's marriages; indeed, the marriages between Pratts and Blantons are frequent and difficult to sort out! On January 14, 1876, Alexander R. Pratt (1832), one of her sons, filed his Bond in Washington County, Missouri, as Administrator of the estate of Nancy Blanton, deceased, who died intestate. He states that the heirs of the estate are: Alexander R. Pratt; Jane Blanton, wife of Henry Blanton; Sarah Blanton, wife of John A. Blanton; Mary Blanton, wife of Alfred Blanton; Jacob H., Fanny (Sarah Frances), R. A. (Rinard A.), and Nancy Pratt, children of James Pratt, deceased; Catherine, Alexander Absalom, Augustus, Queen, Isabella, Susan, Benjamin, Sarah and Louisa Blanton, children of Alex and Nancy M. Blanton; and Susan Ausell (Hansel?), residing in Crawford County; and Lorenda Hull, wife of Ira Hull, residing in Laclede County.

Early in this study, we have discussed the geographic relationships between the counties of southwest Virginia, and the eastern counties of Tennessee. It is apparent that the Pratt families moved about in these areas, and into Kentucky and Missouri, and other areas accessible to them by river or original buffalo and Indian trails. Henry Pratt, Jr. and Nancy Carter had nine children, the first eight born in either Monroe or Greene Counties, in Tennessee; the last child born in Washington County, Missouri:

1. Susan A., born August 4, 1821 in Greene County, and died of pneumonia December 22, 1881 in Crawford County, Missouri at the home of her son, John. Married to Henry H. Hansel (or Ausel), born about 1805, and had eight children:
   a. John W., born 1843
   b. Sarah Jane, born 1845
   c. Henry H., born 1849; married Nancy J.; three children:
      (1) Gilbert L., born 1885
      (2) William E., born 1890
      (3) Ethel J., born 1892
   d. Mary E., born 1850
   e. Benjamin W., born 1853
   f. Beverly, born 1855
   g. Lawrence A., born 1857
   h. Sterling Pierce, born 1860

2. James, born September 30, 1822 in Greene County; died June 25, 1874 at Anthonies Mill in Washington County, Missouri, where he is buried. His will, dated June 22, 1874, is found in the will records of the county. He names his wife and children, leaving specific bequests to each of them. From the will, it is apparent that he was a farmer of reasonable means for the times, with various livestock and property. There is no mention of slaves in the will. He was married to Catherine Kimberlin, born 1828. She was married second October 17, 1875 to Alexander Absalom Blanton (1830), widower of James' sister, Nancy Maria Pratt (1830). The family of James and Catherine appears in the 1840, 1850, 1860 and 1870 census of Washington County, Missouri, in Johnson Township. They had four children:
   a. Jacob Henry, born 1848; married Sarah Elizabeth Pinson and had six children:
      (1) William H., born 1871; married to Susan

        (2)   Charles E., born 1872

        (3)   Lilly B., born 1873

        (4)   Maggie C., born 1880

        (5)   Carrick N., born 1880

        (6)   Minnie Ann

b.   Sarah Frances, born 1852; married John Milton Harmon, born 1852. Two children:

        (1)   Della M., born 1877; married to Walter Franklin Isgrig, born 1872.

        (2)   Effie Catherine, born 1885

c.   Rinard A., born 1856; married Julia A. Scott and second to Theodosia R. Gruell. Two children:

        (1)   Irene, born 1898

        (2)   Mary C., born 1899

d.   Nancy Young, born 1856; married James Page Harmon, and had eight children:

        (1)   John, born 1884

        (2)   Stephen, born 1885

        (3)   Lizzie, born 1887

        (4)   Elmer, born 1889

        (5)   Thadius, born 1892

        (6)   Ava, born 1897

        (7)   Raymond, born 1905

        (8)   Oral, born 1908

3.   Lorenda, born c.1828 in Greene County, Tennessee; married March 16, 1848 in Crawford County, Missouri, to Samuel Campbell, according to Book A in that county. However, the will of her mother names her as Lorenda Hull, wife of Ira Hull, then residing in Laclede County, Missouri, suggesting a second marriage.

4.   Nancy Maria, born July 10, 1830 in Monroe County, Tennessee; died January 27, 1873 in Washington County, Missouri, and buried at Blanton Cemetery in Hamilton Hollow. Married in Crawford County, Missouri, October 14, 1849 to Alexander Absalom Blanton, born November 11, 1830 (or September 7, 1829); died April 29, 1888 (or April 3, 1882). Data provided to me includes these duplicate dates. After the death of Nancy Maria, Alexander was married second October 17,

1875 to Catherine Kimberlin Pratt (1828), widow of James Pratt (1822), Nancy Maria's brother. There is a family Bible in the possession of Lucille Reed of Oklahoma (a granddaughter of the couple), which provides valuable information. Nancy Maria and Alexander had ten children, all born in Missouri, who will be discussed in the following chapter under the name of the father of the children.

5. Alexander R., born March, 1832 in Greene County, Tennessee and married to Mary Kimberlin, born 1835, of whom more

6. John Absalom, born January 14, 1834 in Monroe County, Tennessee; died June 27, 1890 at Sullivan, Franklin County, Missouri. The date of birth is from his tombstone in Buffalo Cemetery, Sullivan, Meramec Township. Married March 24, 1853 in Washington County, Missouri, to Mary Caroline Blanton, born July 24, 1829. She was his cousin, daughter of Cynthia Ann Pratt (1810) and Absalom Blanton (1802). The family appears in the census of 1860 for Liberty Township, in Missouri as house number 702; in the 1870 census for Crawford County, Missouri in Boone Township as house 73; and in the 1880 census for Franklin County, Missouri in Meremac Township. Ten children, born in Missouri:

   a. Nancy C., born 1882
   b. Malinda Jane (or Lorinda Jane), born c.1855; married to Isaac Campbell, born 1838, and had six children:
      (1) Nancy J., born 1882
      (2) David G., born 1883
      (3) Andrew Jackson, born 1885
      (4) John E., born 1888
      (5) James S., born 1891
      (6) Laura Jane, born 1897
   c. Mary F., born 1857
   d. Henry Absalom, born 1859; married to Cynthia Anna Missey, born 1862, and had six children:
      (1) Mary C., born 1885
      (2) John A., born 1887
      (3) Alexander, born 1890
      (4) James W., born 1892
      (5) Francis C., born 1894

        (6)   Minnie A., born 1898

  e.   Alexander, born 1861

  f.   James A., born 1865

  g.   Lila, born 1867

  h.   Matilda Ellen, born 1868; married John Stephen Blanton, perhaps as his second wife (see following the marriage of John Stephen Blanton, perhaps the same individual, to Sarah Ann Blanton, born 1858), and had three children:

        (1)   Homer

        (2)   Orville

        (3)   Grace

  i.   John Absalom, Jr., born 1870, and married to his cousin, Phoebe Blanton, daughter of John Stephen Blanton and Sarah Ann Blanton (1858). Two children:

        (1)   Henry, born 1893

        (2)   William, born 1897; married Thelma Blackburn.

  j.   Elizabeth, born 1875; reportedly married Lohmann. She appears in the household of her brother, Alexander, in the 1900 census for Meramac Township, Sullivan City, in Franklin County, Missouri. There, she is stated to be 22 years old and a widow, with the surname Cain, and a son Alexander Cain, born c.1895.

7.   Sarah Ann, born c.1834 in Monroe County, Tennessee; and married August 10, 1851 to John A. Blanton, born 1830. She died between 1880 and 1889, when her husband married second to Emma J. See also the sketch of her husband in *Goodspeed's History of Franklin, Jefferson, Washington, Crawford and Gasconade Counties, Missouri*, 1970 reprint of the 1888 edition. It is stated there that he was a blacksmith and wagon-maker, born May 1, 1830 in Monroe County, Tennessee, the fourth of fourteen children born to Joshua and Bethanie Harmon Blanton. John A. Blanton and Sarah Ann Pratt Blanton lived on a ninety-acre farm, and had fifteen children; seven sons and eight daughters. When the Civil War began, he enlisted in the Confederate Army under General McBride and took part in the battle of Pea Ridge and others. He was discharged in 1862 and returned to Sullivan. The family appears in the 1860 census of Liberty Township, in

Crawford County; the 1870 census for Johnson Township, in Washington County; and in the 1880 and 1900 census for Sullivan Village, in Franklin County; all in Missouri. The children were all born in Missouri, fourteen of them being:

a. Charles H., born 1853; married Sada Wilson
b. Alexander, born 1854; married Ruth M. Whitinger and had two children:
    (1) Carl, born 1895
    (2) Hattie, born 1904
c. Emily J., born 1855
d. Susan, born 1857; married Joseph Classil.
e. Sarah Ann, born 1858; married John Stephen Blanton and had five children:
    (1) James Edward, born 1873
    (2) Phoebe; married her cousin, John Absalom Pratt, Jr. (1870), which see
    (3) Annie, born 1877; married John Henry Simmerly.
    (4) Nancy; married Enloe
    (5) Maude; married Louis Cardwell.
f. Virginia D., born 1861; married William H. Hulsey.
g. Bethany, born 1863
h. John Wesley, born 1865; married Rosa M. Two children:
    (1) Arthur, born 1892
    (2) Earl, born 1894
i. Nancy, born 1867
j. James E., born 1872
k. Stephen, born 1875
l. Edward, a twin
m. Phoebe, a twin; married John H. A. Pennock.
n. Frederick, born 1878

8. Mary Elizabeth, born August, 1836 in Monroe County, Tennessee; died 1902 in Johnson Township, Washington County, Missouri. Married March 24, 1853 to Albert Sevier Blanton, with Valentine S. Carter presiding as the local minister of the Methodist Church. Albert was born April 4, 1831 in Tennessee, and died at the home of his son, Albert, Jr., near Sullivan, May 15, 1913. The first name, Albert, has also been reported variously as Elbert or Alfred, but Albert appears to be correct.

14

The family appears in the 1860 and 1870 census for Johnson Township, Washington County; the 1880 census of Meremac Township, town of Steelville, Crawford County; and the 1900 census of Johnson Township in Washington County; all in Missouri. Albert appears in the 1910 census of Meremac Township, Franklin County, in the household of his son-in-law, Albert W. Fraseur. According to his obituary there were twelve children, although we can here report only nine:

a. Susan Jane, born 1854; married James Martin Claspill.
b. Absalom, born 1857; married Clara Key.
c. Nancy, born 1858; married Charles Brandt, born 1850, and had six children:
    (1) Walter, born 1882
    (2) Bertha, born 1883
    (3) William, born 1886
    (4) Albert, born 1888
    (5) Reginald, born 1892
    (6) John, born 1895
d. Mary Ellen, born 1860; married Harvey J. Simmons. Her father's obituary lists Ellen Fraseur as a surviving daughter, which reflects her second marriage to Albert W. Fraseur. Three children born to the first marriage:
    (1) Phoebe; married White.
    (2) William S., born 1891
    (3) Carl H., born 1895
e. Sarah Ann, born 1865; married to Michael Edward Dace and had three children:
    (1) Elizabeth
    (2) James M.
    (3) O. E.
f. Martin Van Buren, born 1867; married to Anna Burton, born 1887. Five children:
    (1) Lois Grace, born 1907; married George Doyle.
    (2) Minnie Etta, born 1909; married Thomas Everett Doyle.
    (3) Leo Franklin, born 1910
    (4) Daisy Muriel, born 1912, and married to Homer Woodcock.

     (5)   Walter Sanford, born 1917; married to Fern Marie Herron, born 1921.

g.   Delila Catherine, born 1870, and married to John Nelson Souders.

h.   Albert Sevier, Jr., born 1872; married Alice M. Garner, born 1876, and had five children:
    (1)   William, born 1895
    (2)   Addie, born 1897
    (3)   Annie, born 1899
    (4)   James, born 1905
    (5)   Eva, born 1908

i.   Lucy A., born 1878; married Moss

9.   Matilda Jane, born October 20, 1842 in Washington County, Missouri; married there January 5, 1857 to Henry Hubert Blanton, her cousin, born February 23, 1837, son of Absalom Blanton (1802) and Cynthia Ann Pratt (1810). Their family will be discussed in the following chapter under the name of the father of the children.

Alexander R. Pratt
1832-1912

This son of Henry Pratt, Jr. (1800) and Nancy Carter Pratt, was born in March, 1832, in Monroe County, Tennessee, and died in 1912 at Cherryville, Crawford County, Missouri. Married June 28, 1856 in Washington County, Missouri, to Mary Kimberlin, born 1835 in the county at Anthonies Mill. The service was performed by Valentine S. Carter, a minister of the Methodist Church; reported in Book B, page 181, Marriage Records of the county. Her father was Rinard Kimberlin, born c.1806 in Virginia, and died between 1886 and 1900 in Johnson Township, Washington County, Missouri. Her mother was Frances Peters, born c.1805 in Virginia, daughter of John Peters (1788). Alexander and Mary were parents of eight children, listed first following. As reported in Marriage Book I, page 223, Alexander was married second August 20, 1885 in Hamilton, Washington County, Missouri, to Mrs. Catherine Adeline Dugan, by whom he had two children, listed last.

16

His family appears in the 1860, 1870 and 1880 census of Johnson Township, Washington County, with his wife and children. He appears in the 1900 census of Boone Township, Crawford County, apparently as a widower, with three of his sons; and again at the age of 77 in the household of his son, Henry W. Pratt, in the 1910 census of Boone Township. According to a family story, he died of a heart attack while rocking in a chair at the home of his daughter, Polina. The roads were icy and the family could not get a wagon up the hills to take him home to Sullivan, so he was buried in the Freeman Cemetery outside Cherryville, Missouri. One of his grandchildren reported that Alexander was a very big man; six feet, four inches tall; and weighing about 240 pounds. He was a blacksmith, an auctioneer, and ran a threshing separator. He reportedly went on the goldrush of 1849 to California, perhaps in the company of his father, Henry Pratt, Jr. (1800). His children were:

1. Mary Ellen, born 1857; married to James Frederick Studdard, born 1854. They had five children:
   a. John A., born 1878; married Susan West and second Jane Boyer.
   b. Katherine; married Sylvester Ward.
   c. Franklin, born 1886, married Emma K. Brewer, born 1886
   d. Newton; married Bessie Griffith.
   e. Pearl; married Walter Allen.
2. Michael, born 1860
3. Stonewall Jackson, born 1861; married Mary Louise Taylor, born 1863; and had five children:
   a. Taylor Edward, born 1890
   b. Archie J., born 1894
   c. Alicia Maria, born 1896
   d. Aspasia Louise, born 1899
   e. Ralph Alexander, born 1901
4. Frances Minerva, born 1867; married to David P. Campbell, born 1837, and had eight children:
   a. Maggie, born 1890
   b. Myrtle, born 1893
   c. Hattie, born 1895
   d. Minnie, born 1897

e.	Frederick, born 1900
f.	Howard, born 1902
g.	Harrison, born 1904
h.	Raymond, born 1907
5.	Polina, born 1865; married to Thomas Livey Callahan, born 1856, and had eight children:
   a.	Cora E., born 1888
   b.	William Harrison, born 1889
   c.	Maud Lee, born 1891
   d.	Arthur H., born 1892
   e.	Effie, born 1895
   f.	Bessie H., born 1896
   g.	Sarah, born 1899
   h.	Jesse C., born 1904
6.	Henry Winslow, born September 6, 1868 at Hamilton Hollow in Washington County, Missouri; died March 24, 1914 at Vilander, in Crawford County, Missouri. Married January 29, 1893 to Mary Laura Magdalene Missey, born July 20, 1874 at Bourbon, Crawford County; died there April 17, 1938. They had eight children:
   a.	Columbus Benjamin Alexander, born November 1, 1893 at Catawissa, Franklin County; died July 27, 1947 at Bourbon, Crawford County. Married April 12, 1919 at Catawissa Rue Flavilla Johnson, born January 19, 1894 at Bourbon; died there June 26, 1983. At least one son:
      (1)	Floyd Theodore, born January 6, 1927 at Bourbon; married March 1, 1947 at St. Clair in Franklin County, Missouri, to Delores Virginia Brown, born October 31, 1925 at St. Louis, Missouri; died March 1, 1981 at Los Angeles, California. They were divorced, and had at least one son:
         (a)	Floyd Thomas, my correpondent for this family, born January 3, 1948 at St. Louis, and married there August 14, 1972 to Bonnie Kathleen Bach.
   b.	Jesse Lee, born 1895; married Nadine Mae Skaggs, born c.1905.
   c.	Albert Paris, born 1897; married Mary Shepard.

d. Virgil Ranson, born 1899; married Eula Viola Richardson, born 1909

e. Henry Arthur, born 1902; married Beulah Cross and second Hazel Stall Darnell.

f. Ruth Jane, born 1904; married Rufus Allen Graddy, born 1887

g. Mary, born 1907

h. Orville Hayes, born 1911; married Mary Olive Mallow, born 1917; second Marie Virginia Parsley, born 1917.

7. Rhinehart, born 1875
8. Minnie, born 1876; married George W. Richter, born 1872
9. Carac Francis, born 1888; married Olivea Jane Jarvis, born 1892 and had three children:

a. Elwin Richard, born 1921; married first Dorothy Graddy and second Betty Wright.

b. Orville Carac, born 1928; married Eileen Helen Evans, born 1931

c. Vera Virginia, born 1931, and married James Stanislaus Thebeau, born 1922.

10. Cleveland, born 1892

CHAPTER 4

Cynthia Ann Pratt
1800/10-1850/52

This daughter of Henry Pratt (pre/1765) was born between 1800 and 1810, probably in Greene County, Tennessee. Her father and other family members have been discussed in Chapter 2, and Chapter 3 was devoted to the descendants of her brother, Henry Pratt, Jr. (1800). Cynthia died between 1850 and 1852 in Washington County, Missouri, where many members of the family lived. She was married April 16, 1825 in Greene County, Tennessee, to Absalom Blanton, born c.1802 in Knox County, Kentucky, a son of John Blanton; and died March 4, 1872 in Hamilton Hollow, Washington County, Missouri, where he is buried in the Blanton family cemetery.

After the death of Cynthia, her husband married secondly to Nancy Carter Pratt (1800), widow of Cynthia's brother, Henry Pratt, Jr. Several of the children from each family intermarried. In fact, the relationships between the Pratt and Blanton families in this branch are difficult to untangle; there are several instances of marriages between widows and widowers, involving members of both families, and two members of the same family.

It is known that the Pratt and Blanton families travelled together by wagon train from Tennessee to Missouri. Family legend states that as they were crossing the Tennessee River, they came upon a Cherokee village, and one of the Blanton men spotted a squaw nursing her papoose on a log. He boasted that he could shoot her from a great distance, and proceeded to do so, killing the Indian woman. Several miles from the village, the wagon train was overtaken by a large band of Cherokees, who stated that they would kill every individual in the train if the man responsible for the killing was not turned over to them. In order to save the party, the man who had fired the shot was given to the Indians, obviously over his vigorous objections. Several miles later, the Blanton man was seen running to catch up with the wagon train and, from a distance, appeared to be covered with red paint. As he neared the train, it could be seen that the Indians had skinned him alive and that the "paint" was his own blood. He died before reaching the wagons. It is not now clear whether this Blanton belonged to the Joshua Blanton group, or the Absalom Blanton group, both of whom were in the party.

The family of Absalom Blanton appears in the 1830 census of Sumner County, Tennessee, and the 1850 census of Washington County, Missouri. He and Cynthia had nine children:

1. James, born 1826 in Greene County, Tennessee; died October 9, 1898 in Miller County, Arkansas. Married in Washington County, Missouri November 8, 1849 Margaret Green Goforth, born 1833; second to Nancy A. Adams; and third to Nancy H. Stevenson.

2. Elizabeth, born 1827 in Greene County, Tennessee; died February 22, 1916 in Boone Township, Crawford County, Missouri. Married to John D. Allen; the family appears in the 1860 census of Liberty Township, Crawford County, with six children, all born in Missouri:
   a. Eliza A. 1846
   b. Catherine F. 1848
   c. John D., Jr. 1850
   d. Elizabeth 1853
   e. Mary 1855
   f. Henry 1858

3. Alexander Absalom, born September 7, 1829 in Greene County, Tennessee; died April 3, 1882 at Hamilton Hollow in Washington County, Missouri. Some reports list his birth date as November 11, 1830, and death April 29, 1888. Married October 14, 1849 to Nancy Maria Pratt in Washington County, Missouri. She was his cousin, born July 10, 1830 and died January 27, 1873, daughter of Henry Pratt, Jr. (1800). She is buried in the Blanton cemetery at Hamilton Hollow with other members of the family. They had ten children, all born in Missouri. After her death, he was married second October 13, 1875 to Catherine Kimberlin Pratt (1828), widow of James Pratt (1822), brother of his first wife. The ten children were:

a. Catherine J., born July 28, 1850; married Charles Bowles and had a daughter:
    (1) Nancy, married to Cutwright.
b. Alexander Absalom, Jr., born May 31, 1854; married to Eliza Jane Dace, and had two children:
    (1) Rilla, married to H. H. Graham.
    (2) Ralph M.
c. Absalom, born April 2, 1856; married Ellen Jackson, and had three children:
    (1) Lottie; married Mahlon E. Keyes.
    (2) Arthur "Joker"
    (3) Duel
d. Augustus, born March 2, 1858
e. Nancy Maria, born November 11, 1859; died January 27, 1873. Married William Keys, born 1855; five children:
    (1) Rosie May, born 1887; married John Harvey Reed.
    (2) Birdie; married Hedgeman Asbridge.
    (3) Thomas; married Malissa Neff.
    (4) Theresa; married Alexander Bailey.
    (5) Eva; married Miller, and second Hogan.
f. Isabel, born January 8, 1862; died April, 1901. Married to James H. Eads.
g. Louisa, born March 11, 1864; married to John H. Clark, born 1859, and had seven children:
    (1) Jesse, born 1884
    (2) Elsie, born 1890
    (3) Charles, born 1892
    (4) Carrie, born 1893
    (5) Albert, born 1894
    (6) Alice, born 1896
    (7) Minnie, born 1908
h. Susan, born June 19, 1866
i. Sarah F., born January 15, 1869
j. Benjamin Franklin, born November 11, 1870

4. Mary Caroline, born July 24, 1829 in Missouri; died March 21, 1916 at Sullivan, Franklin County, Missouri, and buried in the Buffalo cemetery. Married March 24, 1853 in Washington County, Missouri, to John Absalom Pratt, her cousin, born

January 14, 1834, and died June 27, 1890; son of Henry Pratt, Jr. (1800). Their family is discussed in the previous chapter under the husband's name, and will not be repeated here.

5. Albert Sevier, born April 4, 1831 in Greene County, Tennessee, and died May 15, 1913 at Sullivan in Franklin County, Missouri. Married March 24, 1853 to Mary Elizabeth Pratt, his cousin, another of the children of Henry Pratt, Jr. She was born August, 1836 in Monroe County, Tennessee, and died 1902 in Johnson Township, Washington County, Missouri. They reportedly had as many as twelve children, nine of whom have been reported in detail in the previous chapter under their mother's name, which see.

6. John Allen, born 1829 in Missouri; married Margaret Blanton, born 1832. Their family appears in the 1870 census of Johnson Township, Washington County, Missouri, next door to his father and his brothers. Children, born in Missouri:
    a. Cynthia A. 1854
    b. Nancy C. 1857
    c. Austin 1864
    d. John E. 1866
    e. Charles H. 1869

7. Henry Hubert, born February 23, 1837 in Missouri, and died January 21, 1908. Married to his cousin, Matilda Jane Pratt (1842), another of the daughters of Henry Pratt, Jr. (1800). The family appears in the 1860 and 1870 census for Johnson Township, Washington County; and in the 1880 census for Meremec Township, in Franklin County; both in Missouri. Eight children, born there:
    a. Henry W., born 1858
    b. James, born 1861; married Ada Hill, born 1862, and had six children:
        (1) Effie, born 1887
        (2) Ida, born 1890
        (3) Jesse, born 1893
        (4) Howard Browning, born 1894; married Sarah Ann Coleman, born 1898
        (5) James Irvin, born 1898; married Margaret.
        (6) Esther Marie, born 1902

23

c. Valentine, born 1863
d. Welsey B., born 1864
e. Jesse Van Buren, born 1869; married Nellie Elizabeth Edwards, born 1876, and had a son:
  (1) Lloyd Jess, born 1903; married to Fannie Eliza Brown, born 1906
f. Wiley, born 1871
g. Charles Edward, born 1873
h. William, born 1876

8. William Wesley, born March, 1834 in Missouri; died August 2, 1902 at Bonne Terre in St. Francois County, Missouri. He was married October 8, 1867 in Franklin County to Mary Ann Blanton, born c.1847. They appear in the census of 1870 for Johnson Township, Washington County; and the 1900 census for Meramec Township, Sullivan City, Franklin County; all in Missouri. Children, all born in Missouri:
a. Charles W., born 1868
b. Sarah A., born 1872
c. Catherine Jennie, born 1878
d. Luther, born 1881
e. Robert Lee, born 1884
f. Bethany

9. Martin Van Buren, born 1841 in Missouri.

CHAPTER 5

Oliver Pratt
c.1784-1832

This son of Henry Pratt (pre-1765), was born between 1784 and 1794, as reported in the census of 1810 for Washington County, Virginia, with a female of the same age range in his household. Marriage Register 2, page 359 of the county reports the marriage of Oliver Pratt to Mary Fulks on July 5, 1810. She was a daughter of Nicholas and Nancy Botts Fulks, originally of Augusta County, Virginia. The Fulks families will be discussed in further detail in Chapter 6, following.

On August 16, 1819, Oliver Pratt purchased 253 acres of land from Margaret Denniston *"in the Rich Valley of the Holston River"* for three hundred, thirty-three dollars and thirty-three cents. On December 13, 1819, he conveyed 63 acres of this property to Rebecca Pritchett, and described it as being *"on the south side of Cove Creek Ridge."* That deed was signed by Oliver Pratt and Polly Pratt, his wife, both with their mark. In several places in the deed, the wife of Oliver is said to be Polly, which is apparently the name by which she was commonly known, as a nickname, rather than her given name of Mary.

Oliver Pratt appears as head of household in the census of 1810 and 1820 for Washington County, Virginia. The following chart of census records demonstrates the probable family of Oliver and Mary Fulks Pratt, according to those records, and with the addition of at least two children born after the census of 1820. Keep in mind that in this period, only the name of the head of household was listed; we have furnished the names of the children from other sources.

It would appear that in 1810 Oliver and his wife had a boarder or the brother of one of them living with them, of roughly the same age. Again, in the 1820 census, there is a female in the household of about the same age as Mary living with them, who is not one of their children. An evaluation of the census records of these early years indicates that a large number of households contained listings of individuals not members of the family with whom they lived.

Individual	1810	1820	Known Name
Oliver	1784-1794	1775-1794	Oliver
Male # 1	1784-1794	-	Unknown
Male # 2	-	1810-1820	Nicholas H.
Male # 3	-	1810-1820	William Henry
Male # 4	-	1810-1820	Madison
Male # 5	-	-	Isaac Thompson
Wife	1784-1794	1794-1804	Mary (Polly)
Girl # 1	-	1794-1804	Unknown
Girl # 2	-	1810-1820	Elizabeth C.
Girl # 3	-	1810-1820	Unknown
Girl # 4	-	-	Nancy Fulks

The last few years in the life of Oliver Pratt are shrouded in mystery, and I have thus far been unable to untangle the web. In the Order Book for Smyth County, Virginia, there is an entry reporting that, on September 19, 1833, the Overseers of the Poor had bound out Henry Pratt, "*son of Oliver Pratt, deceased,*" to William Humes, to learn the trade of spinning cotton yarn and making machinery. On that basis, we had assumed the death of Oliver between about 1830 and 1833.

Some years ago, I received information from another researcher, which stated that Oliver had gone to Hawkins County, Tennessee, where he filed for divorce from his wife Mary, there called Polly, stating that *Polly had run off with Mr. Orndorff.* In the fall of 1986, I went to Rogersville, in Hawkins County, where I rather quickly found the court record of Saturday, April 12, 1828, reporting on the petition of Oliver Pratt for divorce from Polly Pratt. On that date, Polly failed to appear and the court ordered publication in the *Knoxville Register*, calling on her to appear at the next term of court, or the matter will be heard *ex parte* and a decree entered accordingly.

The clerk of court was very understanding, and permitted me to spend nearly an entire day alone, searching through all the boxes of miscellaneous records in the basement storeroom. There were numerous other packets of papers on other divorces during the same period, but none relative to Oliver Pratt that I could discover. No record of the statement that Polly ran off could be found, and a search of the *Knoxville Register* issues for the appropriate period revealed no evidence of advertisement, or further action. I am left to wonder what happened in the case and, if the records can be found, are the parties involved "our" Oliver and Mary Pratt?

It is, of course, possible that rather than accept the stigma of a divorce, Oliver was locally reported by family members as being deceased following a possible second marriage in Tennessee, if that be the case. As will be reported later, some of his children were found in the household of his eldest son, Nicholas H. Pratt, in the 1850 census of Smyth County, Virginia. Records of the Mormon library report the death of Oliver in January, 1831, although it should be quickly noted that the family group sheet submitted to the records was prepared many years later by a member of the Pritchett family, establishing a record of the family of Isaac Thompson Pratt and Nancy Emeline Pritchett, his first wife. That same group sheet has an easily proven error in the listing of one of their sons, given there as Glen, rather than the known Oliver (born c.1865), so I am personally not prepared to accept the record of the death of Oliver in 1831, absent any further documentation.

There were, certainly, Pratts in Tennessee, and quite early. From *North Carolina Land Grants in Tennessee, 1778-1791*, we find that Peter Pratt, private in the Revolution, held a warrant for land, assigned to Thomas Blount, for 40 acres on the Tennessee River. One Thomas Pratt also filed for Revolutionary War pension in 1818 in Hawkins County, at the age of 75, for service in the North Carolina Line. From *Early East Tennessee Taxpayers*, by Crrckmore, we find three Pratts in Cocke County, Tennessee in February, 1836: James, Thomas and William.

Entry Book A, page 262, Hawkins County, Tennessee, states that, on April 27, 1829, Thomas Prat (sic) locates and enters 50 acres of land in the county, on the north side of Clinch Mountain, about three quarters of a mile from Clinch River, and on the north side of the river ridge, to include the improvements of the said Prat purchased from Reuben Mabe, and the spring.

The 1830 census for Hawkins County carries a listing for one Oliver Pratt, born between 1780 and 1790. There is a female in the household (perhaps a wife?), born between 1790 and 1800. The age fits that of our Oliver, so it is possible that he received a divorce, and remarried a year or so later, prior to 1830. It is possible also that this is a second Oliver Pratt, of no known connection to our immediate family group. The 1830 census of Tennessee also carried 35 other households headed by members of the Pratt family, in various counties.

There is yet another very important piece of information that was reported to me, and should not be forgotten. In the 1980s, I received a letter from Angelynn McCrary, a lineal descendant of William Henry Pratt (1815), one of the known sons of Oliver and Mary Fulks Pratt. She reported that her Uncle Carl Day Pratt (1891), a grandson of William Henry, clearly recalled the names of some of the children of Oliver known to him personally, most of them nicknames, including: *Nixie*, which is Nicholas H.; *Thompse*, the nickname my grandfather Isaac Thompson carried all his life; *Maddie*, being Madison; *Nanny*, for Nancy Fulks; *Lizzie*, for Elizabeth C.; and *Lexie*, which we now believe to be John Alexander Pratt, born c.1811/12. Carl Day Pratt also reported an Oliver Pratt, Jr., of whom we have no knowledge.

In her letter, Angie noted that she had "always understood" that Oliver was married twice, and that his father was Henry Pratt, who was born in Scotland and immigrated to America, finally settling in southwest Virginia. Dr. Williams and his wife suggest that Henry, father of Oliver, moved into Washington County, Virginia about 1780, when he was in his teens, from New England. They state that evidence indicates that his father was dead and that his mother was remarried, possibly to a Wheeler or a Dennison. Their report contained no information relative to the source of these suppositions, and Dr. Joe Williams has since died, but the information is repeated here for further evaluation.

Angie reports that William Henry Pratt (1815) removed from Virginia to Gilmore, Wolfe County, Kentucky, some time after 1850. He reportedly was accompanied by his brothers, Oliver, Jr. and Madison. She reports that both of these boys were drowned in a crossing of the Kentucky River at flood, although we now know with certainty that Madison survived (if he went at all), and raised a family in Pulaski County, Virginia, as discussed in Chapter 11 of this study. The second drowned brother was more likely Henry, as reported following.

We now know the names of all the children of Oliver Pratt and Mary Fulks Pratt, with the exception of a daughter reported in early census records. The children included:

1. Nicholas H., born March 14, 1811; see Chapter 8
2. John Alexander, perhaps, born c.1811/12; see Chapter 7
3. Elizabeth C., born c.1813; see Chapter 9
4. William Henry, born c.1815; see Chapter 10
5. Madison, born July 1, 1816; see Chapter 11
6. Henry, born c.1820; married September 10, 1841 to Julia Ann Johnson in Smyth County, Virginia. Reportedly drowned in the Kentucky River while travelling west
7. Nancy Fulks, born May 16, 1823; see Chapter 12
8. Isaac Thompson, born August 5, 1827; see Chapters 13 & 15
9. Oliver, Jr., perhaps, if the family legend reported by Angelynn McCrary of the journey to Kentucky is correct.

CHAPTER 6

The Fulks Families

The Fulks families have ancient roots in England and Wales, and probably earlier in Germany. As is usual with many surnames, the name is found in numerous variations: such as Foulkes, Fowkes, Fulke, Foulks, Fouts, Fouques, and others. Some of these are early adaptations, and some are later results of phonetic spelling of the name by a public clerk or other officer, where the owner of the name was unable to read or write.

One report suggests that census records indicate there are approximately seven hundred heads of households in the United States bearing the name Fulks, or something on the order of only two thousand, two hundred and forty individuals. That is probably understated by a fair percentage, with all spelling variations considered, but the fact remains that the name is not that common, compared to many others. For example, there are easily three times as many listings for Hurleys in my local phone book as there are for Fulks, in any of its spellings.

The General Armory, by Burke, listing the hereditary Arms of English families, contains several entries under the variant spellings of the name, with the ancestral Arms described, including:

Fulke, Earl of Anjou
Folke, Foulke, or Fulke, County Stafford
Folkes, Hillingdon, County Norfolk, baronet
Folkes, County Middlesex, granted March 11, 1685
Foulke, or Fulke, Wickwonen, County Worcester
Foulkes, Eriviatt, or Yr Eifiad, County Denbigh; derived from Gronwy Ap-Davydd, usually styled Y Penwyn, one of the few Welsh chieftains who espoused the cause of Edward I, in his conquest of Wales. Gronwy, who descended from Marchudd, living in the ninth century, head of one of the Fifteen Tribes of North Wales.

Foulkes, Reverend Henry Foulkes, DD, Principal, Jesus College, Oxford, 1827

Foulkes, Medland, County Devon

Foulkes, Cilan-yn-Edeirnion, County Merioneth, derived through Morgan Ap Robert, of Branas, in Edeirnion, the ancestor of Hughes, of Gwerclas, Baron of Kymmer-yn-Edeirnion.

One of the more famous, or infamous, members of the family was one Guido Fawkes or, as modern history knows him, Guy Fawkes. In 1605, England was ruled by James 1st, a Protestant. A group of Roman Catholics determined to destroy James and Parliament, so that England could return to the "one true faith."

The plan became known to history as the *"Gunpowder Plot."* On November 5, 1605, as the King was preparing to visit Parliament on his annual State Opening, investigators discovered large stores of gunpowder in the cellar of the building, designed to destroy the King and the assemblage in one vast explosion. An individual was caught and identified as Johnson, later proven to be Guy Fawkes, and he was convicted of the crime and sentenced to death. To this day, November 5 is known in England as *"Guy Fawkes Day"* and there are parades; and figures of the culprit are burned in effigy.

Early Arrivals in America

Filby's *Passenger and Immigration Lists Index* carries entries for a number of members of the family during the early years of colonization in America, including the following, who arrived prior to 1700. Many others are listed, in later years, under other variant spellings of the name, but none under Fulks, as we know it:

Fowke, Gerard: To Virginia, 1650/54
Fowke, Moses: To America, 1661
Fowke, Thomas: To West New Jersey, 1664
Fowke, William: To Virginia, 1646
Fowkes, Richard: To Jamaica, 1685; age 32
Fowkes, Robert: To Barbados, 1671

Fowkes, or Foulke, William: To Virginia, 1624; age 24
Foulke, Thomas: To New Castle, Delaware, 1677
Foulke, Thomas: To Virginia, 1623
Fouks, William: To Virginia, 1623
Foulke, Edward: To Pennsylvania, 1698, with nine children
Foulke, Thomas: To New Jersey, 1677
Foulke, Thomas: To Virginia, 1622

An entry in *Archives of Maryland* states that just six years after the founding of the Town of St. Maries, the Englishmen were abusing treaties and agreements they had made with the Indians. In one protest filed by the Indians, they stated that James Fowkes had refused to make payment for the land he had acquired along the Choptank River, and was improperly cutting timber on Indian land.

Of those immigrants shown above, one is of particular interest, although he can not yet be proven to be related to the Fulks family with which we are here concerned. He is Colonel Gerard Fowke, born in Staffordshire, England; lived in Charles County, Maryland and died c.1669 in Virginia. His ancestry and descendants, many of whom are quite illustrious, are reported extensively in a number of publications, including: *Genealogies of Virginia Families*, from Tyler's Quarterly, Historical and Genealogical Magazine; *Virginia Genealogies, a Genealogy of the Glassell Family*, by Rev. Horace Edwin Hayden, 1973; *Virginia Ancestors and Adventurers*, by Charles Hughes Hamlin, 1975; *Old Churches, Ministers and Families of Virginia*, by Bishop William Meade; and *Colonial Families of the Southern States of America*, by Stella Pickett Hardy, 1981.

Nicholas Fulks
m/1790

My maternal great grandmother was Mary Fulks, daughter of Nicholas Fulks and Nancy Botts Fulks. We have yet to prove a connection to the earlier Fulks families described above. Nicholas and Nancy were married September 28, 1790 in Augusta County, Virginia; surety was Erasmus Jones. A report of their marriage appears in *Records of Augusta County, Virginia, 1745-1800*, by

Lyman Chalkey, Volume 2, page 288. However, on a very recent trip to Staunton, county seat of Augusta County, I found the original marriage bond for this couple. It has been preserved and bound into a book in the office of the Clerk of the Court. Very clearly, the bond was issued September 20, 1790, but it has been torn on one edge, removing the entire last name of Nancy, the bride to be. Nicholas signed with his mark, as did Erasmus Jones. There is an interesting little note at the bottom, reading: "*E. Jones was obliged to make his mark having a hurt on his arm by reason of which he could not write his name.*" The index book in the Clerk's office reports the bond of *Nicholas Fulks and Nancy Jones ?*, with that question mark in the entry. Probably, whoever wrote the index is suggesting that she may have been a Jones, since Erasmus Jones was surety on the bond. Incidentally, if one of my readers attempts to find the bond, in order to obtain a copy, the index entry reports page 44; it is actually on page 53, Volume III, *Restored Marriage Records 1790-1791.* I have not seen an actual report of marriage, which appears to have taken place eight days later, as reported above, where her proper name may appear. The couple apparently moved to Wythe County, Virginia soon after marriage, where they reportedly had as many as nine children, although only their daughter, Mary, is known to me at this time.

In the 1830 census of Washington County, Tennessee, there is one Nicholas Fulks, living alone, between the ages of 70 and 80 years, who is believed to be this individual. As has been discussed in more detail in the previous chapter, Mary, daughter of Nicholas and Nancy Botts Fulks, was married to Oliver Pratt on July 5, 1810. Assuming that she was about twenty-one years of age at the time, she could have been born c.1791, perhaps the eldest child of her parents.

At this point, I am about to do something no genealogist should do, and that is attempt to assemble a family, or part of it, solely on the basis of dates and geographic location. *Please keep in mind that what follows is pure supposition, demonstrating what could have been part of the family of Nicholas Fulks and Nancy Botts Fulks.* Their reported nine children could have included:

1. Mary, perhaps their eldest child, married July 5, 1810 to Oliver Pratt, my ancestor. This is the only proven child of this family.
2. Abraham, appearing in the 1850 census of Wythe County, living alone at the age of 60 years; thus born c.1790. Like the others listed here, his relationship to our Nicholas Fulks, if it exists, is not yet demonstrated.
3. William, appearing in the Mormon IGI records of Wythe County, Virginia, was born c.1804 in Wythe County, and married c.1822 to Elizabeth. He is of an age that he could have been one of the children of Nicholas Fulks and Nancy Botts Fulks, although that is pure speculation on my part. They appear in the 1850 census of Wythe County, with four children, born there, including:
   a. James, born c.1830
   b. Sally, born c.1837
   c. Virginia, born c.1841
   d. Reuben, born c.1847
4. Joseph, born c.1806, also appearing in the 1850 census of Wythe County, Virginia, at the age of 44 years, with a wife, Elizabeth, born c.1813 and a number of children. Purely from a time and geographic standpoint, he could have been a son of Nicholas Fulks and his wife Nancy Botts. Again, pure speculation, but possible. His children included:
   a. Polly, born c.1831
   b. Leah, born c.1832
   c. Emily, born c.1834
   d. Samuel, born c.1837
   e. Alexander, born c.1838
   f. Elizabeth, born c.1841
   g. Sarah, born c.1843
   h. Joseph, born c.1845
   i. Ann, born c.1849

As reported above, Nicholas and Nancy Botts were married in Augusta County, Virginia in 1790. Recently, I made a search of the records in the Courthouse at Staunton, the county seat. Little was found of any importance. In the will records, there are only two listed in the early years. The information, although meager, will be listed here simply for further reference.

One will was that of John Paul Fought, October 9, 1759, will book 3, page 50. He listed a wife Mary Katrine, who received his estate, including the 200 acres during her lifetime, and then to be divided equally between Katrine Clemons, Andrew and Casper Fought. The will was entered for probate August 10, 1762.

The second estate was that of Ludwig Folks, who apparently died intestate. The bond of his administrators was issued November 15, 1758, filed in Will Book 2, page 280. The value of the estate was set at eleven pounds.

Deed books index yielded very little activity during the late 1700s and very early 1800s:

Deed Book 1, page 689: Frederick and Hannah Kister to George Fults, August 17, 1764. For five shillings, 35 acres on the mountain between the south fork and the south branch of the Potomac at a place called the Little Walnut Bottom.

Deed Book 4, page 399: Andrew Fought, yeoman, to Casper Fought, August 19, 1752. Lease for 112 acres of land for one year at 5 shillings, and one ear of Indian Corn on the feast day of St. Michael, the Archangel.

Deed Book 20, page 306: Andrew and Elizabeth Fought to Leonard Miller, May 17, 1774. For 165 pounds, 235 acres in two tracts along the north side of the north river of the Shenandoah.

Deed Book 33, page 235: Henry Eakle, et al, to Casper Faulk, November 25, 1805. For 340 pounds, 108 acres on the waters of the Middle River.

Keeping in mind that our ancestors generally moved in family groups, it is more than likely that Nicholas Fulks and his bride moved to Wythe County with other members of the Fulks family. There were several other Fulks families found in Wythe County during this early period, who are probably related, including the following.

Samuel Fulks
died c.1837

Samuel is found in the IGI records of the Mormon church, with his wife Leah, in Wythe County, Virginia. Considering that the earliest birth date of one of their children is c.1799, it is possible that Samuel could have been a brother of Nicholas, who was married in 1790 to Nancy Botts. Samuel's will is dated March 6, 1837, according to IGI records. He and Leah had children born in Wythe County:

1. Hannah, born c.1799
2. Polly, born c.1800
3. Nancy, born c.1805
4. Joseph, born c.1806; married 1826/30 to Elizabeth K. Peek, born c.1813 in Wythe County, Virginia. They had children:
   a. Polly, born c.1831
   b. Leah, born c.1831
   c. Emily, born c.1834
   d. Samuel Adams, perhaps, born November 22, 1836 in Carroll County, Virginia
   e. Alexander, born c.1838
   f. Elizabeth, born c.1841
   g. Sarah, born c.1843
   h. Joseph, born c.1845
   i. Ann, born c.1849
   j. James R., born August 15, 1855
   k. Nellie, born c.1856
5. Patsy, mentioned in the will
6. William, mentioned in the will

William Fulks
m/1800

This William also appears in Wythe County records of the IGI index, with a wife, Rebecca, born November 10, 1781. He, too, could have been a brother of Nicholas Fulks; pure supposition based on dates, but possible. They had children, all born in Wythe County:

1. Nancy, born November 4, 1801
2. John M., born December 2, 1804; probably married March 4, 1822 to Sally Corrico in Grayson County, Virginia
3. Elizabeth, born February 11, 1807
4. Letitia, born November 12, 1809; probably married March 6, 1830 in Grayson County to Anderson Moore.
5. Sally Ann, perhaps, born c.1822

Nicholas Fulks
1831-?

This Nicholas appears in the IGI records of Wolfe County, Kentucky, born about 1831, and married there c.1863 to Nancy Tutt, who was born about 1843. Once again, we have no proof of a connection to the families being researched, but the name is a familiar one, and family members are known to have lived in the areas where Virginia, Tennessee and Kentucky come together. They had a number of children, all of whom were apparently born at or near Compton, in Wolfe County, Kentucky:

1. Laura, born c.1864; married perhaps twice. There are marriages reported in Wolfe County of Laura Fulks in 1885 to Bud Savage, and in c.1891 to Stephen N. Tutt; either or both could be this individual.
2. Kelly, born April 22, 1868; married October 16, 1890 to Alice Catherine Hanks, and had children, all born at Compton, in Wolfe County, Kentucky:
   a. Columbus Nicholas, born August 10, 1891
   b. Jane, born September 16, 1896
   c. Dewey Lavander, born May 6, 1898; married December 23, 1921 at Winchester, Clark County, Kentucky, to Ila Mae Ford, and had children:
      (1) James Andrew, born December 23, 1923 at Slade, in Powell County, Kentucky
      (2) Ray Lavander, born May 20, 1925 at Slade
      (3) Paul, born August 1, 1926 at Winchester
   d. Ernest, born March 26, 1900
   e. Kelly Lloyd, born April 20, 1903
   f. Andrew Jackson, born September 2, 1905

g.   Bertie Alice, born February 5, 1908
3.   Nancy W., born c.1869
4.   Jake, born c.1871; married c.1896 to Lilly Tutt
5.   Weyland, a daughter, born c.1873; married c.1894 to George Robinson.
6.   Sara, born c.1875
7.   Christopher Columbus, born March 6, 1876. He is reported by Mormon IGI records as having married Lillie Foster Tutt in Wolfe County, but see also report (from IGI) of marriage of his brother Jake to Lilly Tutt.

William Fulks
1761-

This member of the family appears in the Mormon IGI records for Tennessee, where he was married c.1782, although his wife's name is not there listed; only that she was born c.1765. They are shown with six named children. The children included, at least:
1.   Achsah, born c.1783; married March 7, 1804 to John Marlow in Sumner County, Tennessee.
2.   Orran, born c.1786
3.   William, born c.1786; married 1811 to Rebecca, and had at least two children, born in Sullivan County, Tennessee:
     a.   Thomas S., born c.1812
     b.   Samuel L., born c.1819
4.   Alfred, born c.1795
5.   Wilson, born c.1797
6.   Temperance, born c.1790; married c.1814 Vardiman Halsel.

Andrew J. Fulks
m/1874

Andrew also appears in the records of Sullivan County, Tennessee, married c.1874 to Mary Frances Hicks, and had at least two daughters, born there:
1.   Ellen, born March 23, 1875
2.   Margaret, born c.1877

Thomas Fulks
1828-

This individual also appears in the Mormon IGI records, where he was reportedly married c.1843, probably in Tennessee, to Charity Jackson. They had at least eleven children, the first of whom was born in Tennessee, and the rest in Monroe County, Kentucky. While this Thomas and the Nicholas Fulks (1831) who was reported above, were only three years apart in age, and by that measurement could possibly have been brothers, the counties of Kentucky in which they lived were quite far apart. Monroe County is a border county on the line of Tennessee, opposite the counties of Macon and Clay in that state. Wolfe and Powell Counties are half-way across the state to the north from there and east of the modern city of Lexington. In any case, the family of this Thomas Fulks and his wife Charity Jackson included:

1. W. S., a son, born c.1844 in Tennessee
2. Mary J., born c.1847 in Monroe County, Kentucky, as were the rest of the children
3. S. A., a daughter, born c.1848
4. John S., born c.1852
5. Gilly S., a daughter, born April 29, 1854
6. Lucetta C., born c.1856
7. Jarod J., born c.1860
8. Henrietta, born c.1862
9. Hester A., born c.1863
10. Elsy W., born c.1864
11. Lettie J., born c.1866

The Marriage Register, Book 1, Washington County, Virginia, contains references to three marriages of as yet unidentified Fulks family members:

William Green Fulks, son of John Henry and Margaret Fulks of Johnson County, Tennessee; married October 28, 1878 Martha Ellen Bridgeman. He was 19; the bride was 15 years of age.

John Fulks, son of William Green and Martha (above) married October 12, 1898 Anna Mosier. He was 17; she was 32.

Catherine Fulks married May 18, 1814 William Marshall.

CHAPTER 7

John Alexander Pratt
1811-1879

John Alexander is referred to in a newspaper account dated February 11, 1932, which unfortunately had no information as to the location of publication. The caption refers to Boone County, which is apparently in Indiana. There, it is said that he moved from Knoxville, Tennessee, to the area in 1830, with his wife and twelve children. That is obviously hardly possible, since he would have been only nineteen years old at that time! It is more than likely that he perhaps moved to Indiana as a young man, after which he met and married his wife, and had his large family. He was described there as Captain John A. Pratt, who was married to Talitha Cumi Clements, daughter of Philip Andrew Clements and Mary (Polly) Hyland Clements. She was born May 1, 1820 in Montgomery County, Kentucky, and died January 1, 1890 in Boone County, Indiana. The Clements family moved to the area from Kentucky in 1832, and located near Old Union Church, building a log cabin on a farm owned by Clay Baumgardner.

The article described an old hammered-barrel rifle originally owned by Captain John A. Pratt, and then in the possession of the tenth of his twelve children, Philip A. Pratt, born 1853 and died 1945; living in 1932 at Cloverdale, also in Indiana. There is reference also to a powder horn, made from the horn of one of the oxen drawing the family wagon of Philip Clements. One of the team died enroute and was replaced by a cow from the family herd.

There is some reason to believe that John Alexander Pratt was another of the sons of Oliver Pratt (1784-1832). There is one problem, however, that being the reported birth of John Alexander on September 18, 1811 in Greene County, Tennessee, and the fact that Nicholas H. Pratt, a proven son of Oliver, was born March 14, 1811 in Wythe County, Virginia. There could be an error in one of the dates, of course; that of John Alexander is taken from Mormon

Church records, and that of Nicholas from family records and tombstone inscription.

In any case, as we reported earlier, Angelynn McCrary, who is a lineal descendant of William Henry Pratt (1815), another of Oliver's sons, reported that her Uncle Carl Day Pratt (1891), a grandson of William Henry, clearly recalled the names of some of the children of Oliver known to him personally, most of them nicknames, including: *Nixie*, which is Nicholas H.; *Thompse*, the nickname my grandfather Isaac Thompson Pratt carried all his life; *Maddie*, being Madison; *Nanny*, for Nancy Fulks; *Lizzie*, for Elizabeth C.; and *Lexie*, which we now believe to be John Alexander Pratt, born c.1811/12. Carl Day Pratt also reported an Oliver Pratt, Jr., of whom we have no knowledge. We have reported this piece of important information earlier, but it is worthy of repeating here in this context. Angie had also stated that she had always been led to believe that Oliver was married twice. However, all of his children that we have proven were born after 1811, and it was about 1828 that *some* Oliver Pratt (perhaps ours) instituted divorce proceedings in Hawkins County, Tennessee. That being the case, if Angie is correct and Oliver was married twice, John Alexander may have been a son from his first marriage, in Tennessee, born before any of his other proven children, born in Virginia.

According to a letter in 1983 from Sara Ruth Thomas Buck (1915) (Mrs. Henry Edison), then living in Indianapolis, Indiana, John Alexander Pratt had a total of sixteen children, of whom thirteen lived to maturity and married. She also says that he was born September 8, 1811 in Greene County, Tennessee, and died November 4, 1879 in Boone County, Indiana. He and Talitha Cumi Clements were married July 15, 1838, by John H. Clements, brother of the bride. Their children, all born in Jackson Township, Boone County, Indiana, were:

1. Mary Frances, born April 23, 1839; died February 1, 1863. Married to Henry Meyer, born c.1836 at Detmold, Germany.
2. Louisa Elizabeth, born May 24, 1840; died May 24, 1920. Married Louis C. Leesemann, born c.1833, also at Detmold, Germany.
3. Clementine Cumi, known as Tine, born November 27, 1841; died July 30, 1888. Married John H. Utterback.

4. Nancy Ellen, born April 6, 1843; died October 26, 1885. Married March 2, 1862 to Samuel S. Blakemore, born October 2, 1838 in Hendricks County, Indiana, and died December 15, 1893 in Boone County. His parents were Thomas Poteet Blakemore (1809-1877) of Lee County, Virginia, and his wife, Narcissa Burdett Warren Blakemore (1811-1854), also of Virginia. They had at least one child:

    a. Irene Cumi, born January 1, 1863 in Boone County, and died August 22, 1953 in Marion County, Indiana. She married in Boone, December 5, 1886 to John Abraham Shelley, born there June 23, 1864; died in Marion County May 27, 1944. He was a son of Isaac James Shelley (1836-1916) and Malinda M. Booker Shelley (1841-1910). They had at least one daughter:

        (1) Mamie Malinda, born September 25, 1887 in Boone County; died August 7, 1981 in Marion County. Married March 15, 1910 to Elmer Ernest Thomas, born January 3, 1888; died January 3, 1962; son of James Henry Thomas (1862-1938) and Elizabeth C. Osburn Thomas (1867-1917). At least one daughter:

            (a) Sara Ruth, my correspondent, born November 25, 1915 in Marion County, and married first in 1939 to Kelly W. Quinlan; divorced 1953. Married second August 16, 1958 to Henry Edison Buck, born August 4, 1924 in Vigo County, Indiana.

5. Louisiana E., known as Lucy, born January 20, 1845. Married January 12, 1873 to Oliver B. McReynolds.

6. Wesley Oliver, born August 10, 1846; died January 27, 1910. Married September 10, 1874 to Mary Etta Marlowe.

7. Henry Lewis, born April 1, 1848; died May 6, 1896. Married to Hanna J. Walls.

8. Marinda Jane, born July 16, 1849; died May 3, 1920. Married January 26, 1871 to John Wesley Courtney.

9. Maranda Margaret, known as Meg, born February 1, 1851; died July 18, 1902. Married first Dr. Stephen Beck and second to George Dodson.

10. Philip Alexander, known as Phil, born May 7, 1853; died August 15, 1945. Married Elizabeth J. Wall.
11. John Finley, born July 18, 1855; died August 17, 1886. Married October 27, 1878 to Sarah McClain.
12. Talitha Hiland, known as Lida, born February 12, 1857; died July 28, 1920. Married to Delbert Southwick.
13. Willard, born December 4, 1858; died May 2, 1876
14. Sarah Lovina, born September 24, 1860; died June 10, 1941. Married to Joseph Coombs.
15. Charles Dow, born April 20, 1864; died May 4, 1864
16. Emma Hathaway, born August 29, 1865; died November 21, 1879.

CHAPTER 8

Nicholas H. Pratt
1811-1891

Nicholas is believed to be the eldest child of Oliver Pratt (1784) and Mary Fulks Pratt. However, see the preceding chapter for a discussion of the possible inclusion in the family of John Alexander Pratt, perhaps from a prior marriage of Oliver, or perhaps from this same family, with an error in the birthdates. In any case Nicholas, according to his tombstone, was born March 14, 1811, probably in what was then Washington County, Virginia, later to become part of Smyth County, formed in 1832. He died July 4, 1891, and is buried in the cemetery of the Rich Valley Presbyterian Church, near Chatham Hill. Married Sarah Thomas, born April 20, 1812; died August 13, 1893, and buried beside her husband. Nicholas appears to have been named for his maternal grandfather, Nicholas Fulks, a fairly standard practice. He and Sarah, known as Sally, had eight children:

1. Laura, born c.1838; married April 8, 1856 Enoch J. McCarty, born c.1818, son of James and Mary McCarty. At least a son:
    a. J. M., known as Bud, married Mabel Golihorn, and had seven children:
        (1) Jack
        (2) Charles
        (3) William, a doctor
        (4) James
        (5) Virginia
        (6) Sidney
        (7) Lucille
2. John Marion, born c.1839, of whom more
3. William Harrison, born October 3, 1840; died February 20, 1910. Nicknamed "Toad," he was married December 25, 1861 to Emma, or Emaline, Carrie Buchanan, daughter of Lolen and Nancy B. Buchanan. She was born October 15, 1842 and died October 28, 1902. No children.

4. George Washington, known as Wash, born November, 1842; died June 9, 1906. Married December 6, 1872 to Olivia Epps Magruder from Roanoke County, Virginia, born c.1852; a daughter of P. H. and Sallie Magruder. He was a Mason and his will, proven at Marion, Virginia, June 21, 1906, indicates that he owned several farms in Rich Valley, Smyth County. They had two children:
    a. Henry Sidney, born October 18, 1873; died August 18, 1884, reportedly as a result of being struck in the head by a ball thrown by a childhood friend. Records at Marion list the cause of death as "brain fever."
    b. Ada Grace, born October, 1874; married 1910 Dr. Albert E. Buchanan, son of Hickman Spiller and Laura Maria Sexton Buchanan. He was born August 21, 1872; died October 22, 1950 in Nebraska. Three children:
        (1) Edna, married Stephens; lived in Parsons, Kansas
        (2) Laura Marie, married Wengert; lived at Fremont, Nebraska
        (3) Warren, lived in Omaha, Nebraska
5. America A., born September 10, 1845, of whom more
6. James Dallas, born September 18, 1848 in Rich Valley, Smyth County, Virginia. Married April 15, 1883 to Lillie Elizabeth Baldwin at Baldwin Farm, Unison, Loudon County, Virginia. He died August 22, 1923; buried in Rock Creek Cemetery in Washington, D. C. His wife died January 25, 1924. They had eight children:
    a. Otway August, born August 8, 1887 at Chatham Hill, in Smyth County, Virginia; died May 12, 1972. Married to Alice Jenkins.
    b. Florence Rosedale, born September 2, 1891 at Rosedale, in Russell County, Virginia; died December 15, 1981. Married first Scott Randolph Riser; had a daughter and was divorced. Married second September 17, 1927 in Beverly Hills, California, to Landon Hammer Phillips, born December 21, 1894 at Bristol, Tennessee; died April 23, 1970. The one child of Florence was:
        (1) Doris, born at Washington, D. C., February 23, 1914. Married October 15, 1939 to Charles John

45

Krueger, born December 13, 1904 at Philadelphia, Pennsylvania, son of Bernhard Krueger and Anna Reiter Krueger. They had a son:

    (a)   Robert Dale, born July 3, 1958 in New York.

c.   Alice Lillian, born January 6, 1894; married Frank Kells, and had a son:

    (1)   James Thomas, born at Greenfield, Massachusetts, and married to Betty Faulkner.

d.   James Alton, born September 23, 1896; married twice. First Lillian Bales, and second Margaret Louise Mays.

e.   Vivian Waller, born December 24, 1898; died January 3, 1899.

f.   Dallas Norman, born November 30, 1899 in Loudon County, Virginia. Married to Louise Smitley; one son:

    (1)   James Dallas, born May 21, 1937 in Washington. Married July 1, 1961 Josephine Mebane Burgwyn, born April 2, 1940; daughter of John Griffin and Mebane Holoman Burgwyn of Roanoke Rapids, North Carolina. Two sons, the first born in Philadelphia; the second at Norwalk, Connecticut:

        (a)   James Glen, born March 12, 1969

        (b)   Stephen Dallas, born October 24, 1972

g.   Samuel Baldwin, born May 28, 1903; married Elizabeth Howell.

h.   Kenneth Orell, born February 19, 1906; married Juanita Batty, and had one son:

    (1)   William James, married December 27, 1981 to Margaret Christina Kern, at Frostburg, Maryland.

7.   Susan, born in June of 1850; died at the age of 5, September 3, 1855 of dysentery; reported in Smyth County death records at Marion, Virginia.

8.   Florence E., born April 25, 1852. Married to her first cousin, George Ringo Campbell, born November 15, 1846; and died June 9, 1926. He was a son of Spottswood Mitchell Campbell (1804) and Nancy Fulks Pratt Campbell (1823). The children of Florence and George Ringo will be discussed in the section devoted to his family, in Chapter 12.

Captain John Marion Pratt
Army of the Confederacy
1839-1905

Hettie Virginia McCready Pratt
1848-1914

John Marion Pratt
1839-1905

This son of Nicholas H. Pratt (1811) was born c.1839 in Smyth County, Virginia, and died in January, 1905. He enlisted into the Army of the Confederacy September 14, 1861 and, on October 7, 1861, was appointed 1st Lieutenant, Co. L, 50th Regt, Infantry, Virginia. On May 20, 1862, he was promoted to Captain and served in that rank for the remainder of the war with Co. E, 23rd Virginia Infantry, Echol's Brigade, Breckenridge's Division. He was reportedly wounded at the battle of Cold Harbor near Richmond, Virginia. Married April 28, 1875 to Hettie Virginia McCready, born c.1848; died July 2, 1914. Six children, all born in Smyth County, Virginia:

1. Edna E., born February, 1876; married September 5, 1906 to Dr. F. M. Eversole. He was a Presbyterian missionary, serving in Korea with his brother-in-law, Dr. Charles Henry Pratt.
2. Laura E., born August, 1877; died August 11, 1893 in Rich Valley, Smyth County
3. Mary K. (or perhaps Mary Virginia), born January, 1879 and died December, 1969. Single, she taught school at Rich Valley High School for many years.
4. Charles Henry, born January 20, 1881 at Saltville; died January 26, 1950 at Fort Worth, Florida. Buried at the Presbyterian Church, Swannanoa, North Carolina. He was a noted minister, missionary and educator. On the occasion of his death, the Louisville Presbyterian Theological Seminary published *Memorials,* a small volume devoted to his life and accomplishments, and including testimonials from colleagues relative to his contribution to their lives and society. At the end of the booklet is a resolution announcing the creation of The *Charles H. Pratt Prize in Field Work,* to be given each year to that member of the senior class who is judged to have made the most outstanding progress in field work during his studies at the Seminary. Charles Henry received a number of degrees: the AB from Kings College in 1902; the BD at Union Seminary in Richmond, 1905; an AM from Princeton University in 1907; an Honorary DD from Kings College in 1917; and the

The Reverend Doctor Charles Henry Pratt
1881-1950

LLD in 1926. He was a pastor, secretary of the Laymen's Missionary Movement, missionary to Korea, secretary of the Committee of Foreign Missions, and held the Chair of Missions and Evangelism at the Louisville Seminary, retiring in May, 1949 as Professor, Emeritus. He was married July 7, 1905 to Pattie Foster Ward at Richmond, Virginia, and was the father of five children:

a. Charles McCready, born June 5, 1909 at Athens, Georgia and married September 7, 1937 to Sara Lane Smith. Two children:

    (1) Charles McCready, Jr., born April 30, 1939 at Richmond; married December 27, 1962 to Helen Louise Forson. Two children:

        (a) Eliot Forson, born June 25, 1971

        (b) Charles Edward, born January 27, 1975

    (2) Sterling Lacy, born February 11, 1946 at Louisville, Kentucky; married August 21, 1971 Valerie Joy Green. He married second September 18, 1988 to Julianne Therese Hahn. Two children were born to the first marriage:

        (a) Katherine McCorkle Lindvahl, born August 23, 1976 at Chicago, Illinois

        (b) Elizabeth Ward Cranston, born May 19, 1982

b. Lanier Ward, born May 30, 1912 at Richmond; died June 4, 1956; married August 24, 1938 Ella Fountain Keesler. Two children:

    (1) Laniel Ward, Jr., married Mary Margaret Melville

    (2) Samuel Keesler.

c. Pattie Virginia, married Joseph Brown Ledbetter, and had two children:

    (1) Pattie Pratt, born May 11, 1942

    (2) Joseph Brown, Jr., born September 1, 1945 married Candy; three children:

        (a) Daniel Alexander

        (b) Molly Lanier

        (c) Jeffrey Brown

d. Ellen, born August 10, 1917 at Franklinton, North Carolina; died October 18, 1992. Married January 7, 1944 to Charles Frederick Wortham. Five children, the first born at Pensacola, Florida; the second at Louisville, Kentucky; and the last three at Richmond, Virginia:

    (1) Ann Lanier, born February 19, 1945. Married at Powhatan, Virginia Gilbert R. Kuper and divorced. Two children, both born at Powhatan:

        (a) Gilbert R., Jr., born June 8, 1972

  (b) Ward Hawkins, born February 18, 1974. In December, 1992, he changed his surname to Wortham, his mother's maiden name.

(2) Charles Frederick, Jr., born June 5, 1946. He is a doctor; married to Jane Woolford at Richmond, Virginia, who was the daughter of William and Elizabeth Woolford of Aylett, Virginia. They have two children, born at Richmond:

  (a) Mary Douglas, born January 6, 1981
  (b) Virginia Pratt, born April 27, 1982

(3) Ellen Randolph, born March 21, 1948. Married at Richmond to John Christian Dwyer, who was born there December 29, 1949, son of Roland W. and Anne Christian Dwyer. They have three children, the first born at Charlottesville, Virginia, the last two at Richmond:

  (a) Philip Hawkins, born February 28, 1972
  (b) Melanie Christian, born September 9, 1974
  (c) Ellen Elizabeth, born January 19, 1976

(4) Marion Pratt, born July 20, 1954. Married first David Gerald Wember and divorced after having two children. Married second on June 24, 1984 at Arnold, Anne Arundel County, Maryland, Douglas Coulson. Her two children were born at Falls Church, Virginia:

  (a) Asa Frederick, born December 29, 1976
  (b) Summer Laurel, born August 6, 1978

(5) Margaret Thomas, born February 11, 1958, and married Craig H. Donor, from whom she was divorced. He was born at Elmyra, New York, a son of Alton and Mary Ellen Donor. They had two children, born at Cherry Point, North Carolina:

  (a) Lawrence A., born November 8, 1980
  (b) Piper Grace, born December 4, 1984

e. Mary Elisabeth, married Philip Thayer. Five children:

 (1) Pamela Ward, married David Richardson.
 (2) Barbara Adin, married Edmund de la Cour and had two children

        (3)   Anna Chittendon, married Scott Diarmid and had two children
        (4)   Elizabeth Lawrence, married to William Behrends and had two children:
            (a) Alden
            (b) Molly
        (5)   Meta Britten, married and had two children.

5. James Marion, born April 22, 1882; died August 17, 1967. He is buried at Rich Valley Presbyterian Church in Rich Valley, Smyth County, Virginia. Married October 9, 1912 to Nannie Lee Gass, born September 22, 1894; died July 18, 1978, a daughter of S. E. and Rose Gass. Five children, all born in Rich Valley, Smyth County:

a.   James Marion, Jr., born September 2, 1918; married June 20, 1942 to Laura Belle Morehead, born October 28, 1921 at Meadow View, Washington County, Virginia, a daughter of Harry L. Morehead. Two children, both born at Radford, Virginia:
        (1)   James Marion, III, born September 10, 1945
        (2)   Judith Lynn, born April 24, 1948; married July 6, 1967 to William Newsome, Jr. Two sons, born at Emporia, Virginia:
            (a) William Todd, born April 3, 1970
            (b) James Brett, born September 25, 1974

b.   Mary Grayson, born September 10, 1913; single.

c.   Elizabeth Tate, born February 21, 1916; married August 12, 1942 to Rawley F. Turner. Two children, first born at Saltville in Smyth County; the second at Roanoke:
        (1)   Rawley Pratt, born August 17, 1946; died February 9, 1967 at Roanoke
        (2)   Philip Lane, born May 1, 1951

d.   Margaret Agnes, born September 11, 1921, and married February, 1943 to Wilkes T. Thrasher, Jr. Divorced after two children were born:
        (1)   Wilkes, T., III, born August 22, 1944 at Saltville; died November 12, 1965 at Oxford, Mississippi
        (2)   James Pratt, born June 9, 1954 at Chattanooga

e. Laura Virginia, born November 3, 1923; married June 21, 1947 to Dr. Walter F. Becker. Two children:
   (1) Walter Francis, born September 12, 1956
   (2) Carol Pratt, born November 7, 1958 New Orleans

6. Margaret L., born August, 1887; married October 11, 1911 to Joseph Burch, born September 17, 1884. She died June 15, 1965 in Hickory, North Carolina. Four children:

   a. Mary Virginia, born July 27, 1912 at Wytheville, Virginia; married Samuel H. Warlick.

   b. Margaret Josephine, born April, 1914 at Chatham Hill in Smyth County, Virginia. Died January, 1975. Married to Charles H. Allison.

   c. Annie Sue, born April, 1917; married first William H. Copenhaver, and second to Charles E. Allison.

   d. Nancy B., born February 27, 1919 at Chatham Hill, and married April 29, 1944 at Hickory, North Carolina, to John James Bannister, born July 10, 1919, son of William C. and Sadie B. Bannister of Richmond. They had two children:
      (1) Margaret Ellen, born at Richlands, Virginia, February 2, 1947. Married April 15, 1972 to Gerald Eugene Parr, son of Clifton Franklin and Lillian France Parr. Two children, born at Richmond, Virginia:
         (a) John Clifton, born December 23, 1977
         (b) Ellen France, born June 25, 1979
      (2) John James, Jr., born December 6, 1945; married October 11, 1975 at Afton Mountain, Virginia, to Sandra Diane Musgrove, born April 1, 1951, the daughter of Williams Jenning Musgrove and Lorene Musgrove.

America A. Pratt
1845-1929

This daughter of Nicholas H. Pratt (1811) was born September 10, 1845 in Smyth County, Virginia, and died January 14, 1929. She was married February 3, 1869 to Daniel Absolum

Troutman, from Troutman, North Carolina. He was born July 20, 1835 in Iredell County, North Carolina, and died March 21, 1918, a son of Henry and Margaret Elizabeth Leonard Troutman. He is buried in the cemetery of the Rich Valley Presbyterian Church in Smyth County, Virginia.

North Carolina Troops, 1861-1865, Volume XI, reports that there were four privates with the surname Troutman in Co C, 48th Regt, North Carolina State Troops, Army of the Confederacy. Each of them was listed as having been from Iredell County, and they are apparently brothers. They include Adam Carmi Troutman, born c.1841, who was captured at Hatcher's Run, Virginia, April 2, 1865, and confined at Hart's Island, New York Harbor. Released June 19, 1865, after taking the Oath of Allegiance. Second, there was Charles A. Troutman, born c.1839, wounded in the right arm at Fredericksburg on December 13, 1862. He was also captured at the battle of Hatcher's Run and confined at Hart's Island until he was released June 19, 1865. There was also John Troutman, born c.1834, enlisted August 1, 1862. He was killed at the battle of Ream's Station, Virginia about August 26, 1864.

The fourth was our subject, Daniel Absolum Troutman, who enlisted March 1, 1862 at the age of 25 years (actually 27 years old). He was wounded at Sharpsburg, Maryland about September 17, 1862, captured at Petersburg, Virginia, October 1, 1864, and confined at Point Lookout, Maryland until released May 14, 1865. Absolum and his brother Adam reportedly managed to bury their brother John, but after their captivity and release, were unable to find the tree under which they had buried him.

Daniel was described as having been a small man, weighing only about one hundred and thirty pounds. He was apparently wiry and strong, however. He rode horseback from Iredell County for about one hundred and forty miles over the mountains into Rich Valley, Virginia, where he met America and, after their marriage, took her back to North Carolina. She was not happy there, and they returned to Rich Valley, where their children were born. At a late point in her life, America went to Nebraska to visit with members of her family, and it is reported that she often sat in her rocker, smoking a clay pipe, and reading her Bible. The children included:

Daniel Absolum Troutman, America A. Pratt Troutman
Their son LeRoy Troutman & the Family Dog
c.1905

1. Estella, born February 3, 1870; died February 24, 1941 and
   buried at Graceland Park Cemetery, in Omaha, Nebraska.
   Married first to William Tell ("Tell") Worley and second to
   Marshall Hendrick. She and Worley moved from Virginia to
   Missouri where Clint and Mary Troutman lived, and later they
   all moved to Nebraska in early 1914. Estella was the mother
   of at least four children:
   a. Carl, married to Sarena, who was said to be one quarter
      American Indian. He was a barber, and they lived in Ne-
      braska and Oklahoma, where Serena died. He married a
      second time after her death. Their children were:
      (1) Verdena.
      (2) Wilburna.
      (3) Captola.
      (4) Carl, Jr.

b. Leona Ann, born June 3, 1903; married February 18, 1924 Charles Jefferson Brewer, born August 15, 1900, a son of James Milton Brewer and Effie May Robinson Brewer. They lived in Bellevue, Nebraska, where he was a carpenter, and had several children, including:
   (1) Howard Robert, born December 3, 1924; died December 10, 1925 at Omaha, Nebraska
   (2) Beverly June, born July 5, 1928; died May, 1979 at Dawson, Nebraska. Married May 14, 1961 to Loren DeWeese Noa.
   (3) Charles Dean, born June 23, 1935, and married October 22, 1966 Laurel Ann Elscher, born June 9, 1942. They lived at Gretna, Nebraska, and have two children:
      (a) Jason Dean, born November 30, 1968
      (b) Tricia Elaine, born June 19, 1971
c. Ethel, married James Craneck (or Kranek), and had twin daughters, one of whom died. The other was:
   (1) Maureen, married to Donald Danewood. They are makers of clocks in Quitman, Missouri. They have children, including:
      (a) Cindy
      (b) Roy
      (c) Dale
      (d) Donald
d. Dale, born c.1902; married to Verna. Moved to Oregon, where he had several children, including:
   (1) Naomi, who died young
   (2) Kenneth
2. Bessie J., born January 10, 1874; died March 12, 1881
3. John William, known as Bud, born December 23, 1874, of whom more
4. Clifton P., born June 22, 1876; died September 28, 1880
5. Mary E., born September 12, 1878; died September 8, 1880
6. Daniel; married Carrie Sexton.
7. James Henry, married Susie Olinger and died during 1969; both are buried at Marion, Virginia. They apparently had no children, but raised two as their own:

a. Frances, born to Edna Neal, who died young and is buried in Rich Valley, Virginia

b. Harold Clifton, born c.1916 to Virginia Totten Troutman, widow of John William Troutman, who was a brother of James Henry.

8. Walter Clinton, born December 16, 1887, of whom more

9. Lee Roy, born August 8, 1891; died October 13, 1919 from tuberculosis, single.

10. Daisy Virginia, married to William Tell ("Will") Worley, who was a nephew of William Tell ("Tell") Worley, who married her sister, Estella. Her husband was born January 20, 1884; died September 11, 1973. They were divorced and she left the children with her husband, moving to California, where she was married secondly to Les Fogleman. The five children, all but Lee Roy later lived in California (he remained in Saltville, Virginia) were:

a. Marvin Jackson, who had a daughter:
    (1) Marva Lee, married and had a daughter:
        (a) Barbara, married to Jay Dunlap

b. Thelma, married and had a daughter:
    (1) Dierdre

c. William Tell, Jr., married Eunice Machaido, and had one daughter:
    (1) Sharon, married Larry Friesen and had a son and one daughter, who was:
        (a) Stephanie

d. Harold Eugene, married Cloretta Johns; two daughters.

e. Lee Roy, married Katherine Louise Patrick; two sons:
    (1) Edward Lee, born October 9, 1937; married Carol and had three children:
        (a) Bryne Lee, born January 20, 1969
        (b) Mark Evan, born August 18, 1973
        (c) Steven Ashley, born September 3, 1974
    (2) James Clinton; married Judy and had two children:
        (a) William Patrick, born January 29, 1966
        (b) Pamela Jill, born December 22, 1972

Walter Clinton Troutman
1887-1949

This son of Daniel Absolum Troutman (1835) and America A. Pratt Troutman (1845), was born December 16, 1887 in Smyth County; died July 24, 1949, and was buried at Winside, Nebraska. Married October 27, 1909 to Mary Ann Waggoner, born in Smyth, and died March 24, 1964 at Winside, Nebraska. She was daughter of Elie Waggoner and Rachel Havens Waggoner. They lived for a time in Virginia, Missouri and Nebraska. Children:

1. Neville America, born August 22, 1910; married October 31, 1942 to William Maxwell Lamson, born March 18, 1906; died January 29, 1979 at Neligh, Nebraska, a son of William Aloysius Lamson and Emma Theresa Rogers Lamson. They had two sets of twins:
    a. William Maxwell, Jr., born June 28, 1943; married in 1966 to Michaela Wright
    b. Mary Virginia (Ginger), born June 28, 1943, and married in 1963 to Gary John Wilkins.
    c. Jack Alan, born May 27, 1949, and married in 1979 to Sharon Reeves.
    d. Jill Ann, born May 27, 1949; married in 1980 to Michael D. Gran.
2. James Gordon, born September 24, 1911; died July 25, 1977 at Winside, Nebraska. Married May 29, 1938 Ruth Ressiquie Schindler, born December 19, 1906; died July 5, 1971 at Winside, daughter of Albert August Schindler and Una Maybelle Ressequie Schindler. Two children:
    a. Connee Sue, born July 2, 1939; married June 26, 1960 Leon Glen Handke and divorced January 14, 1983. Married second Harold Dean Willis. There were four children born to the first marriage:
        (1) Lane Thomas, born August 31, 1961, and married June 15, 1985 Linda Susan Ford. Two children:
            (a) Philip Thomas, born February 20, 1987
            (b) Garret Paul, born May 13, 1989
        (2) SueAnn Kay, born July 31, 1964
        (3) Lee James, born April 17, 1970

(4)   Luke David, born June 27, 1977

b.   Ruth Ann, born September 17, 1941, and married August 12, 1962 to Larry Bruce Bartels, born May 10, 1939, a son of Roy and Florence Fix Bartels. They lived in Lincoln, Nebraska, and had three children:

(1)   Laura Ann, born April 13, 1965

(2)   Melissa Jo, born June 18, 1967

(3)   Michelle Marie, born May 23, 1969

3.   Carl Justin, born December 4, 1912; married Dorothy Martha Fleer, and lived at Winside, Nebraska. Seven children:

a.   Gary Eugene, born c.1933; married April 3, 1958 Betty, who died October 10, 1983 of lung cancer. They lived in Dysart, Iowa, and had three children:

(1)   Beth, born c.1959; married August 12, 1989 Ralph Johnson. She holds a doctorate from the University of Iowa (1988); he is a professor in the psychology department of the university.

(2)   Mark, born 1961; married June 9, 1984 to Genise Dostal. They lived in Rochester, Minnesota, and had one child:

(a)   Allison Marie, born September 25, 1988

(3)   Juli, born 1965; married June 3, 1989 Dave Norby and lived in West Des Moines, Iowa.

b.   Darrell Clinton, born January, 1935; married to Shirley Barner. He was a Naval Academy graduate, and a career naval officer, retiring in 1985. They had children:

(1)   Brent, born 1960, and married August 21, 1982 to Tamara Stillwell.

(2)   Brenda; married March, 1983 to James Bell.

(3)   Clint, died at about one year of age

(4)   Dara

c.   Judith Karen, born May 30, 1939. She was a nurse in the Peace Corps in Managua, Nicaragua.

d.   Dwight Dean, born September 12, 1945; married to Judy and lives in Omaha, Nebraska, where they had children:

(1)   Matthew Carl, a twin, born March 29, 1982

(2)   Michael John, a twin, born March 29, 1982

e.   Kirk Douglas, born 1948; a teacher in Ralston, Nebraska

f.   Lynne, married Robert Walker; he is a farmer and she is
     a teacher, lived at Winside, Nebraska. Children:
     (1)   Darren, born 1970
     (2)   Jennifer, born 1972
g.   Gregg, married to Carla; lived in Omaha, Nebraska, and
     had children:
     (1)   Jared, born 1979
     (2)   Kylie Ellen, born September 22, 1982
4. Verne Clinton, born April 13, 1914; married May 4, 1940 to
    Norma Lois McIntyre, born July 16, 1922 in Smyth County,
    Virginia, daughter of John Martin McIntyre and Fannie Mae
    Myers McIntyre. They lived in Virginia, Nebraska, Florida
    and Missouri. They had children:
    a.   Vance Gordon, born March 10, 1941; married September
         26, 1959 to Jane Elizabeth Land; divorced May 2, 1965.
         She was born January 14, 1940, daughter of John Land.
         He married second February 2, 1967 to Marie Annette
         Vezina, born October 9, 1946 in Quebec, daughter of
         Paul Eugene and Juliette Savard Vezina. Vance had one
         child from his first marriage; three from the second:
         (1)   Teresa Jane, born January 7, 1961, and married
               October 30, 1981 to K. Andrew McCall.
         (2)   David Clinton, born October 29, 1968
         (3)   Sonya Chantale, born June 19, 1972
         (4)   Linda Danielle, born February 21, 1983
    b.   Verna Lois, born August 14, 1943; married December
         29, 1959 Ronald James Bolz; divorced August 2, 1985.
         He was born January 23, 1943 in Stanton County, Ne-
         braska, son of Otto August Bolz and Helen Aimee Kinne
         Bolz. They had three children:
         (1)   Joseph Ronald, born March 27, 1960 at Daytona,
               Florida; married October 11, 1986 to Sheila Gaye
               Stiltner, born April 1, 1966, daughter of Sidney E.
               and Ocie Bentley Stiltner. They had one child:
               (a) Daniel Aaron, born April 8, 1987
         (2)   Jeffrey Scott, born September 3, 1961 at Norfolk,
               Nebraska.

      (3)   Bret Philip, born November 25, 1963 at Norfolk, Nebraska; married April 1, 1989 to Gina Marie Avino and lived in Omaha, Nebraska. She had a daughter, Autumn, born c.1984 from a previous marriage.

  c.   Zola Mary, my correspondent for this family, born May 9, 1946; married March 2, 1969 to Myron E. Noble. He was born October 30, 1946, son of Ethod E. and Winona Butler Noble. Lived at Anderson, Indiana; three children:

      (1)   Jay Samuel, born September 14, 1976 at Indianapolis, Indiana

      (2)   Sarah Michal, born october 16, 1978 at Marion, Virginia

      (3)   Lee Daniel, born August 10, 1982 at Anderson, Indiana

  d.   Regina Gwen, born November 5, 1947 in Wayne County, Nebraska; married November 9, 1969 to Joe Rodney Snowden, born March 11, 1947, son of Roscoe and Nellie Field Snowden. Divorced October, 1987, and had one daughter:

      (1)   Meghan Brooke, born December 19, 1977

5.   Virginia Ovella, born March 5, 1916 and married October 27, 1946 to Leo William Nielsen, born April 20, 1911, a son of Christian J. and Bertha Elizabeth Hansen Nielsen. They have two children:

  a.   Leo William, Jr., born September 8, 1947, and married Rogene Mary Siert, born December 7, 1946. He was a maritime lawyer in St. Louis, Missouri; two children:

      (1)   Kathryn Gene, born May 13, 1981

      (2)   Sarah Siert, born January 31, 1984

  b.   Stewart C., born September 6, 1952; married August 9, 1980 to Lori Brown, born June 24, 1956. He was given only the middle initial "C" as being representative of both his grandfathers: Clinton and Christian. He made documentary movies in California, and was divorced in October, 1989. Two children:

      (1)   Jessica Leigh, born November 30, 1981

      (2)   Clint James, born December 19, 1983

John William Troutman
1874-1910

This son of Daniel Absolum Troutman (1835) and America A. Pratt Troutman (1845), was born December 23, 1874 in Smyth County, Virginia, and died there December 20, 1910; buried at the Presbyterian Church Cemetery in Rich Valley. He was married to Virginia "Jenny" Totten, and they had six children. After his death, Jenny had a seventh child, who was raised by her brother-in-law, James Henry Troutman and his wife, Susie Olinger Troutman. The children were:

1. Hallie Mae; married to Albert Lehmkuhl and had children:
   a. Allan; married Betty
   b. Madeline R., born March 24, 1921; married June 7, 1944 to Albert Meyer, born November 11, 1915, son of Fred W. Meyer and Emma Douse Meyer. They lived at Randolph, Nebraska, and had children:
      (1) Roger L., born December 31, 1946; married April 27, 1984 to Roxanne Black, born October 22, 1953, and had a son:
         (a) Jordan Carl Albert, born January 30, 1989
      (2) David G., born January 19, 1950
2. Eula L., born April 16, 1900, died December 8, 1972. Married April 1, 1916 to Reese B. DeBord, born March 3, 1897, son of Andrew B. DeBord (1849) and Susan Marion Elizabeth Pratt DeBord (1857). They had children:
   a. Charles
   b. Mildred
   c. Kenneth, married Della and had children:
      (1) David, born October, 1946; married Linda Sherfey and divorced c.1988. Children:
         (a) Aaron David, born August, 1975
         (b) Ashley, born January, 1977
         (c) Amber Nicole, born March, 1980
      (2) Sharon; married and had one son:
         (a) Joshua
   d. Phyllis
3. Wilma, married Harry Kennerson and died in childbirth

4. Ernest, married Margaret; lived in Glade Spring, Virginia, and had children:
   a. Bernard
   b. Betty Jane
5. Hazel; married Louis Christoferson, and had children:
   a. Shirley; married Harold Rush
   b. Robert; married first Kathy, and second Lynn
6. Glenna V., born September 30, 1906; died April 21, 1915
7. Harold Clifton, born c.1916, probably in Missouri; married to Virginia, but had no children. Raised by his uncle, James Henry Troutman and his wife Susie Olinger Troutman. He was a barber for many years in Chilhowie, Virginia.

CHAPTER 9

Elizabeth C. Pratt
1813-1873

This daughter of Oliver Pratt (1784) and Mary Fulks Pratt, was born c.1813 in what was then Washington County, Virginia, to become Smyth County in 1832, and died May 15, 1873. She was married July 2, 1839 to Basil Talbert, born November 8, 1806; died September 10, 1882, son of Charles Talbert and Elizabeth McReynolds Talbert. In 1986, Dr. Joseph E. Williams of Emory and Henry College, and his wife, Eleanor Talbert Williams, who is a descendant of this family, prepared an unpublished manuscript entitled *Too Early To Be A Talbert*. The small booklet is a colorful narrative sketch of Elizabeth C. Pratt Talbert, her life, ancestors, and descendants.

They submit that, in about 1830, when Oliver Pratt either died or moved away from Smyth County, his daughter, Elizabeth C., was only about seventeen years old, and the oldest of the six unmarried children of the family. The Williams' suggest that perhaps Elizabeth moved into the household of the Andrew Shannon family, and earned her keep by helping with the work of the house. Andrew was a son of John Shannon and Ann Marshall Shannon. John was a son of Robert Shannon, who reportedly brought his family from Ireland in the late 1700s, and settled in Washington County, Virginia.

William Marshall, a brother of Ann Marshall Shannon, was married to Catherine Fulks, apparently a sister of Mary Fulks, mother of Elizabeth C. Pratt, so there was at least a distant family relationship. Whether or not Elizabeth actually lived with the Shannon family, it appears that in the five years between 1833 and 1838, she had three children. According to the Williams narrative and family folklore, there appears to be strong reason to believe that Andrew Shannon was the father of these children.

Dr. Williams reports that family stories recall that Andrew Shannon, a member of a prominent and well-to-do family of the period, offered Basil Talbert a dowery of forty acres of land for each of the three children, and Elizabeth, as well as a cow for each child, if he would marry her.

In any case, Elizabeth C. Pratt was married to Basil Talbert, and they raised the first three children, as well as the seven born to their marriage, living in White Rock Cove just north of McCready's Gap, in Smyth County, Virginia. Basil Talbert was said to be the grandson of another Basil, who migrated with his wife and five children from Maryland to the Saltville area around 1780, where he held a large land grant, owning many slaves and lots of livestock. Elizabeth has been described as being intelligent, small and delicate of build, but able to work long, hard hours, and dedicated to teaching her children what she considered to be right and wrong. She is buried in the Talbert family cemetery; Basil is buried in the McCready cemetery. She was reportedly the mother of as many as ten children, the first three listed apparently having been fathered by Andrew Shannon, but carrying the Talbert name. Eight of the children were:

1. Andrew J., born in December, 1833 at Rich Valley, in Smyth County, Virginia; died April 1, 1917 and buried on the family farm at Glenford, in Washington County, Virginia. Married December 23, 1858 to Martha Elizabeth Whitaker, who died September 25, 1922, daughter of James Whitaker and his second wife, Nancy McReynolds. An early ancestor of James Whitaker was Jabez Whitaker, who was reportedly a large land-owner on the eastern shore of Virginia, a member of the House of Burgesses, inventor of the split rail fence, and opened the first guest house for visitors to Jamestown. Andrew J. served in the Confederate forces for a time, and then hired James Mulhausen as his replacement. In his army records, Andrew is described as being six feet, two inches tall, fair complexioned, light hair and gray eyes. Mulhausen apparently did not finish the enlistment, and Andrew was held responsible. He reportedly took his family to Lawrence County, Ohio in 1863 to avoid service, where they remained until about 1873, when he returned to Virginia. He had five children:
   a. Robert Luther, born January 22, 1860 at Elkhorn Branch in Virginia; died September 8, 1928. Married December

15, 1887 to Dixie Bailey, who died during the birth of their only child, a stillbirth. On April 23, 1895, he was married to Letitia Virginia Foster, born 1865, a daughter of John George Foster and Cynthia Margaret Bourne Foster. She was a teacher, and evidently taught in both Wythe and Washington Counties. She died of tuberculosis August 14, 1922 at Catawba Sanitarium. She and her husband are buried in Maiden Cemetery. Two children:

(1) Marcus Aurelius, born December 2, 1900 and died June 30, 1960, just one month after his youngest child graduated from Emory and Henry College. He was married to Mary Elizabeth Thompson, and had six children, one of whom was:

(a) Eleanor, who married Dr. Joseph E. Williams

(2) Cynthia Elizabeth, born c.1902. Married to Hope Shewbridge and moved to Richmond, where she died suddenly in 1955. No children.

b. James, born 1862 on Elkhorn Branch, and died c.1892. Married a Texas girl from whom he was divorced after one son, who was raised by his paternal grandparents:

(1) Frank Lee, born c.1885; served in the first world war in the Navy. Married an Irish girl, Ebba Kelly, and died at about thirty years old, leaving two children:

(a) Harry

(b) A daughter

c. Harry, born c.1865 in Ohio; married c.1895 Laura Ayers and had four sons and three daughters. They lived at Glenford until their children reached high school age, when they removed to Bristol, Tennessee. Children were:

(1) Pierce, who was not a strong child, and spent his early years driving his father's horse and buggy. He attended Emory and Henry, and worked as a pharmacist

(2) Grace, attended business college, married, and had a daughter, who was a nurse

(3) Zoe, died rather early

> (4) Mable, in 1987 a nurse in Kansas. Her husband was warden at Leavenworth prison
>
> (5) Joe, died at age 22 of appendicitis
>
> (6) Harry, Jr.; married and moved to Jacksonville, Florida, where he taught school, and became a full-time radio sports announcer
>
> (7) A son

d. Margaret, born 1870 in Ohio; married Whitley Hayter and lived near Meadowview. He was killed by a train during a blizzard, while walking home. Two children:

> (1) Harry, a doctor, who practiced in Abingdon, where he was well-respected and influential in establishing recognition for the local hospital.
>
> (2) Myrtle, who apparently never married

e. John, died at about the age of two years

2. Elizabeth, born c.1836

3. Mary Ann, born 1838; married first January 3, 1859 George Collins, and second on January 10, 1866 to Alex Homes.

4. Oliver, born c.1840; killed in action at battle of Cold Harbor near Richmond, serving in Confederate forces

5. Nancy C., born c.1842, and married January 10, 1866 to John Hogston.

6. James, born c.1845; also killed at Cold Harbor

7. Thomas Thompson, born c.1848; married 1866 to Emma Catherine, and was the grandfather of Isaac Henry (Tony) Talbert and Walter Talbert, the brothers who married two of the daughters of Charles Edward Pratt (1873), a son of Isaac Thompson Pratt (1827), who was a brother of the mother of Thomas Thompson Talbert, our subject here. Thomas and his wife moved into Washington County, into the Holmes cabin in River Hills on Bear Wallow Branch. His parents lived with him until his mother's death. About 1877, they all moved back to White Rock Cove, where his father, Basil, died. The home of Tony Talbert stood on this farm.

8. Findlay, about whom nothing is known

CHAPTER 10

William Henry Pratt
1815-1902

This son of Oliver Pratt (1784) and Mary Fulks Pratt, was born about 1815, according to census records, in what was then a part of Washington County, Virginia, in 1832 to become Smyth County. In the census of 1850, he appears in the household of his brother, Nicholas H. Pratt, stating that he is employed as a boat-builder. The reader is referred to *Smyth County History and Traditions*, by Goodridge Wilson for some fascinating reading relative to the origins of Chatham Hill in Smyth County, and the commerce of the region. Much of that information was discussed in the introduction to this study.

William Henry left Smyth County some time after 1850 and settled on Gilmore Creek, in Wolfe County, Kentucky. It is said that two of his brothers; Henry Pratt (1820) and Oliver Pratt, Jr.; went with him, and both of them were said to have drowned while crossing the Kentucky River in flood. As discussed earlier, that does not quite fit other information. It appears that he was actually married twice, first to Rachel Stamper, perhaps before he left Smyth County, by whom he had seven children. He was married second to Cindy, and they had one daughter.

1. James Charles, born June 18, 1853; died February 28, 1901. His wife was a Graham, born November 18, 1859, and died January 17, 1884. Both are buried in the Graham cemetery on Gilmore Creek, close to Hazelgreen. He apparently married again after the death of his wife, and his second wife either had been married before, with a son; or married again after his death, and had a son. Three children born to the first marriage:
   a. Kelly, born March 15, 1878; died January 17, 1884
   b. Molly; married Bailey and died September, 1920
   c. Clarence, born 1882, of whom more

William Henry Pratt
1815-1902

2. Oliver Marion, born January 12, 1862 at Gilmore, Wolfe County, Kentucky. He was married twice and had fifteen children, the first two being from his first marriage to Louellen Little, and the remaining thirteen from the second marriage to Fanny Osborne. The children, apparently all born at Gilmore Creek, Wolfe County, Kentucky, were:
    a. Elizabeth
    b. Dora
    c. Grace, born May 19, 1887; died 1952.
    d. Marion Kelly, born April 7, 1888; died January 6, 1893
    e. Sarah Maude, born November 22, 1889
    f. Carl Day, born December 9, 1891
    g. Nora Esther, born November 6, 1893
    h. Ura Bayne, born August 12, 1895
    i. Cora Adeline, born July 12, 1897
    j. Pearl, born May 24, 1899
    k. Rausie, or Rose, born April 1, 1901
    l. William Henry, born April 25, 1903
    m. Wardie H., an infant death, March 4, 1905
    n. Wilson, an infant death, October 3, 1906
    o. Clifton Jackson, born November 8, 1907
3. Elizabeth, born in Gilmore, Kentucky; first married Henry Banks, and had four children. He was killed while log rolling, and she married Ike Bach; then Jerry Brewer, and finally Bill Spencer. She died March 15, 1930. Her four children were:
    a. Asbury; married and had a number of children, including:
        (1) Leona
        (2) Walker
        (3) Verlin
        (4) Orville
        (5) Orbin
        (6) Montgomery
        (7) Lumy
        (8) Lenis
        (9) Clifford
        (10) Linda
        (11) Gladys
    b. Leck, who also had a large family, including:

          (1)   Calvin
          (2)   Ollie Profitt
          (3)   Cleary Mullins
          (4)   Pecola Trent
          (5)   Roy
          (6)   Asbury
    c.   John, married his cousin, Frances Puckett; children:
          (1)   Cora
          (2)   Anna; married York
    d.   Floyd
4.   Mary; married John Bush
5.   Savannah, about whom nothing is known
6.   Adeline; married Green Puckett, and had two children:
    a.   Green, Jr.
    b.   Frances, married her first cousin, John Banks; see above
7.   Margaret; married Logan Bach, and had children, including:
    a.   Courtney
    b.   Harlan; married and had at least thirteen children

Clarence Pratt
1882-1972

This son of James Charles Pratt (1853) was born 1882 in Gilmore County, Kentucky, and died 1972. Married May 8, 1903 to Mahalia Rose at Compton, in Wolfe County, Kentucky. She was a daughter of Clay Rose of Lee City, and died April 18, 1953 in Cleveland, Texas. Clay Rose was a son of Robert Rose, who was born c.1818 in Pennsylvania, and moved with his parents to Owsley County, Kentucky about 1820. Robert Rose moved to Morgan County about 1836, where he married Henrietta McQuinn, daughter of Alex McQuinn.

In 1969, Robert Wayne Pratt (1938), a grandson of Clarence Pratt, prepared a series of notes from his grandfather's recollections, which provide an interesting insight into the life of Clarence, and the times during which he lived. Some of those notes are reported here for interest and color, just as they were written, in the first person, as though Clarence were speaking:

Clarence Pratt (1882) and Robert Wayne Pratt (1938)
c.1970

I helped my daddy build a house that still stands in Kentucky. My father willed me a team of mules and the Lee City property, but gave it to my stepmother for as long as she desired. She had another boy by another man, and gave the property to him. He sold his interest to Uncle Ol. I got a mare and a saddle for my interest. Your grandmother and I were married in 1903. She was 17 and I was 21. We were married in Compton and moved to Lee City. We had a little trouble getting married because her old man was Clay Rose, a known drinker. The J. P. sent a note to Clay, since he knew him also and the note got sent back, OK.

Clarence and his brother-in-law, Bruce Lewis, who married Honey Rose, went into the grist mill business until Bruce was killed in a fight. Then, Clarence went into the lumber business hauling timber with his mules from the mouth of Quicksand Fork of the river. His leg was nearly cut off under a rail car, but *"we prayed and the doctor sewed, and it got better!"* After that, he started hauling, and made about $9,600 and apparently bought a store in Lee City. At that point, he was rather well-to-do, with eight or ten mules working, a store and a sawmill, which he bought with Henry Chancy and Clay Lawson. After his partners appeared to have messed up on a contract, he moved the sawmill to Whitesburg close to the head of the river. He reported that there were long lines for soup in Huntington, West Virginia during the panic of 1907, which did not appear to affect him. He had owned two farms and sold out for ten thousand dollars, and in 1922, bought a big farm in Kentucky, putting down twenty thousand in cash, but lost it all during the great depression.

Clarence moved to West Texas some time after 1922, where he sold goods to the oilfield workers, and operated a fleet of dump trucks for the CCC outfits in East Texas. Finally, he had a store in Cleveland, Liberty and Arp, Texas. His son, Clifford, had the store at Livingston, Texas for years, but apparently failed in the operation. Clarence and Mahala Rose had five children:

1. Clifford, born February 19, 1905; died July 4, 1978
2. Charles Elwood
3. Thomas, a Baptist minister
4. Pearl, married to Autery
5. Clarence, Jr., born March 23, 1918 at Lothair, Kentucky, and killed in action during the second world war, while serving as a bomber pilot over Italy, November 30, 1944. Married May 10, 1937 to Marian Horton at Jacksonville, Texas. One son:
   a. Robert Wayne, my correspondent, born October 13, 1938 at Galveston, Texas. He taught auto-mechanics at the Aldine High School in Houston, holding a masters degree in Vocational Administration. Married three times: first April 6, 1957 at Jacksboro, Texas, Willie Rose Whitsett; second August 28, 1967 Gayle Louise Coe at Marathon, Texas; and third October 7, 1977 at Houston to Kathleen

Jones. Two sons from the first marriage; and one from the second:

(1) Robert Wayne, Jr., born January 14, 1958 at Jacksboro, Texas; married April 4, 1987 at Brazoria, Texas, Margaret Pasztor, born August 20, 1957. One child:

(a) Taylor Nicole, born February 21, 1989 at Lake Jackson, Texas.

(2) William Gary, born May 27, 1960 Odessa, Texas. Married first October 8, 1977 at Wellborn to Nancy Redmon, by whom one child was born. He was married second January 23, 1988 to Elizabeth Marshall Millican, Texas, born July 8, 1967, and had a son. The children were:

(a) Teri LaNell, born November 25, 1978 at Bryan, Texas.

(b) Weston Lee, born 1994

(3) Coe DeWayne, born August 16, 1972

Clarence Pratt, Jr.
1918

Clarence Pratt
1882

CHAPTER 11

Madison Pratt
1816-1893

This son of Oliver Pratt (1784) and his wife, Mary Fulks Pratt was born in old Washington County, Virginia, July 1, 1816, in an area that was to become part of Smyth County when it was formed in 1832. Madison died January 6, 1893 and is buried in the old Newburn Cemetery, located on the west side of Virginia Route 682, between the towns of Newbern and Dublin, in Pulaski County, Virginia. Married January 16, 1840 in Montgomery County, Virginia, to Elizabeth Fisher (Book A, pages 269 & 400), daughter of Adam Fisher. All of the later records relative to Madison and his descendants are found in Pulaski County, which was formed from Montgomery in 1839, just prior to his marriage, but before the records were kept in the new county. The family is shown in the census of 1850, 1860, 1870 and 1880 for the county, and are tabulated as follows (with the addition of a known middle initial or name by the author):

Individual	1850	1860	1870	1880	Birth
Madison	34	43	54	62	1816
Elizabeth	30	40	50	60	1820
James A.	8	18	-	-	1841
George T.	7	17	-	-	1843
Mary Susan	6	15	-	-	1844
Joseph	5	13	-	-	1845
Harriett E.	4	12	-	-	1848
William	1	10	-	-	1850
John F.	-	8	19	-	1851

As can be seen from the above, the census reports, taken in ten year intervals, frequently do not reflect ten year aging for each individual. In the 1870 census report, daughter Harriett E. was still in her father's household, with her husband, Joseph D. Chumbley, and their infant daughter, Elizabeth.

Also in the household in 1870 were three persons, apparently not family members: Gilford Dudley born c.1842; Harriett Dudley, born c.1855; and Gordon Howell, born c.1860. In the 1880 census, there was one William Walker at the age of nine (born c.1871), living with Madison and Elizabeth. As we have reported elsewhere, it was not at all uncommon in these early years to find non-family members living in the household; the researcher should keep that in mind during the early census years when only the head of household was listed by name.

Births and Deaths, 1853-1871, by Clarita H. Morgan, lists a son, Robert G. Pratt, born April 26, 1853. In several records found, Madison is listed as a blacksmith. On June 4, 1866, he bought 84 acres of land, for two hundred dollars (Deed Book 3, page 651). On January 31, 1885, for twelve hundred dollars, he bought the interest of Joseph D. and Harriett E. Chumbley (his daughter and son-in-law) in a tract of 71 and 1/4 acres, whereon Madison then lived. He also bought, in Deed Book 3, page 660, dated September 10, 1866, *"one still, 14 tubs, seven hogs, 200 bushels corn in the field, one growing crop buckwheat."*

His Bond is reported in Deed Book 3, page 179; Deed Book 3, page 301, and Deed Book 3, page 553, in the amount of $5,000, assuring his service as Constable of the County of Pulaski, to which he was elected for successive two-year terms, effective on July 1, 1858, 1860 and 1862.

In Deed Book 5, page 47, dated March 4, 1870, Madison filed for homestead exemption, and the list of his personal property reported there is listed following as a matter of some interest to the reader. Compare Madison's personal belongings, and its value to that of your own in today's world.

Valuable

LAND

FOR SALE!

Pursuant to a decree of the Circuit Court of Pulaski county, entered at the November term, 1895, thereof in the chancery cause of Wall's executor against M. Pratt's heirs and others, I will, as Special Commissioner in said cause, on

Monday, May 4, 1896,

on the premises, proceed to sell at public auction to the highest bidder all that certain tract of land lying on the south side of the Macadam road in "'Possum Hollow,'"Pulaski county, Va., containing in the aggregate 72 acres more or less being the same tract of land conveyed to M. Pratt by J. D. Chumbley and wife by deed of record in the clerk's office of the County Court of Pulaski county in Deed Book No. 10, page 371, subject to the dower of Elizabeth Pratt in sixteen acres of said land upon which the house formerly owned by M. Pratt is located, assigned to her as her dower. The purchaser will get the reversion in this sixteen acres, that is he will get the sixteen acres subject to the life estate of Mrs. Pratt therein.

This is a fair quality of upland and has some good timber upon it. It is located on the Macadam road, a great thoroughfare of the county and state, and lies about three and a half miles distant from the town of Pulaski, the county seat of Pulaski county, and about three and a half miles southwest of Newbern, Va., and about one-half mile distant from Macadam Flag Station on the Cripple Creek Extension of the N. & W. R. R., near which point a school is located. Persons desiring to buy a desirable farm will do well to examine this property.

TERMS OF SALE.

Costs of suit and sale cash in hand; the residue upon a credit of one, two and three years, the purchaser giving interest bearing bonds with good security for the deferred payments.

J. C. WYSOR, Special Commissioner.

March 11, 1896.

I, J. N. Bosang, Clerk of the Circuit Court of Pulaski County, certify that the bond required of Special Commissioner J. C. Wysor by the decree rendered in said cause at the November term, 1895, of said court has been duly given.   J. N. BOSANG, Clerk.

March 11, 1896.

Item	Value
lease of 150 acres for one year	$ 100
lease of 40 acres for one year	80
3 horses	425
4 cows	100
2 yearlings	35
18 sheep and 6 lambs	48
8 hogs and 8 pigs	32
1 old waggon	25
1 new waggon	140
1 jersey waggon and harness	75
2 big plows, old	5
2 double bull tongues	4
2 single bull tongues	2
2 double trees	4
2 single trees	1
2 harrows	8
500 pounds bacon	85
200 bushels corn	170
4 bushels buckwheat	2
1 stack hay	10
25 dozen (?) oats	7
household furniture	150
2 saddles	22
2 guns	5
2 watches	40

In Will Book 4, page 390, dated February 11, 1893, there is a report of the appraisers of the estate of Madison Pratt, listing his personal property, with values, totalling one hundred, forty-nine dollars and ninety-five cents in value.

In Will Book 4, page 427, dated February 18, 1893, can be found a listing of the Sale Bill of personal property of Madison Pratt, made by J. A. Pratt, his Administrator (probably his eldest son, James A. Pratt). It is rather lengthy, and lists the name of each item sold, the amount, and the purchaser. It will not be repeated here, but should be of interest to anyone interested in the way our ancestors lived, and the tools and equipment needed to conduct a small farming operation. The total of the sale amounted to one hundred, fifty-three dollars and seventy cents, close to the appraised value stated above.

After the death of Madison, a claim was filed on December 7, 1894 against the estate. Papers relative to the claim can be found in a box labelled *Closed Cases 1900* in the Courthouse at Pulaski. The papers show that the property consisted of the 71 and 1/4 acres tract on Macadam Road. Various family members are mentioned, and the widow's dower was to be cut out. The remainder of the lands, located in Possum Hollow in Pulaski County were sold at public sale on Monday, May 4, 1896, for the sum of $1,350. It was of some interest to the author to notice in the files that the fee for surveying was $4.50, since I am a Professional Land Surveyor. It has been a little over thirty years since I dissolved my partnership in the business, and at that time, our fee would have been in the one thousand dollar range for the boundary survey. Modern engineers, with all their fancy equipment, would charge several thousand dollars for the same service.

From the various records noted, and from family recollections, Madison Pratt had at least eight children:
1. James A., born June 25, 1841, of whom more
2. George Thomas, born January 5, 1843, of whom more
3. Mary Susan, born c.1844; married at Pulaski on January 27, 1865 to Thomas J. Hall, born c.1844, son of R. and J. A. Hall. He was born in Montgomery County; the marriage is reported in Marriage Register 1, page 5, line 2.
4. Joseph, born c.1845, perhaps deceased before 1880. Married Nellie, probably a daughter of Brooks Archibald. The census of 1880 for the county carries the Archibald family, and those in the household include Nellie Pratt, listed as a daughter at age 26, with three children listed as grandchildren, one of them being Laura, born c.1878. It would appear that Joseph died prior to the census, leaving a wife and three minor children, who then lived for a time with her father. In that the fourth listed child was born some time in 1880, Nellie Archibald Pratt must have been expecting the child at the time of her husband Joseph's death. The four children were:

a. Arthur, born c.1871
b. Laura, born c.1874, named in the Chancery case relative to the estate of her grandfather, Madison Pratt.
c. Mamie, born c.1878
d. Edith E., born c.1880; married at age 16 on March 11, 1896 to Clyde Hall, aged 20 (born c.1876). Marriage Register 1, page 64, line 21, reports their marriage, and states that he was born in West Virginia, son of T. (middle initial indistinct) Hall and his wife Susan Hall. It should be noted that Mary Susan Pratt was married to Thomas J. Hall. It is possible that Clyde Hall was their son, and that he and Edith E. Pratt were first cousins.

5. Harriett E., born c.1848; married Joseph D. Chumbley, born c.1850, and had at least one child:
a. Elizabeth, born c.1869

6. William, born c.1850

7. John F., born c.1851, and married twice. Marriage Book 1, at page 40, reports his married November 18, 1874 at age 23 to Cynthia A. F. Hall at age 20, daughter of T. B. and Catherine Hall. In Book 1, page 55, John F. Pratt, age 27, widower, is reported married February 23, 1879 to Jennie L. Dobbins, age 22, a widow. Her parents are listed as James and Nancy Garnand. See also Marriage Book A, pages 269 and 400. John F. had at least two daughters, both born to his first marriage:
a. Bettie, born c.1875; married at age 21, October 7, 1896 to William David Lowman, age 31 (born c.1865), son of David and Catherine Lowman. See also Marriage Book 1, page 65. At least four daughters:
   (1) Lillian, married Flora; lived in Roanoke c.1987
   (2) Lena, married P. R. Bates; lived in Bluefield, West Virginia c.1987
   (3) Ruby, single, lived in Johnson City, Tennessee in 1987
   (4) Blanche L., born July 23, 1897 at Pulaski and died March 13, 1987 in Greeneville, Tennessee, and buried at Highland Memory Gardens in Dublin, Virginia. She taught school for many years at Jefferson Elementary School in Pulaski, Virginia.

Married to Robert W. Brown, with two sons from his first marriage: Robert W., Jr., and Frank W. At least two daughters were born to Blanche:

 (a) Elizabeth McCormick; married Smith, and in 1987 lived in Greeneville, Tennessee.

 (b) Edith; married P. W. Dwyer. In 1987, lived at Jacksonville Beach, Florida

 b. Maggie, born c.1883; married at age 24, February 27, 1907 to Oscar S. Hall, age 24 (born c.1883). His parents were George and Emma Hall.

8. Robert G., born April 26, 1853 in Pulaski County, Virginia; died from inflammation of the brain, April 17, 1859

James A. Pratt
1841-1911

This son of Madison Pratt (1816) was born June 25, 1841 in Pulaski County, Virginia. He died June 20, 1911 and is buried in the Allison cemetery high on a hill near the intersection of Interstate highway 81, and State Route 100, south. He was married twice: first, on May 29, 1865 to Margaret J. Chumbley, born c.1841; second on July 6, 1870 to Sarah J. Sloan Sayers. She was born May 4, 1835; died February 28, 1915, and is buried beside her husband. She was a widow at the time of their marriage, having two daughters from that union: Mary W., born 1863; and Joanna D., born 1861. James is listed in the census reports of 1870, 1880 and 1900 for Pulaski County. As the records show, he was a man of considerable means, with servants. In the 1870 report, his real estate is valued at $12,510 and his personal property at $4,130.

James A. Pratt served in the Army of the Confederacy during the War Between The States. He was enlisted by Captain William J. Jordan at Newbern, Virginia, September 9, 1861. He entered Co. F, 54th Regt, Virginia Infantry as 3rd Sergeant. On May 13, 1862, at camp near Dalton, Georgia, he was elected 2nd Lieutenant of Co. F, 54th Regt, Virginia Infantry, Reynold's Brigade, Stevenson's Division, Hood's Corp, Army of Tennessee. Some time prior to February 28, 1865, he was elected 1st Lieutenant, and served in that capacity for the duration of the war.

Lieutenant James A. Pratt
1841-1911
Army of the Confederacy

The Muster Roll of April 16, 1864 reports that he was at home on 24 days leave of absence by order of General Johnson. It is an interesting coincidence that, on May 31, 1864, little over a month later, my great grandfather, James F. Hurley, wrote a letter to his wife (the last we are aware of prior to his being killed in action before Jonesboro, Georgia in October, 1864) from the same camp in Dalton, Georgia, while serving the Confederacy.

James A. Pratt was apparently not wounded, and was perhaps paroled with his company at the end of hostilities. In the Archives at Washington, we found a Requisition for Clothing and Camp Equipage, by James A. Pratt, Lieutenant, Commanding. It requests issuance of three jackets, twenty-four pairs of pants, two woolen shirts, ten cotton shirts, 1 blanket, twenty-six pairs of shoes, fourteen pairs of trousers, one camp kettle, thirty-nine tin cups, and six mess pans. In the home of his granddaughter, Jean Pratt (1910), I found the photo of James A. Pratt in his Confederate uniform.

Census records for the James A. Pratt household indicate the size of his family:

Individual	1870	1880	1900	Birth
James A. Pratt	29	38	58	1841
Sarah J. Pratt	35	45	65	1835
Joanna D. Sayers, stepdau	9	19	-	1861
Mary W. Sayers, stepdau	7	17	-	1863
Minnie J. Pratt	-	8	-	1872
James H. Pratt	-	6	-	1874
Edward T. Pratt	-	4	-	1876
Charles Sayers Pratt	-	3	23	1877
Price G. Pratt	-	1	21	1878
Susan C. Calfee, house help	21	-	-	1849
Richmond Montgomery, black labor	12	-	-	1858
Rachel Jonston, mulatto	30	-	-	1840
Sarah, mulatto	9	-	-	1861
Rose, mulatto	5	-	-	1865
John, mulatto	3	-	-	1867
Alexander, mulatto	1	-	-	1869
2 servants under age of 10	-	X	-	-
3 servants, no age stated	-	-	X	-

James A. Pratt prepared his will on May 18, 1907, found in Will Book 6, page 268, Pulaski County, Virginia. It provides that all his property is to go to his wife for her natural life, and upon her death, it is to be equally divided between their filve children, listing each of the children, and where they were residing at the time. James A. Pratt had two children born to his first marriage, and five to the second:

1. Robert M., born October 20, 1866; apparently died young
2. A still-birth girl, March 1, 1869
3. Minnie J., born c.1872; married September 4, 1888 to Charles C. Allison at Pulaski, Virginia (Marriage Register 1, page 44, line 73), son of Hiram and Sarah Allison. Two children:
   a. Walter W., born c.1901, and in 1987 owned the farm on which the family cemetery is located
   b. Sarah Jane, born c.1892; married a man named Early, and in 1986 lived in Galax, Virginia at about age 94
4. James H., born c.1874; married October 7, 1896 at Pulaski to Virginia Gannaway, born c.1871 in Wythe County, Virginia, a daughter of T. M. and M. A. Gannaway. The census of 1900 for Pulaski carries the family, including two servants. They had at least one daughter and a son:
   a. Annie V., born October, 1897; married Harry H. Price.
   b. Thomas G.; deceased by 1986
5. Edward T., born c.1876. His will is found in Book 16, at page 549, dated August 3, 1944, in Pulaski County, Virginia, listing his wife and a son. Married to Daisy B., born c.1875 and had one son:
   a. Brooks, born c.1903; in 1944 lived at Galax, Virginia
6. Charles Sayers, born February, 1877. Married November 4, 1903 at Drapers Valley, Pulaski County, Virginia, to Ruby Honaker, born c.1877, daughter of S. P. Honaker, and Susan J. Honaker. See Marriage Register 1, page 86, line 86. His will is found in Will Book 14, page 562, dated March 15, 1939 and probated June 7, 1939. Papers filed with it provide names, addresses and ages of each of his heirs. Children were:
   a. Agnes, born c.1904; married to Felts.

b.   Stuart Sayers, born c.1907; married August 25, 1931 to Jane Castell of Abingdon. They lived on a farm in Draper Valley and had at least one son:

(1)   Donald Stuart

c.   Jean, born c.1901, single; owned and operated the family farm of about 289 acres, raising sheep and beef cattle, and lived in the original home built by her father.

d.   Sam H., born c.1912; married March 28, 1932 to Ruth C. Sloan, born c.1909, daughter of D. C. and Lillian A. Cassell Sloan. See Marriage Register 1, page 192, line 31. Will Book 16, page 153, dated December 3, 1942, has a report of Virginia S. Sloan, Administratrix of the estate of Ruth Sloan Pratt, deceased, in which she was also named guardian of the children of Sam and his wife, Ruth. She is probably a sister of Ruth. The children were:

(1)   David, born c.1934

(2)   Jane Calvin, born c.1935

7.   Price Gilmer, born August 9, 1878, and died July 2, 1960. He was married October 17, 1906 at Drapers Valley to Sarah Margaret Wood, daughter of W. J. and M. E. Wood (Marriage Register 1, page 98, line 113). She was born November 14, 1883 and died February 13, 1966. His family is reported in *Southwest Virginia Families*, by David B. Trimble. His wife's parents are there identified as being William James Wood (1841-1902) and Mary Ellen Allison Wood (1853-1922). At least the following children were born to the marriage:

a.   Charles G., married Callie.

b.   James A.

c.   Richard B.

d.   Lewis T. died July 31, 1964, married Elizabeth Whitman.

e.   Price Gilmer, Jr.

f.   Sarah Ellen, born c.1908, married April 2, 1930 Marvin M. Gardner at Pulaski, Virginia, born c.1905 in Carroll County, Virginia, son of D. M. and Cora Hurst Gardner. They had children, including, at least:

(1)   Denny Pratt

(2)   Mack

g.	Margaret, born c.1913; married September 25, 1933 to George Bentley Simmerman at Pulaski, Virginia, born c.1904 in Wythe County, son of Thomas Edward and Mamie Elizabeth Hansom Simmerman. Children:
	(1)	George Bentley, Jr.
	(2)	Betty Pratt
h.	Mary Sue; married Harold W. Baker and had children:
	(1)	Harriet.
	(2)	Harold W., Jr.
	(3)	Jeffery
i.	Louise; married Marvin King.

George Thomas Pratt
1843-1913

This son of Madison Pratt (1816) was born January 5, 1843 in Pulaski County, Virginia and died July 16, 1913. Marriage Register 1, page 9, line 33, reports his marriage December 24, 1868 to Esther M. (properly Mary Easter) Sayers, born November 2, 1841; died November 4, 1911, daughter of John Thompson Sayers and Rachel Grayson Sayers. He is first found in the 1870 census in the household of his mother-in-law, Rachel Sayers, then a widow. At that time, Rachel Sayers was listed at age 46, born c.1824; George T. is shown at age 28, with his wife, Mary E. at age 27, and their first-born son, John S., at one year. The household included other children of the Sayers family: Joanna, age 24; Susan J., age 22; Annie E., age 17; Fannie P., age 16; Helen H., age 14; and Maggie, age 9. In the census of 1880, George T. appears as head of household, with his wife and four children.

George T. Pratt served in the Confederate Army during the War Between The States, with some distinction. He enlisted March 14, 1862, at Newbern, Virginia, under Captain Gardner. He was enrolled as private, Co. C, 4th Regt, Virginia Infantry, and appears on the company muster rolls from that time through late 1864. He was wounded in the left leg at the battle of Fredericksburg, December 13, 1862, but by the report of February 28, 1863, had returned to duty. On July 3, 1863, he was severely wounded at the battle of Gettysburg, while serving in the Stonewall Brigade under Brigadier General James A. Walker.

George had been at Chamborazo Hospital in Richmond, and on July 22, 1863 was transferred to White Sulphur Springs, suffering from disease, *vul solopet*. In a report dated January 9, 1864, signed by J. William Walls, Surgeon, his wound is described as follows: *"...the ball entering wrist of left hand, traversing the palm and severely injuring and requiring amputation of middle and ring fingers, the little finger of said hand is useless on account of rigid contraction of its flexor muscles; he is unfit for active duty. I respectfully recommend him for light duty."*

On September 23, 1864, George wrote a letter to General S. Cooper, Adjutant & Inspector General: *"I was wounded at Gettysburg, Penn & as appears by the accompanying certificate of a Med Board am unfit for duty as a soldier in the field. I joined the Reserves of Pulaski Co., Va. and was, on the 13th day of August, 1864, elected 1st Lieutenant of the Pulaski Reserves, as appears by the accompanying Certificate of Maj. J. B. Dorman, Commanding Rendevouz of Reserves at Dublin, Virginia, and therefore respectfully ask to be discharged from the army as a private in Co. C, 4th Va Inf Regt."*

The record contains the certificates as noted by George, one of them from Commanding Colonel stating that: *"...he is a young man of decided gallantry and with a little experience would no doubt make an officer of respectability."* George was discharged on February 1, 1865, and served thereafter as a Lieutenant in the Pulaski Reserves. His discharge states that he was five feet, ten inches tall, fair complexion, blue eyes, light hair, born in Newbern, Virginia, 22 years of age, and a blacksmith.

The children of George T. Pratt and Mary Easter Sayers Pratt included:
1. John L. S., born October 17, 1869, and died July 19, 1892; married July 5, 1890 to Belle A. Smyth. Against his father's wishes, John found employment in the zinc mine on New River, where he was later killed. He had a daughter:
   a. Pearl M., born August 1, 1891; died February, 1894

2. Robert Madison, born April 23, 1871; died c.1941. Married December 26, 1900 to Nora Belle McAuley, born October 18, 1873; died April, 1943, and had a son:
   a. Charles Sayers, born September 11, 1907, of whom more
3. Walter Cable, born January 11, 1874, of whom more
4. Gertrude Bertha, born March 24, 1876, of whom more

Charles Sayers Pratt
1907-1980

This son of Robert Madison Pratt (1871) was born September 11, 1907 at Bristol, Virginia, and died there September 3, 1980. Married March 5, 1930 at Abingdon, Virginia, to Lucille Willie Smith, born August 20, 1909 in Sullivan County, Tennessee; died January 8, 1988 at Bristol, Tennessee. Some of my readers may not be aware that Bristol is a city that straddles the line between Tennessee and Virginia, partially in each. Three children, born at Bristol, Virginia:

1. Charles Sayers, Jr., born October 3, 1938; died September 7, 1967 in Washington County, Virginia. Married to Iva Alma Booth, born there, and had two children:
   a. Martha Lucille, born July 30, 1961; married to Dave Kolstedt and had two children:
      (1) William
      (2) Robert
   b. Charles Sayers, III, born February 9, 1967; married Lisa and had a son. Married second Teresa Shaffer. His son:
      (1) Charles Sayers, IV.
2. Robert Bascom, born February 7, 1940; married August 19, 1961 at Bristol, Virginia, to Elizabeth Sue Smith, born February 27, 1943 at Cripple Creek, Virginia, and had children, born at Bristol, Virginia:
   a. Genoa Ruth, born February 8, 1963; married April 23, 1988 at Kingston, Tennessee to Edward Atwood, born January 1, 1960.
   b. Lenora Rhea, born August 12, 1964; married September 24, 1988 at Kingsport, Tennessee, Bruce Rutledge, born April 20, 1958, and had children, born there:

      (1)   Morgan Leah, born June 13, 1990

      (2)   Jamie Caroline, born July 15, 1993

3.   Rebecca Isabella, born October 2, 1943; married July 7, 1962 at Bristol, Virginia, to Bruce Washington Hodgson, Jr., born February 20, 1942 at Anawalt, West Virginia. Children, born at Bristol:

   a.   Lisa Darlene, born March 11, 1964; married November 15, 1986 at Bristol to Mark Scott Cofer, born December 4, 1963.

   b.   Anthony Dewayne, born March 18, 1966, and married December 21, 1991 at Gelena, Alaska to Laura Beth Dailey, and had children:

      (1)   Andrew James, born June 21, 1994 at Shaw AFB, South Carolina

      (2)   Michael Bruce, born September 9, 1995 at Sumter, South Carolina.

   c.   Janice Dawn, born August 16, 1968; married August 15, 1993 at Bristol to Kevin Ron Helbert, born December 3, 1966, and had a child:

      (1)   Kolton Parker, born February 16, 1994

Walter Cable Pratt
1874-

This son of George Thomas Pratt (1843) and Mary Easter Sayers Pratt (1841), was born January 11, 1874. Married May 20, 1908 in Sullivan County, Tennessee, to Sallie Nancy Cowan, the daughter of Mahlon Susong Cowan and Addie Margaret Delaney Cowan. Four children:

1.   Mahlon Walter, born March 10, 1909 in Washington County, Virginia; died c.1975 at Radford, Virginia. He was married in Sullivan County, Tennessee to Nina Ann Wilson, born May 6, 1905 in Johnson County, Tennessee. She operated Piedmont Market, a small neighborhood grocery and deli, and reportedly served the best chicken salad in town. He was a barber, having a shop nearby.

2.   James Winifred, born December 7, 1909 Washington County, Virginia; married at Bluff City, Tennessee, Virginia Haworth,

born c.1916 in Sullivan County, daughter of Cecil Haworth. They had a son:

a. James Stephen, born June 29, 1955

3. Edyth Adelaide, born July 25, 1913 in Sullivan County, and married at Wytheville, Virginia to Vernon Foster Derey, born April 4, 1904 at Bristol, Virginia; died there c.1975, a son of Samuel Derey and Zelia Campbell Derey. Three children:

a. Clifford Walter, born January 30, 1942; married August 12, 1967 in Franklin County, Virginia, to Jessie Diane Fralin, born there June 30, 1944, daughter of Ernest W. Fralin and Grace Tatum. They had children:

(1) Celeste Tatum, born November 24, 1971 at Knoxville, Tennessee

(2) Walter Leaton, born December 31, 1974 at Richmond, Virginia

b. Sally Jane, born July 6, 1944 at Bristol, Virginia; married February 3, 1967 at Knoxville, Tennessee, to Benjamin Cross, born July 8, 1940 at Bristol, son of Harry Cross and Gertrude Step. Children were born at Waynesboro, Virginia:

(1) Nell Pratt, born September 27, 1968

(2) Spencer Benjamin, born September 10, 1972

c. Jill Pratt, born March 22, 1959; married 1979 at Bristol, Tennessee, to Brian K. Brinser, born there 1958; and had children:

(1) Will Foster, born about 1981

(2) Sarah Elizabeth, born January 22, 1985

(3) Emily Jeanette, born July 16, 1988

4. Walter Haven, born February 14, 1916 in Sullivan County, Tennessee; married at Bristol, Tennessee, Frances Peters, born there about 1918, and had a son:

a. John Michael, born about 1953

Gertrude Bertha Pratt
1876-1956

This daughter of George Thomas Pratt (1843) and Mary Easter Sayers Pratt (1841), was born March 24, 1876 in Pulaski

County, Virginia; died January 28, 1956 at Abingdon, Washington County, Virginia. Married in Washington County August 3, 1897 to Connally Litchfield Lee, born there April 21, 1862, and died there September 8, 1901, son of James Mobley Lee and Amanda Jane Hayter Lee. Connally had tuberculosis, and went west for his health, homesteading 160 acres in easter Colorado, but returned to Virginia. They had one son, listed first following, and she married second March 1, 1903 in Washington County to his brother, Henry Morgan Lee, born there October 19, 1855; died there November 16, 1918. They had five children. Gertrude is buried between her two husbands in the Lee Cemetery in Poor Valley. The six children were all born in Washington County, Virginia:

1. Robert Edward, born December 29, 1898; died August 31, 1984 at Coldwater, Michigan. He was a graduate engineer of TriState College in Indiana, where he met his wife. Spent most of his professional career with the Army Corps of Engineers; chief engineer in building Loring Air Force Base in Maine, and a dam in Walla Walla, Washington; later a permafrost expert in Alaska. Married September 29, 1928 in Huntington, West Virginia, to Lena Mary Elliott, born June 1, 1903 in Steuben County, Indiana, and died October 25, 1989 at Elkhart, Indiana, the daughter of John H. Elliott and Jenny Brattin Elliott.

2. James Thomas, born June 26, 1903, of whom more.

3. Ralph Hamilton, born August 25, 1905; died September 24, 1972 at Orlando, Florida. Married Nola Belle Thompson, born September 9, 1906; died February 29, 1972 at Orlando. He had tuberculosis, spending the last years of his life in a sanitarium; he was a master mechanic; loved children, but had none of his own.

4. Infant son, born January 8, 1908; lived four days

5. Howard Hampton, born May 10, 1909; died April 4, 1983 at Bristol, Virginia. As a young man, Howard sought work in the north, but decided to join the Army instead, and was sent to Panama as a surveyor's assistant. He also served in the Amazon, where he contracted malaria, and was transferred to West Point for the remainder of his service. Married October 15, 1931 at Blountville, Tennessee, to Anna Kate Pippin, born

February 10, 1905 at Stonega, Virginia and died November 16, 1985 at Raleigh, North Carolina; the daughter of Elijah Thomas Pippin and Frances Gordon Shelton. She was a graduate of the University of Virginia, and held a masters in library science from Peabody, and was a teacher for forty-four years in Virginia and Tennessee school systems. They had children, born Washington County:

a. Howard Hampton, Jr., born August 21, 1933; died September 28, 1984 at El Monte, California. Married September 6, 1955 in Bristol, Tennessee, to Josie Anne Sangid, born November 22, 1936 in Tazewell County, Virginia; daughter of Nasaib Berkat Sangid and Nellie Mae Phipps. Two children:

   (1) Howard Hampton, III, born June 29, 1956, Bristol, Tennessee; died November 8, 1965 Los Angeles

   (2) Christopher Nasaib, born September 10, 1966 Los Angeles, California; married May 28, 1990 at Winnipeg, Manitoba, Canada, to Tracey Lynne Kotschorek, born there November 14, 1965; the daughter of John Kotschorek and Ivey Jean Atchison. Two children, born Upland, California:

      (a) Erin Lynda, born May 8, 1992

      (b) Tyler Remington, born July 30, 1994

b. Shirley Ann, born March 6, 1935. A graduate of Mary Washington College, she was a teacher for several years before working for IBM in California, from which she is retired. She bought and restored the old Granny Lee house built by her grandparents.

6. Henry Morgan, Jr., born January 1, 1912; married February 17, 1941 in Mountain City, Tennessee, to Virginia Powers. He married second June 4, 1946 at Lebanon, Russell County, Virginia to India Lorena Rambo, born August 23, 1909, graduate of Radford College, and daughter of Otho Holland Rambo and Mary Ellen Edmondson Rambo.

James Thomas Lee
1903-

This son of Connally Litchfield Lee (1862) and Gertrude Bertha Pratt Lee (1876), was born June 26, 1903 in Washington County, Virginia, and died July 7, 1979 in the county at Abingdon. Married September 19, 1922 at Bristol, Tennessee, his third cousin, Fannie Vernon Scyphers, born November 13, 1904 and died March 21, 1978 at Abingdon, daughter of Calvin Martin Scyphers, Jr., and Minnie Vernon Buck Scyphers. James Thomas operated a country store, and served for a number of years on the Washington County School Board. They had children, the second born at Bluefield, West Virginia; the rest in Washington County, Virginia:

1. Catherine Vernon, born November 20, 1925, and married November 20, 1948 at Tazewell, Virginia, to James Samuel Dickenson, born there July 12, 1921; son of James William Dickenson and Viola Jane Kinzer. Three children, born at Bristol, Tennessee/Virginia:
   a. Deborah Catherine, born September 3, 1953; married in Washington County, Virginia, August 31, 1974 Stephen Roger Moretz, born May 16, 1953 at Dante, Virginia; son of Daniel Moretz and Billie Jean Isenhour. Deborah is a teacher and a graduate of East Tennessee State. A daughter:
      (1) Rebecca Elizabeth, born May 10, 1980
   b. Fannie Karen, a nurse, born July 17, 1956; married in Washington County, Virginia, August 6, 1977 John Gary Pledger, born January 9, 1955 at Manhattan, Kansas; son of Huey Pledger, Jr. and Dorothy Jane Bamford. They had children, born at Abingdon:
      (1) John Eric, born March 29, 1983
      (2) Erin Danielle, born June 16, 1985
   c. James Samuel, Jr., born August 7, 1965; married May 3, 1994 at Salem, Virginia, Valerie Michelle Motley, born September 25, 1968 at Roanoke, the daughter of James Hershel Motley and Lera Odessa Stalnaker.
2. Dorothy Helen, born November 29, 1927; died October 28, 1965 at Abingdon, Virginia. Married March 13, 1948 at

Tazewell, Virginia, Stafford Clayborn Taylor, born June 27, 1920 in Washington County, Virginia; son of Judge Hutton Taylor and Cora Duncan. Children:

a. Joan Lee, born May 26, 1950 at Bluefield; married December 19, 1969, Washington County, Virginia, Tony Wayne Worley, born March 15, 1948 Bristol; son of Noah Estel Worley and Esther Akers. They had children:

(1) Cynthia Lynn, born February 24, 1971 Fort Worth, Texas.

(2) Kristi Lee, born May 17, 1980 Abingdon, Virginia

3. Jack Thomas, born January 25, 1932; married November 8, 1950 in Washington County to Vivian O'Dell Duncan, born there January 7, 1932, daughter of George Duncan and Madge Kate Warren. They had children:

a. Gregory Neal, born September 16, 1956 at Lynchburg, Virginia; married May 30, 1981 at Rich Creek to Paula Kay Whitlow, born January 31, 1959, Pearisburg, Giles County, Virginia; daughter of Willard Wanlas Whitlow and Pauline Ida Syres Whitlow. They had children, born at Blacksburg:

(1) James Thomas, born September 30, 1987

(2) Amber Pauline, born January 13, 1992

b. Michael Thomas, born April 25, 1958

4. Janie Sue, born February 15, 1939; married September 10, 1957 in Washington County, Virginia, to James Ruddy Duty, born November 3 1935 in Russell County; son of James Russell Duty and Lydia Shoemaker Gilmer. Children, born at Abingdon, Virginia:

a. Sarah Jo, born October 27, 1964; married June 15, 1985 in Washington County to Gale Bradley Webb, born there September 20, 1961; the son of Gale Webb and Shirley Wise. A child, born at Abingdon:

(1) Whitney Lee, born July 29, 1990

b. Kimberly Lee, born May 26, 1968; married December 9, 1989 at Bristol to Matthew Samuel Gibson, born March 7, 1968 Kingsport, Tennessee; son of Franklin D. Gibson and Mary Jane Kay. Daughter, born Abingdon:

(1) Lauren Kay-Lee, born January 8, 1994

c. Jeffery Ruddy, born February 4, 1971; died July 24, 1987 at Abingdon. Married to Phaedria Penelope Taylor, born November 16, 1970 at Marion, Virginia. A son:
    (1) Jeffery Brandon, born February 9, 1988, Abingdon seven months after his father's death

5. Patsy Carol, born August 24, 1942; married December 31, 1965 in Washington County, Virginia, Allen Randolph Parris, born September 18, 1942 at Meadowview, Virginia; son of Floyd Oliver Parris and Mildred Humphrey. They had three children, born at Kingsport, Tennessee:
a. Tamara Carol, born April 3, 1967; married July 25, 1987 in Washington County, Virginia, to Warren Arthur Cole, born January 9, 1965 at Nashville, Tennessee; the son of David Austin Cole and Carolyn Blankenhorn.
b. Allen Randolph II, born May 3, 1971, married September 18, 1993 in Washington County to Betsy Jean Alexander, born August 18, 1974 at Abingdon; daughter of William Russell Alexander, Jr. and Brenda Whitehead.
c. Kevin Lee, born July 10, 1976

6. James Donald, born September 30, 1945; married June 17, 1966 at Mountain City, Tennessee, to Glenda Darlene Parris, born February 17, 1948 at Meadowview, Virginia; daughter of Floyd Oliver Parris and Mildred Humphrey. Children, born at Abingdon:
a. Sharon Arlene, born October 30, 1967; married June 1, 1991 in Washington County, Virginia, to Edward Tildon Farmer, born March 20, 1967, Abingdon; son of Archie Tildon Farmer and Linda Smith. He has a degree in accounting from Emory and Henry, and Sharon holds a masters from Radford University. Two children, born at Abingdon, Virginia:
    (1) Justin Sean, born January 22, 1993
    (2) Zachery Ryan, born September 27, 1994
b. Christopher Donald, born August 17, 1971

CHAPTER 12

Nancy Fulks Pratt
1823-

This daughter of Oliver Pratt (1784) and Mary Fulks Pratt, was born May 16, 1823 in what was then Washington County, Virginia, later to become Smyth County in 1832. She was named for her maternal grandparents, Nicholas Fulks and Nancy Botts Fulks, and was married January 16, 1846 to Spottswood Mitchell Campbell, born September 7, 1804; died July 6, 1885.

The Campbells were among the more important families of southwest Virginia, and indeed, of the Colonial period in general. They were among the earliest settlers of the Holston country in what later became Wythe and Smyth Counties, Virginia. Among the early families were Colonel (later General) William Campbell (1745), who commanded the mountain men at the Battle of Kings Mountain during early October, 1780, where a British force of superior numbers under Colonel Ferguson was soundly defeated. Ferguson, himself, was killed in the action, partly due, it is said, to the fact that he wore a silver whistle around his neck to signal his men, and a Virginia sharp-shooter used it as a target, killing the Colonel instantly. Reportedly, the whistle was given to Colonel Campbell as a souvenir of the engagement. William Campbell was but one of seven colonels who brought forces together for the battle, including his brother, Colonel Arthur Campbell. However, recognizing his superior leadership capabilities, the others elected Colonel William to command the whole force.

Of the battle of Kings Mountain, in his major work, *Ashe County, A History*, Arthur L. Fletcher stated that "*the most spectacular service by the mountain men came at the Battle of Kings Mountain which marked the beginning of the end for the British in the original thirteen colonies and in all of America south of Canada.*" The reader is urged to read Fletcher's book for an in-depth look at the overall history of the region from the earliest days to the recent present.

As to the Campbell family in general, if at all possible, anyone interested in this important group of individuals should obtain a copy of *Ancestors and Descendants of James Arthur Campbell (1877-1963)*. It was compiled by Mary Frances Campbell, in 1995 living at 685 Park Boulevard, Marion, Virginia 24354. It was privately printed, primarily for family, but I would think that she surely placed a copy of it in the Smyth County Library at Marion.

In her study, Mary Frances traces the descent of the Campbell Clan from its early origins with Dougal Campbell, born at Inverary in Argyleshire, Scotland; the ancestral home of Clan Campbell in the highlands. Although precise dates are not given, it appears that Dougal was born late in the 1500s. The book includes a drawing of Inverary Castle, home of the Duke of Argyle, Chief of the Clan Campbell. Early in the 1600s, the family removed to Ireland, and are found in that country thereafter, until the early 1700s, when they are found in America.

No effort will be made here to duplicate the work of Mary Frances Campbell, but it may be of interest to follow the direct lineage that reaches down to Spottsswood Mitchell Campbell, the first of the clan to marry into the Pratt family, through his second wife, Nancy Fulks Pratt.

Spottswood Mitchell Campbell was born September 7, 1804 in that part of old Washington County, Virginia, which in 1832 became Smyth County. It was there that he married first August 12, 1834 to Nancy D., and secondly, January 2, 1846 to Nancy Fulks Pratt, born May 16, 1823, daughter of Oliver Pratt (1784) and Mary Fulks Pratt, married 1810. By his first wife, he had five children: Rush S., born c.1835; Elizabeth D., born c.1837; Emily B., born June 20, 1839, who married Charles M. Sexton and had children; Louise S., born c.1841; and Mary Adaline, born c.1844. By his second marriage, he had six, who will be listed here following as members of the Pratt lineage.

Spottswood's father was Captain John Campbell, III, born May 12, 1768 in Washington County, Virginia, and his wife Dorcas Tate, daughter of General William Tate and Nancy Mitchell.

Captain John Campbell, III, was a son of Captain John Campbell, II, born c.1738, perhaps near Londonderry, Ireland. It is

County, Pennsylvania, in company with members of the Buchanan families. It is difficult, at best, to determine the precise movements of families in this early period. It is reported historically that in 1748, when Colonel James Patton explored the region, and found the Cumberland Gap, his party included his own son-in-law, John Buchanan; Charles Campbell (apparently son of Colonel Patrick Campbell (1696), brother of Captain John Campbell, II; and the father of Colonel William Campbell). At the time, John Buchanan was Deputy Surveyor for Augusta County, Virginia, and during the trip, large tracts of land were laid off for Patton, Campbell and Buchanan.

In 1758, another Captain John Campbell (1741), son of White David Campbell, bought the *Royal Oak* grant, now the site of the city of Marion, Virginia, from John Buchanan. The following year, he and his brother, Colonel Arthur Campbell (1743) and their sister, Margaret Campbell (1739), moved there to establish a home, and a house of worship.

To continue our lineage study, Captain John Campbell, II (1738) was a son of John Campbell, born November, 1674 at *Drumboden*, seven miles from Londonderry, Ireland. He reportedly immigrated to America in 1726, where he settled on the Sweet Ara, in Lancaster County, Pennsylvania. In 1730, he purchased a large tract of land in Orange, later Augusta County, Virginia, and moved there with his family.

John of 1674 was one of the five known children of Duncan Campbell, born 1645, and his wife Mary McCoy.

Duncan was a son of Andrew Campbell; who was a son of Hugh Campbell; who was a son of Patrick Campbell; who was a son of Duncan Campbell; who was a son of Dougal Campbell of Inverary, Argyleshire, Scotland. Little details are available relative to the early generations reaching back to the late sixteenth century.

Suffice to say that members of this illustrious family are found in numerous references during the early years of the development of America, in the service of the British Crown during the Colonial period; in American service during the Revolution; and in civil service after that time. Among their ranks, they included prominent military leaders, governors, judges, teachers and religious leaders;

active in agriculture, business and civic pursuits. We can all be justly proud to call them kin.

Spottswood Mitchell Campbell and his wife, Nancy Fulks Pratt Campbell, had a number of children, including:
1. George Ringo, born November 15, 1846, of whom more
2. John, born c.1849
3. James M., born c.1851
4. Jerome B., born c.1854
5. Henry P., born c.1858
6. Nora C., born c.1859

George Ringo Campbell
1846-

This son of Spottswood Mitchell Campbell and Nancy Fulks Pratt Campbell was born November 15, 1846 in Smyth County and died June 9, 1926. He was a master carpenter, building the Chatham Hill and Riverside Methodist church buildings, as well as a remodeling job on the Rich Valley Presbyterian church. He built several homes, including houses on the Elgin Green farm, the J. M. Pratt farm, and the Charlie Clark farm. Married June 9, 1873 to his first cousin, Florence E. Pratt, born April 25, 1852 at Rich Valley, daughter of Nicholas H. Pratt and Sarah Thomas Pratt (Nicholas was a brother of Nancy Fulks Pratt). They had four children, all born at Chatham Hill, Smyth County, Virginia:
1. William Enzer, born April 13, 1875, of whom more.
2. James Arthur, born September 16, 1877, of whom more.
3. Harry Eugene, born September 21, 1880, of whom more.
4. Gertrude Mae, born November 13, 1882; died March 6, 1970. Married three times: first to Herman Buchanan; second May 25, 1914 to George W. Burnop, by whom she had the two children; and third to John H. Burnop. Her children were:
   a. Florence Elizabeth, born January 22, 1916 at Abingdon, Virginia; married March 26, 1937 Vernon H. Neel, born June 6, 1910; died March 15, 1988. Two children:
      (1) William Campbell, born February 11, 1944, and married June 18, 1965 to Evangeline Kay Atwell, and had one son:

        (a)   John Campbell, born May 22, 1971 Augusta, Georgia

   (2)   Elizabeth Gail, born August 29, 1950, and married first August 21, 1969 to Ronald Hubble, and was divorced after having a son. Married second October 20, 1992 to Samuel D. Vernon. The son:

        (a)   Chad Eric, born September 7, 1971 at Marion

b.   George Campbell, born October 25, 1918 at Chatham Hill, Virginia; died February 14, 1986. Married in 1945 to Jean McLarnon, and on December 26, 1964 to Helen Martin. No children.

William Enzer Campbell
1875-1936

This son of George Ringo Campbell (1846) and Florence E. Pratt Campbell (1852) was born April 13, 1875 at Chatham Hill, Virginia, and died September, 1936. Married to Virginia Blackwell, born September 3, 1889; died January 9, 1989. Seven children:

1.   Eva, born May 31, 1905 at Broadford, Virginia; married to Fred Martin, born 1912; died 1969. Two children:

a.   Nancy, born June 24, 1931, and married April 17, 1949 to Jack Allen Hudson. Four children:

   (1)   Jack Allen, Jr., born January 15, 1950; married first Tina Nelson; divorced. Married second Susan Weaver. One son from first marriage:

        (a)   Christopher Allen, born March 7, 1971

   (2)   Carol Sue, born July 27, 1952; married June 8, 1968 to Robert Fitchko. Two children:

        (a)   Bryan Anthony, born April, 1969

        (b)   Amy, born December 25, 1975; married Scott Keheley.

   (3)   Teresa Ann, born January 17, 1956; married first September 5, 1974 to Alan Dean. Second to David L. Berry and had two children:

        (a)   Sarah Elizabeth

        (b)   Erin Ann

        (4)   Cynthia Jo, born August 29, 1957; married John Edward Stringer, who had two children from prior marriage. One son:

           (a)   Seth Edward.

   b.   Peggy, born May 14, 1934; married December 2, 1956 to Robert Owens. Divorced; two sons:

       (1)   Michael Eugene, born October 28, 1957

       (2)   Mark Todd, born July 2, 1967

2.   Mary Helen, born February 12, 1907 at Broadford; died October 2, 1987. Married May 25, 1935 to Gilmer Helton. No children.

3.   William H., born October 15, 1910; died December 25, 1944. Married first November, 1933 to Lillian Ross and second to Florence Lynch. One daughter from his first marriage:

   a.   Nancy Jean, married Steve Quillen; three children:

       (1)   Ira

       (2)   Richard

       (3)   Suzanne; married Mays and had two children

4.   George, born March 14, 1922 at Chilhowie, Virginia, and married to Myrtle Powers. They had children:

   a.   Sandra; married Randy Patterson, and had children

   b.   Brenda, married to Jack Farrell and had children

5.   Inez, born January 9, 1925 at Chilhowie; married to Jack Fitzgerald, who died 1953; and second to Edward Carter. Two children, from the first marriage:

       (1)   Julian Ray.

       (2)   Katherine Ann.

6.   Louise, born October 12, 1927 at Chilhowie; married August 2, 1952 to William Hankla. They had two children, born at Marion, Virginia:

   a.   Kenneth Boyd born December 18, 1956; married August 20, 1983 to Donna Sturgill. One son:

       (1)   Christopher Mark, born November 28, 1990

   b.   Kathy Lou, born July 17, 1963 at Marion; married June 26, 1993 to Edwin C. Sheffield, Jr.

7.   Jane, born January 9, 1931 at Chilhowie; married to Paul W. McGee, Jr., born 1919; died 1993. One son:

a. Paul Gregory, born April, 1958 at Marion, Virginia, and married Dora Arnold. One daughter:
    (1) Marie, born May 15, 1990

James Arthur Campbell
1877-1963

This son of George Ringo Campbell (1846) and Florence E. Pratt Campbell (1852), was born September 16, 1877 at Chatham Hill, Smyth County, Virginia, and died March 28, 1963. Married January 27, 1910 Margaret Louise Buchanan, born April 16, 1887 and died December 22, 1959 at Chatham Hill. She was a daughter of Felix Grundy Buchanan and Florence Dunn Sanders Buchanan. See also reports on this family in *Southwest Virginia Families*, by David B. Trimble. They had twelve children, born at Chatham Hill:

1. Florence Kathryn, born February 7, 1911, and married April 20, 1938 to Lonnie Edsel Munroe, born February 9, 1914 or 1916, at Sylacauga, Alabama, son of Lonnie B. Munroe and Pearl Vest Munroe. They had two children:
    a. Margaret Jean, born October 26, 1940; married first October 13, 1962 to Henry Clay Pruner, Jr. and divorced. Married second Robert Reeves and divorced. One child born to the second marriage:
        (1) Daniel Munroe, born April 16, 1966; married at Las Vegas, Nevada, July 4, 1994 to Melody Lynn Milam, born July 7, 1965 at Nashville, Tennessee, daughter of Travis Milam and Lynda Long Milam.
    b. Joseph Edsel, born December 17, 1945
2. James Clyde, born November 13, 1912; died May 23, 1995. Married April 18, 1941 at Little Rock, Arkansas, to Frances Elizabeth Stout, born August 31, 1916, daughter of W. I. and Elta Coopwood Stout. Two children, born at Little Rock:
    a. James Clyde, Jr., a doctor, born July 26, 1944; married April 11, 1970 to Kathy Cooper, born April 23, 1945 at Berkeley, California, a daughter of Dr. James Oliver Cooper and Mary Cecilia Cohen Cooper. Two daughters:
        (1) Lisa Marie, born November 28, 1970 at Portland, Oregon.

        (2)   Kerry Lynn, born October 8, 1974 at Jackson, Mississippi

b.   Ellen Louise, born February 13, 1947; married January 4, 1969 at Little Rock, Arkansas, to Bruce Allen Wankel, born November 18, 1947 at Lincoln, Nebraska, son of Ronald Allen Wankel and Jane May Duffield Wankel. Two sons, born at Kingsport, Tennessee:

        (1)   Andrew Meade, born November 20, 1971; married July 16, 1994 to Jennifer Ann Sparger, born May 20, 1972 at Richmond, Virginia, daughter of H. Merritt Sparger, Jr., and Ann Grim Sparger.

        (2)   Mark Allen, born January 23, 1975

3.   George Allen, born February 22, 1915; died December 15, 1990. Married March 22, 1940 to Mary Graham Gass, born April 20, 1919 at Chatham Hill, daughter of John M. and Louise Buchanan Gass. Four children, and divorced 1965. Married second July 22, 1982 Helen Jolene Parks Campbell (1932), widow of his brother, Jackson Pratt Campbell (1931). His children were:

a.   Rosemary Gass, born June 3, 1942 Elizabeth City, North Carolina. Married Donald Ivon McDowell, born February 25, 1932 at Owensboro, Davies County, Kentucky, son of William Bertram McDowell and Eileen Ward McDowell.

b.   James Allen, born March 22, 1945 New York City; died May 22, 1946

c.   George Sanders, born June 2, 1949 Alexandria, Virginia; married March 23, 1974 Carol Sanders, born September 15, 1953; divorced with one son:

        (1)   Gabe Sanders, born September 6, 1976 Donalson, Davidson County, Tennessee

d.   Martha Jo, born August 13, 1953 at Saltville, Virginia; married first May 8, 1977 to James Curtis Maloyed, son of J. B. Maloyed and Cookie Hatfield Maloyed; divorced. Married second April 26, 1987 James Clyde Dancy, born July 16, 1947 at Marion, Virginia, son of Blaine James Dancy and Bessie Olivine Price Dancy. One child born to the first marriage:

      (1)   Ashley Jo, born January 27, 1981 at Marion

4.   Jean Elizabeth, born September 24, 1916; died January 18, 1979. Married first to Leon Noel on October 23, 1937, who was born May 31, 1913 and died July 18, 1961. Married second March 9, 1970 Dr. Herbert A. Ellis and divorced. Two children born to the first marriage, both at Marion, Virginia:

    a.   Carol Jean, born December 29, 1944, and married June 24, 1967 Prince George's County, Maryland, to William Seaman, Jr., born January 30, 1945, son of William and Helen Ernst Seaman. Three children born in Gainesville, Florida:

        (1)   William Scott, born October 18, 1971; married October 22, 1994 to Christine Cynthia Gaudiosi at Pompano Beach, Florida

        (2)   Ashley Elizabeth, born October 7, 1973

        (3)   Amy Hope, born July 27, 1975

    b.   Margaret Elizabeth, born September 28, 1946; married August 9, 1968 to Dr. Thomas Frederick Wert, III in Prince George's County, Maryland. Divorced, after two sons were born in Washington, D. C.:

        (1)   Christopher Thomas, born July 30, 1972

        (2)   Gregory Leon, born June 14, 1975

5.   John Buchanan, born November 17, 1918; married December 19, 1942 to Mary Frances Price, born March 29, 1921 at Roanoke, Virginia, daughter of Howard Orin Price and Eunice Harriet Enochs Price. Five children, born at Saltville, Virginia:

    a.   John Buchanan, Jr., born November 22, 1943; married June 12, 1976 to Arleen Jean Plecenick, born October 11, 1947 Pittsburg, Pennsylvania, daughter of John Andrew Plecenik and Anna Toth Plecenik. One daughter:

        (1)   Courtney Anne, born November 3, 1983 Roanoke

    b.   David Price, born June 25, 1947, and married November 27, 1971 at Alexandria, Virginia, to Marilyn Nossen, born April 1, 1949 at San Francisco, California, daughter of Richard A. Nossen and Virginia Mae Milewski. Three children, born in Richmond, Virginia:

        (1)   David Price, Jr., born July 14, 1976

        (2)   Elizabeth Christine, born May 2, 1979

        (3)   Kristen Victoria, born January 24, 1984

    c.   **Margaret Sanders**, born June 10, 1953; married in Rich Valley, Virginia, September 20, 1975 to James Wallace Emery, Jr., born April 29, 1952 at Dallas, Texas. They had four children:

        (1)   Erin Elaine, born June 24, 1979 Brunswick, Maine

        (2)   Sean Patrick, born July 21, 1982 at Jacksonville, Florida

        (3)   Margaret Lynn, born March 3, 1988 at Monterey, California

        (4)   Molly Campbell, born July 1, 1990 at Fredericksburg, Virginia

    d.   James Howard, born August 16, 1955. This child is shown incorrectly as Jane Howard, a girl, in *Southwest Virginia Families*, by Trimble. Married June 12, 1982 in Rich Valley to Myra Lynn Neeves, born January 13, 1957 at Bristol, Virginia, daughter of Roy Lee Neeves and Verna Mae Calhoun Neeves. Two sons, both born at Marion, Virginia:

        (1)   William Hal, born April 15, 1986

        (2)   Jonathan Roy, born February 6, 1989

    e.   Virginia Lynn, born June 4, 1959; married April 2, 1983 in Rich Valley to Barry Clay Robinson, born December 17, 1957 at Roanoke, son of Sterling Rupert Robinson, Jr. and Barbara Ann Burnett Robinson. Three children, born at Marion, Virginia:

        (1)   Dana Lynn, born March 11, 1986

        (2)   Kelly Marie, born May 9, 1990

        (3)   Andrew Clay, born June 14, 1995

6.   **Grundy Sanders**, born June 10, 1921; died April 22, 1987. Married May 15, 1948 (or May 18, 1955) at Blountville, Tennessee to Daphine Lee Whillock, born March 10, 1923 at Marion, Virginia, daughter of Robert Lee Whillock and Maggie Lee Powell Whillock. Four children, born at Marion:

    a.   Sandra Lee, born February 14, 1956 at Marion; married May 19, 1984 at Marion to William Kevin Elswick, born July 25, 1957, son of William J. and Eleanor Cole Elswick. Two children, born at Marion:

       (1)   Brandon Lee, born July 19, 1988

       (2)   Whitney Shea, born May 13, 1991

  b.   Richard Noel, born January 27, 1957; married August 2, 1986 in Rich Valley, Vida Fullen, born January 2, 1962, daughter of William and Mildred Call Fullen. Divorced.

  c.   Stillbirth, September 20, 1959

  d.   William Claude, born October 5, 1961; married July 16, 1988 Dorothea Shouse, born March 4, 1968 Wilmington, North Carolina, daughter of Robert Nelson Shouse and Ellen Marie Herndon Shouse. Divorced; one daughter:

       (1)   Ellen Marie, born December 31, 1989 at Marion

7.   William Harold, born April 5, 1923; married May 15, 1948 at Kingsport, Tennessee, to Imogene Ann Redwine, born March 20, 1924 at Clinchport, Virginia, daughter of Charles Henry Redwine and Nettie Catherine Falin Redwine. One child:

  a.   Susan Beth, born February 27, 1949 at Kingsport, and married first to John S. Jones, born August 3, 1949 at El Dorado, Kansas, son of Walter S. and Alberta Hawkins Jones. Married second June 21, 1992 to Thomas Reeves Floyd, born December 19, 1955 at Lynchburg, Virginia. One son born to the first marriage:

       (1)   Jason Campbell, born March 6, 1972 at Marion

8.   Margaret Ann, born December 6, 1924; died November 11, 1925.

9.   Julian Arthur, born March 22, 1926; died July 19, 1977. Married October 21, 1951 to Doris Imogene Snapp, born November 6, 1927, a daughter of Charles Gilbert and Beulah Juiton Eads Snapp. Three children:

  a.   Sandra Keele, born May 31, 1953 at Chilhowie, Virginia. Married first December 21, 1968 to Danny Ray Ashley, son of Ray Gentry Ashley and Betty Johnson Ashley; divorced. Married second June 30, 1971 David Michael Lester, son of Melvin Cecil Lester and Billie Jean Campbell Lester. Divorced May 27, 1987. A son born to the first marriage, and a daughter to the second, both using the Lester surname:

       (1)   Terrence Patrick, born May 23, 1969 at Abingdon, and married July 1, 1989 to Renee Denise Abshire,

who had a daughter from a prior marriage. One
son born to this marriage:

    (a)   Faith Denae (LaFleur), born August 29, 1987
at Lake Charles, Louisiana

    (b)   Aaron Michael, born August 9, 1990 at
Frankfurt, Germany

  (2)   Brittany Campbell, born December 31, 1976 at
Rocky Mount, North Carolina

b. Gilbert Leon, born June 22, 1957 at Abingdon. Married
November 19, 1980 to Janet Heath, born August 22,
1960 at Abingdon, daughter of James Daniel and Parlee
Yarber Heath. One daughter:

  (1)   Crystal Leann, born June 8, 1981 at Abingdon

c. Alaine Juiton, born August 11, 1959 at Abingdon;
married first June 2, 1979 to David Neely and divorced.
Married second November 20, 1982 Dennis Blain Forrester, Jr., born December 5, 1945 at Glade Spring,
Washington County, Virginia, son of Dennis Blaine and
Mary Elizabeth Dyson Forrester. Two children, born to
the second marriage at Abingdon, Virginia:

  (1)   Julian Blake, born August 13, 1984

  (2)   Alea Shea, born June 1, 1990

10. Charles Meade, born August 24, 1928; married September 14,
1951 at Chatham Hill, Virginia, to Annie Carolyn Gwyn, born
May 7, 1929, daughter of John M. and Ivy Madeline Travis
Gwyn. Six children:

a. Thomas Meade, born July 22, 1953 at Johnson City,
Tennessee. Married first June 21, 1975 to Jo Ann Delp, a
daughter of Joe and Patsy Harris Delp. Divorced, with
one son. Married second August 28, 1983 to Kim Ratliff,
born August 23, 1962, daughter of Joseph Jackson Ratliff and Martha Elizabeth Clapp Ratliff. The son was:

  (1)   Thomas Meade, Jr., born November 14, 1976

b. James Arthur, 2nd, born September 9, 1954 at Marion,
Virginia. Married August 15, 1987 at Roanoke, Virginia,
to Jane Leonard, born November 9, 1960 at Roanoke, a
daughter of Clarence E. and Alice Morgan Leonard. Two
sons, born at Roanoke:

        (1)   James Arthur, III, born February 6, 1989

        (2)   Jonathan Everett, born February 14, 1991

c.   Catherine Travis born October 19, 1956 at Marion, and married November 27, 1982 to Richard H. Ellett. They were divorced.

d.   Nancy Caroline, born January 15, 1958 at Marion, and married June 23, 1989 to Terry R. Hawthorne, born July 13, 1953 at Chilhowie, son of Charles Walter and Annie Ruth Adams Hawthorne. Two children born at Abingdon:

        (1)   Sarah Catherine, born November 21, 1990

        (2)   Stephen Campbell, born March 11, 1993

e.   Charles Edward, born September 18, 1960 at Marion and married February 9, 1986 Janet L. Gross born November 4, 1962 at Marion, daughter of Joseph Vance Gross and Mildred A. Little Gross. Two sons, born at Abingdon:

        (1)   Joseph Meade, born September 5, 1986

        (2)   Justin Edward, born June 3, 1988

f.   Sarah Ellen, born December 27, 1962

11. An unnamed boy, stillbirth in 1931

12. Jackson Pratt, born November 13, 1931; died January 25, 1980. Married August 5, 1955 at Blaine, Tennessee, Helen Jolene Parks, born July 6, 1932 at Grant, Grayson County, Virginia, daughter of Bays E. Parks and Hattie Holdaway Parks. After her husband's death, Helen Jolene married his brother, George Allen Campbell (1915). Four children, first three born at Marion, the last at Abingdon, Virginia:

a.   Robert Jackson, born August 25, 1957; married June 11, 1983 at Rich Valley to Rhonda Lynn Hopson, born July 3, 1964 at Washington, D. C., daughter of Noah Hopson and Patsy Elizabeth Keesee Hopson. Two children, born at Marion, Virginia:

        (1)   Kristen Nicole, born December 31, 1983

        (2)   Josey Robert, born November 3, 1986

b.   Anne Elizabeth, born January 26, 1959; married June 28, 1986 to Joseph William Boone, born August 31, 1952 at Newnan, Georgia, son of Daniel Walter Boone, Jr., and Winifred Tremble Glover Boone. Two children, born at Atlanta, Georgia:

      (1)   Joseph William, born June 2, 1989

      (2)   Anne Cameron, born October 4, 1990

c.   Raymond Arthur, born December 5, 1960; married January 1, 1985 to June Ella Waddell, born September 6, 1965 at Marion, daughter of Thomas Holmes Waddell, Jr. Two sons, born at Marion, Smyth County, Virginia:

      (a)   Jack Pratt, born December 4, 1987

      (b)   Gary Raymond, born April 4, 1989

d.   Laura Sue, born June 4, 1967

e.   An unnamed son, born January 3, 1934; lived four days

Harry Eugene Campbell
1880- 1969

This son of George Ringo Campbell (1846) and Forence E. Pratt Campbell (1852) was born September 21, 1880 at Chatham Hill, Smyth County, Virginia, and died April 17, 1969. Married November 22, 1905 to Emma Frances Shuffelbarger, and had eight children. Reportedly married second to Mary Jones. Children were:

1.   Emma Florence, born December 23, 1907; died January, 1990. Married September 2, 1931 to Frank Holcomb Maxey, born October 24, 1910. They had two children:

a.   William Frank, born March 26, 1934 in Washington, D. C.; married September 5, 1959 to M. Susanne Lyons. Three children:

      (1)   William Eric, born September 23, 1960

      (2)   Michele Susanne, born September 13, 1961

      (3)   Jenifer Kathleen, born February 17, 1966

b.   Harry Eugene, born August 23, 1935, and married April 17, 1954 Karen E. Thompson. Two children:

      (1)   Robert Eugene, born July 9, 1955

      (2)   William Harry, born June, 1959

2.   Eloise, born March 11, 1910; died September 25, 1910

3.   Mary Louise, born July 11, 1912; married February 3, 1932 to Charles Taylor. Two other marriages: to Joe Tabor and to William Nutter. One daughter, born to Taylor:

a.   Betty Tate, born November 27, 1932; married July 11, 1952 at Woodlawn, Virginia, a distant cousin, William

Cook Neal. He was born July 6, 1931, and their family will be presented in Chapter 13 of this study, as part of the first family of Isaac Thompson Pratt (1827).

4. Edgar, born November 3, 1914; married December, 1935 to Ruth Deskins, and had one son:
    a. James Allan, born August 12, 1936; married Doris Ann Caudill. Two children, born in West Virginia:
        (1) Kimberly Ann, born January 16, 1964
        (2) Kellie Alane, born June 6, 1968
5. Nellie, born September 21, 1919; married August 31, 1946 to Peter Gangi. Three children born at Baltimore, Maryland:
    a. Lynn Campbell, born March 21, 1948; married Edward Wintermyer, and had two children:
        (1) Adam Gangi, born July 29, 1983
        (2) Ashleigh Lynn, born July 5, 1988
    b. Gary Frank, born July 20, 1949; married October, 1975 to Janice Marie Wilhelm. Two children:
        (1) Brian Michael, born April 6, 1980
        (2) Amy Marie, born December 28, 1984
    c. Terry Jean, born December 30, 1956; married in September, 1973, to Donald Wayne Canoles.
6. Dorothy, a twin, born August 26, 1921; married August, 1941 to Herman Baldwin. One daughter:
    a. Nancy Lee, born April 21, 1942; married first to Nelson and second to Ronald Leroy Stevens. Four children from the first, and one child from the second marriage; all seem to use the Stevens name:
        (1) Daniel Scott, born July 7, 1959 in New York
        (2) Diane Lynn, born October 14, 1960
        (3) Richard Dean, born May 6, 1962 and married to Michele Marie Brown. One daughter:
            (a) Heather Daun, born November 5, 1981
        (4) Mark Allen, born September 3, 1963; married first Linda Formica and divorced, one son. He married second Glenda Dimeler; a daughter:
            (a) Dustin Matthew, born September 21, 1989
            (b) Sara Ann, born October 27, 1994

        (5)   Ronald Douglas, born October 26, 1965, and married to Elke Hoffman. Two children:
           (a) Phillip LeRoy, born May 17, 1991
           (b) Gina Lee, born March 30, 1993

7. Harry Eugene, Jr., a twin, born August 26, 1921 and died January, 1948 in the Phillipines

8. Margaret, born February 1, 1924; married February, 1946 to Charles Robert Whitaker, Jr. Two sons:

  a.   Randall Dean, born October 25, 1951

  b.   Charles Robert, III, born July 24, 1955

Isaac Thompson Pratt
1827-1909

CHAPTER 13

The First Family of Isaac Thompson Pratt
1827-1909

This son of Oliver Pratt (1784), and his wife, Mary Fulks Pratt, was born August 5, 1827 in what was then Washington County, Virginia, and later became part of Smyth County when it was formed in 1832. He was my grandfather, was married twice, and was the father of eighteen children. His daughter, Josephine Davis Pratt Hurley, my mother, born when he was in his sixty-ninth year, recalls that she had understood that her father was born in a small log house near the Ellendale School which she attended. The house, if indeed that is where it stood, is long since gone; the Ellendale School building was recently still standing on the Buchanan farm, far back from the road, in a poor state of repair, most recently being used for the storage of hay.

Isaac Thompson was orphaned at an early age, perhaps as young as three to six years, and was apparently raised by his oldest brother, Nicholas H. Pratt. Called Thompie, he could neither read nor write, nor could his father and mother before him, each of them appearing at various times in public records with their mark. The name of Isaac Thompson appears on land records of Smyth County on at least eight different occasions:

August, 1880: Book 13, page 292. Isaac Thompson Pratt and Joseph P. Pratt (probably his son) obtain a one-acre lot at Chatham Hill on the east side of the road.

June 7, 1884: Book 21, page 547. W. M. Davis and his wife convey 150 acres of land to I. T. Pratt and James M. Pratt. The latter could have been James Madison Pratt, son of Isaac Thompson, although that young man died just twenty days after the date of the deed.

April 27, 1885: Book 16, page 240; a deed of trust. States that I. T. Pratt is then living on a farm of 149 and 1/2 acres, known as the old James Miller tract, as it was deeded to him by W. M. Davis.

June, 1896: Book 27, page 593. T. G. Buchanan and his wife, Florence D.; and I. T. Pratt and his wife, Nannie J.; deed a tract of land to John A. Lamie, next to I. T. Pratt's land.

May, 1900: Book 29, page 325. I. T. Pratt and wife N. J. Pratt convey 43 acres to Crabtree for $400, being part of the land of I. T. Pratt.

December, 1904: Book 1, page 450. Deed of trust for 50 acres on which I. T. Pratt then resides, being part of the old Cox land. Released in a margin entry.

June 1, 1900: Will Book B, page 339. The will of I. T. Pratt refers to the land known as the Cox farm, on the North Fork of the Holston River in Smyth County. In Deed Book 11, page 163, dated September 11, 1830, Oliver Pratt, his father, deeded 200 acres of land to Benjamin Cox. This may be part of the same tract. That land was adjacent to other lands conveyed by Oliver Pratt to Rebecca Pritchett. The first wife of Isaac Thompson Pratt was Nancy Emeline Pritchett, who was probably related to Rebecca. If that is true, the small farm on which Isaac Thompson lived at the time of his death may have come through the Pritchett family inheritance.

We know that at the time of death in 1909, Isaac Thompson was living on a farm of about 55 acres, on which my mother and other family members were born. The little farm is near the larger property owned in later years by his son, Charles Edward Pratt, and the original house is long since gone. I understand that no one lived on the property after his family left it about 1914, when it was sold to Charles Edward by my grandmother.

The barn that grandfather built still stands, with the original massive hewn timbers, notched, fitted and pegged. The area where the house stood is generally planted to corn, and after the spring rains, fragments of broken items work their way to the surface. My youngest son and I have visited the farm, and have collected numerous pieces of broken glass and pottery frangments, an old hinge, a table fork, a buckle, a brick, and a small shirt button, obviously from family possessions.

In the Introduction to this study, I described the industry of Chatham Hill, involving the movement of goods down the Holston River on the spring floods. Local family tradition holds that Isaac

Thompson took part in this enterprise as a young man. He was short of stature, perhaps only five feet, six inches tall, but broad of chest, and quite strong. As a young man, he apparently enjoyed a good brawl, and an occasional drink. One of the stories that I have heard states that grandfather and two friends had made the boat trip down-river, perhaps into Tennessee, had sold their cargo and their boat, and were walking home. Along the way, they saw a black man approaching them on the path. Remember that this was before the Civil War, and not too many black people lived in this area, either slave or free. Grandfather had apparently had a nip or two from the jug, and encouraged his friends to cause a bit of grief for this man, and to run him off the path, but they declined. The two went ahead, leaving Isaac Thompson to his own devices. Some time later, they waited a bit, and he caught up to them, looking much the worse for his encounter, bruised and bleeding. And with that, he said to them, *"fellows, I shall never fight nor drink again!"*

Mother reports that her father never did either again, although he did chew tobacco on occasion. However, my son and I found the bottom of a half-pint bottle on the little farm. It has the words, *Paul Jones*, clearly printed into the bottom of the bottle, so someone on that farm had at least that one small bottle of whiskey!

In checking through grandfather's life, there is one interesting little coincidence worthy of mention. His marriage bond to Nancy Jane Lowder was dated July 15, 1885; his last birthday that he celebrated was August 5, 1908; and he died on June 16, 1909. Each of those important dates in his life was on a Wednesday.

He was first married April 4, 1850 to Nancy Emeline Pritchett who was born May 19, 1832. Their marriage bond was dated April 3, 1850, and signed by Isaac Thompson Pratt with his mark, and by William D. Pritchett, bondsman. That would probably be William DeCalb Pritchett (1824), brother of Nancy Emeline. For those of you who may not be familiar with the practice, in the early years marriage bonds were issued prior to marriage, presumably to ensure that the groom would go through with his commitment. This particular bond is recorded in the public records of Smyth County, Virginia, is fairly typical of others, and reads in its entirety:

Know all men by these presents that we Isaac T. Pratt and Wm D. Pritchett of Smyth County are held and firmly bound unto the Commonwealth of Virginia in the sum of one hundred and fifty dollars, to which payment well and truly to be made to the said Commonwealth we bind ourselves our heirs executors and administrators jointly and severally by these presents. Witness out hands and seals this 3rd day of April, 1850. The condition of the above obligation is such that whereas there is a marriage shortly intended between said Isaac T. Pratt and Nancy Pritchett, now if there be no lawful cause to obstruct the same, then this obligation to be void. Otherwise to remain in full force and virtue. Signed, sealed and delivered.

Nancy Emeline was one of the daughters of John Anderson Pritchett (1794) and Nancy Hilton Albert Johnston Pritchett. In the genealogical library of the Mormon Church in Salt Lake City, there are family group sheets of the Pratt family filed by Susan J. Pritchett Joplin, a sister of Nancy Emeline, listing their parents. There are numerous entries in the International Genealogical Index of the church relative to the children of John Anderson Pritchett and his wife Nancy, including references to the birth and marriage of their daughter Nancy Emeline to Isaac Thompson Pratt, although in some of those records, his name is erroneously listed as Elisa Thompson Pratt.

Nancy Emeline died of cancer June 2, 1883, and is buried in the cemetery of the Rich Valley Presbyterian church. On a visit there in the 1980s, I found the stone marking her final resting place lying near the church. I moved it to its proper position beside her husband, whose second wife rests on the other side of his grave. There were eleven children born to the first marriage of Isaac Thompson Pratt, all at Chatham Hill, Smyth County, Virginia:

1. John Geddings, born March 24, 1851; died March 31, 1884. Married August 29, 1879 to Annie Liza Lowder, daughter of George Washington Lowder (1830) and Lorena Butler Patrick (1832) Lowder. She was born October 11, 1861 at Tazewell, Virginia and died October 22, 1954 in Salem, Oregon. After the death of John Geddings, Annie Liza married secondly to George Washington Farris, and their children and descendants will be reported in the study devoted to the Lowder families. It is of some importance to note here that after the death of his first wife, Nancy Emeline Pritchett, mother of these eleven

Annie Liza Lowder Pratt
Wife of John Geddings Pratt

children, Isaac Thompson Pratt was married second to Nancy Jane Lowder (1858), older sister of Annie Liza Lowder; who thus became her sister's stepmother-in-law! John Geddings was father of two children, born at Chatham Hill:

a. Joseph W., born July 4, 1880; died October 29, 1885
b. Georgia, born March 23, 1882; died January 24, 1918 of a ruptured appendix. Married April 12, 1905 to James Duskey; no children.

2. William Warfield, born June 21, 1853; died January 22, 1879
3. Joseph Parley, born October 23, 1855, single, died June 14, 1883, of consumption
4. Susan Marion Elizabeth, born December 8, 1857, of whom more
5. Henry Thompson, born April 2, 1861, of whom more
6. James Madison, born 1862, single; died of consumption June 27, 1884
7. Oliver, born October 26, 1865, of whom more
8. Nancy America, born May 28, 1868, of whom more
9. Thomas McClure, born October 8, 1870; died c.1883
10. Charles Edward, born December 15, 1873, of whom more
11. Harrison Campbell, born April 3, 1876, of whom more

Susan Marion Elizabeth Pratt
1857-1911

This daughter of Isaac Thompson Pratt (1827) from his first marriage, was born December 8, 1857 at Chatham Hill, in Smyth County, Virginia, and died September 27, 1911. Married February 3, 1875 to Andrew B. DeBord, born November 16, 1849; died June 6, 1936, son of John and Sarah DeBord. The two are buried at Ridgedale church cemetery, Rich Valley, Virginia. Nine children, all born at Chatham Hill:

1. William John, born c.1876, died 1946. Married to Louise Buchanan, born 1898; died March 30, 1930. Seven children:
   a. Glen, married Mary Purdie
   b. Mable, married Pat White
   c. Edna
   d. Curtis, married Mary Synovec

e. Alda
f. Donald
g. Opal, married Leo Dickess
2. John Thompson, born November 29, 1878; died March 24, 1953. Married December 6, 1905 Emaline McCready, and had ten children:
   a. Susan Margaret, born 1907; married Walter Ferguson and had at least one child:
      (1) Gary Walton
   b. Nannie Virginia, born 1909; single
   c. Ethel Marie, born 1911; married Wallace Necessary, and had two children:
      (1) Judith Ann, married Frosher
      (2) Robert T.
   d. Walter Beattie, born December 6, 1913; died December 24, 1969. Married Grace Justice and had a child:
      (1) Beattie Lee
   e. Raymond Lee, born 1916; died 1968. Married to Lee Etta Buchanan, and had three children:
      (1) Raymond Lee, Jr.
      (2) Jeffrey Blake
      (3) John William
   f. William B., born 1918; single
   g. Mary Ovella, born 1920; married H. F. Clear, Jr., and had one daughter:
      (1) Beverly Rose, married Goodman
   h. Robert Edward, born 1922; married Jane Porter, and had five children:
      (1) Martha Henderson
      (2) Nancy Virginia
      (3) Emily Jane
      (4) Robert Edward, Jr.
      (5) David Porter
   i. Edith Glenna, born 1924; married James T. Gardner, and had three children:
      (1) Andrew T.
      (2) James Hugh, a twin
      (3) Emma Sue, a twin

Left: George Wiley DeBord (1890-1963)
Right: William John DeBord (1876-1946)

j. Harold Eugene, born 1926; married Gail Skibba, and had two children:
   (1) Deborah Jean
   (2) Joseph Michael

3. Nannie R., born March 14, 1881; died December 14, 1950. Married May 30, 1911 W. H. Buchanan.

4. Thomas P., born March 3, 1884, died May 28, 1899, reportedly from choking on a piece of arborvitae he was chewing.

5. Henrietta, born August 26, 1887; died November 24, 1916. She married William V. Olinger.

6. George Wiley, born June 19, 1890; died December 13, 1963. Married March 12, 1913 to Pearl Buchanan, born August 16, 1890, daughter of Thomas Theopolus Buchanan and Cynthia Bise Buchanan. See page 21, *Southwest Virginia Families*, by Trimble. Four children:
   a. Woodrow Wilson, born January 2, 1914; married June 18, 1940 to Vera Murray, born June 11, 1917, and died February 5, 1981. Buried at Ridgedale.
   b. Louise Miller, born October 9, 1915; married April 16, 1938 to Ray Caldwell.
   c. Opal, born September 22, 1917; married February 2, 1939 to G. B. Ross.
   d. Mariam, born October 9, 1928; married June 11, 1951 to J. C. Williams, III

7. Henry H., born February 6, 1893; died November 3, 1969, single. Buried at Ridgedale Church, as are all his brothers and sisters, with the exception of William John DeBord

8. Mattie S., born October 6, 1895; died December 19, 1895

9. Reese B., born March 3, 1897; married April 1, 1916 to Eula L. Troutman, born April 16, 1900; died December 8, 1972, a daughter of John William Troutman (1874). Their children are listed under that family, to which the reader is referred.

Henry Thompson Pratt
1861-1912

Martha Loraine Carson Pratt
1866-1942

Henry Thompson Pratt
1861-1912

This son of Isaac Thompson Pratt (1827) and Nancy Emeline Pritchett Pratt (1832), was born April 2, 1861 at Chatham Hill, in Smyth County, Virginia. Married December 26, 1885 to Martha Loraine Carson, who was said to be a first cousin to the famous scout, Kit Carson. She was born December 17, 1866 in Grayson County, Virginia, daughter of William Carson and Mary Elmira Boyd Carson; died February 9, 1942 at Encinal, Texas, where she is buried beside her brother-in-law, Oliver Pratt (1865).

Early in his life, in company with his brother Oliver, Henry Thompson went west to seek his fortune, finally arriving in the gold fields near Cripple Creek, Colorado. The brothers were reportedly successful, each becoming rather well-to-do and respected in their later lives. Alma Lavonne Pratt Rogers, a grand-daughter of Henry Thompson, who now lives in Austin, Texas, reported to me that she still has a gold ring fashioned from the raw gold that Henry Thompson found. He spent the last several years of his life in Warrensburg, Missouri, where he died May 22, 1912, and is buried in Sunset Cemetery.

His obituary was published May 24, 1912 in the *Weekly Standard Herald*, which stated:

"Henry T. Pratt, the well known and popular stockman, died suddenly at his home on North Holden Street Wednesday morning of this week about 6 o'clock. He had been suffering of indigestion several days, but his condition was not considered critical. Wednesday morning he was not feeling as well as usual, and Mrs. Pratt summoned the family physician. The physician arrived, and soon after he stepped into the room Mr. Pratt fell over on the bed and soon expired.

Henry T. Pratt was a native of Smith County, Virginia, and was born forty-nine years ago. When a young man he left his Virginia home and went to Nebraska. He was married December 26, 1885 to Miss Martha Carson, from his old Virginia home, and to this union were born four children, one dying in infancy, the three living being Harry G., Susie, and Carson. The family moved to this vicinity in 1896. Mr. Pratt was an extensive dealer in live stock and widely known, not only locally, but in many sections of the country. His was an active business life. In a business way he visited many sections of the country, and was especially well known on the large markets. He was enterprising, a good citizen, jovial, and popular with those who knew him. His sudden death was a shock to our people, and they deeply sympathise with the bereaved widow and children."

After his death, Martha moved with her children to Encinal, Texas, during the winter of 1915, and lived there until her death. It was near there that Henry's brother, Oliver, operated a very large ranch holding, and she and her family lived in the house in Encinal which he owned. I visited that house during 1980, at that time still occupied by Mrs. Mamie Brown, who knew the family well, and had helped care for them in later years. We know that Martha's son, Kit Carson Pratt, was working on his uncle's ranch when my mother visited there in 1917, although mother did not recall that there were other family members living in Encinal.

Henry Thompson fathered four children, one of them an infant death, and the following three, who survived:

1. Sue Anne, known as Susie, was born November 16, 1890 in Humphrey, Nebraska; died August 25, 1966 at Ridgewood Hospital, Sand Springs, Oklahoma, and is buried there at the Woodland Cemetery. She was reportedly crippled by polio at about age 21, ending a promising career as a singer. Another family report states that she was perhaps injured severely in a riding accident. In any case, she lived with her mother for many years at Encinal, Texas, from about 1915 until the death of her mother in 1942. From then, until the early 1960s, she remained in the Pratt's Encinal house, with Mrs Mamie Brown to care for her, until she moved to Sand Springs to live with her brother, Harry Thompson. She was never married.

Sue Ann (Susie) Pratt
1890-1966

Left to right: Martha Loraine Carson Pratt and her daughter Susie
On Oliver Pratt's ranch south of Encinal, Texas; c.1915
The six-gun was said to be for rattlers.

House in Encinal, Texas
It was here that Martha Loraine Carson Pratt and her children
lived after moving to Texas about 1915.
Picture c.1975

2. Harry Thompson, born June 28, 1893 in Iowa, according to
    the 1910 census of Missouri; died April 8, 1977 at St. Johns
    Hospital, Tulsa, Oklahoma. A major contributing cause of
    death was his history of 25 years of coronary artery disease,
    which is my principal ailment, and which I have been told is
    genetic. Although born many years apart (in fact, Harry was
    two years older than my mother), we were first cousins, so our
    problem may be derived from Pratt genes. The death certifi-
    cate of his wife indicates that she too suffered from coronary
    artery disease with acute congestive heart failure, so one can
    not be sure. The death certificate of Harry's sister, Sue Anne

130

Pratt, also lists arteriosclerotic heart disease. The death certificate of his brother, Kit Carson, also lists coronary occlusion and myacardial failure as the cause of death. Harry was buried at Woodland Cemetery in Sand Springs, Oklahoma, where he had lived for many years, and was there engaged in the real estate business. He was married to Hazelle Lillian Rawson, born April 4, 1895; died February 10, 1981 and buried beside her husband. She was daughter of Charles and Lillian Trimble Rawson, born also in Missouri. One son:

    a.   Charles Rawson, born July 22, 1920, of whom more.

3.   Kit Carson, born August 1, 1900 at Warrensburg, Missouri, and died July 8, 1937 at Marlin, Texas. He was apparently named for the famous scout, who was said to be a cousin of his mother, Martha Carson Pratt. Kit was at times a cowboy on his uncle's ranch near Encinal, a rancher in his own right, a constable, and a businessman. He was perhaps first married to a girl named Pauline from Tulsa, Oklahoma, and married September 3, 1932 at Antlers, Oklahoma to Alma Woodland of Marlin, Texas,

born c.1908, daughter of George Woodland, the owner of extensive ranch land adjoining that of Kit's uncle, Oliver Pratt (1865) near Encinal, Texas. His only child was:

    a.   Alma Lavonne, born October 10, 1935 at Marlin, Texas, and married April 6, 1958 to Harry Foster Rogers from

East Liberty, Pittsburg, Pennsylvania. He was a son of Clarence E. Rogers (1875-1952), and grandson of Alfred Henry Rogers (1852-1932) of Worcestershire, England, who emigrated to America in 1869. From 1984 to 1986, Harry was mayor of Rollingwood, a suburb of Austin, where they made their home. Currently, in 1995, is commanding Colonel of the 2nd Regiment, Austin Greys, Texas State Guard; and officer-in-charge of the Guard of the Republic. They have three daughters:

(1)   Roshay Lavonne, born June 24, 1960 at Vanden-vurg Air Force Base.

(2)   Rosanne Dawn, born March 24, 1962 at Vandenburg; married August 22, 1981 to Horis Tilton Stedman in Marlin, Texas. Two children:
       (a)   Marisha Rose, born December 27, 1986
       (b)   Harris, born February 2, 1990

(3)   Rosemary Faith, born December 23, 1963, Marlin

Family of Alma Lavonne Pratt & Harry Edward Rogers
25th Wedding Anniversary 1983
Left to right: Rosanne Dawn; Lavonne; Roshay Lavonne
Rosemary Faith; Harry

Charles Rawson Pratt
1920-1983

This only son of Harry Thompson Pratt (1893) was born July 22, 1920 at Sand Springs, Oklahoma; died September 20, 1983, and is also buried at Woodland Cemetery with his parents. Married September 6, 1942 at Victoria, Texas, to Patricia Jean Brown, born June 18, 1919 at Tulsa, Oklahoma, daughter of Paul and Emily Nell Brown. Six children:

1. Gretchen Lynn, born December 23, 1944, San Angelo, Texas; married September 2, 1966 Owen Lloyd Pugh, born June 22, 1942 at Burlington, Colorado, son of Lawrence and Helen Pugh. One child:
   a. Patrick Whitney, born March 21, 1972 at Tulsa
2. Christopher Elizabeth, born November 28, 1945 at Tulsa and died there May 20, 1984. Married at Tulsa November, 1963 to Gary Wheeler, born 1944 at Enid, Oklahoma, son of Virgie Wheeler. Three children, born at Tulsa, Oklahoma:
   a. Brian Andrew, born August 9, 1965; married to Donna Lampore, and had one child, born at Tulsa:
      (1) Ryan Christopher, born November 22, 1984
   b. Amy Elizabeth, born March 5, 1972
   c. Jane Ann, born February 28, 1962, and married James Hoover and had two children, born at Tulsa, Oklahoma:
      (1) Jimmy Lee, born February 24, 1981
      (2) Zachary Adam Pratt, born December 9, 1983
3. Courtney Jean, born November 1, 1948 at Tulsa, Oklahoma; married there February 11, 1967 to William Lynch, born November 4, 1946, son of Norman and Gen Lynch. They were divorced January 25, 1979, after three children:
   a. Christopher Carson, born February 17, 1969
   b. Reagan Kathleen, born August 27, 1970
   c. Shane Elizabeth, born May 22, 1973 at Oklahoma City
4. Whitney Carson, born January 6, 1950 at Tulsa and married August 8, 1970 at Sand Springs, Oklahoma to Stephen Austin, born March 23, 1948 at Tulsa, son of Shelby and Augusta Marie Austin. Three children, the first two born at Tulsa, and the third at St. Joseph, Missouri:

133

a. Joshua Steven, born September 30, 1975
b. Amanda Kimberly, born May 25, 1980
c. Adam Christopher, born November 25, 1985
5. Kimberly Patricia, born January 13, 1954 at Tulsa, Oklahoma and married June 4, 1976 at Sand Springs to Michael Perdue, born January 11, 1952, also at Tulsa, son of Carson and Mary Perdue. Two children:
a. Michael Blake, born July 15, 1982
b. Benjamin Rawson, born February 15, 1984 at Tulsa
6. Patrick Brett, born November 21, 1957 at Tulsa, and married January 8, 1983 at Sand Springs to Beth Gardner, born March 31, 1957 at Tulsa, daughter of Fred and Nancy Gardner. They had no children.

Oliver Pratt
1865-1932

This son of Isaac Thompson Pratt (1827) and Nancy Emeline Pritchett Pratt (1832), was born October 26, 1865 at Chatham Hill, Smyth County, Virginia. He and his brother, Henry Thompson (1861), went west together as young men, as reported above in the section devoted to Henry. As reported there, Henry lived for a time in Nebraska, in Iowa, and finally in Warrensburg, Missouri. Oliver made his way to Texas, where he acquired a ranch said to contain as much as 32,000 acres of land near the village of Encinal. That little town is located on the south border of La Salle County, Texas, just above the very large county of Webb. From Encinal, it is about thirty-five miles along Interstate 35, south across Webb County to Laredo near the Mexican border, and it is said that Oliver's ranch covered most of that distance.

It has also been reported that Uncle Oliver had a partner in the ranch and that, during the 1930s, the ranch was lost as a result of drought and bad debts made by his partner, which Oliver honored. I have seen a letter written in the 1980s to Alma Lavonne Pratt Rogers, by a man from Encinal, identified there only as Robert, apparently with a wife named Lorraine. In his letter, Robert writes, *"I left Encinal when only a boy and returned to Encinal after Mr. Coleman had been declared bankrupt, and since your Uncle*

Left to right: Oliver Pratt and his ranch partner, Tom A. Coleman

*Oliver was a partner with Mr. Coleman, the debtors took
everything they could, and this made it almost impossible for your
Uncle to stay in the business. His ranch was sold to Mr. B. B.
Dunbar, and I was told it was 32,000 acres, and he had other
acres leased."* The Mr. Coleman referred to in the letter is believed
to be the same T. A. Coleman mentioned following.

According to a report in *La Salle County, South Texas Brush
Country, 1856-1975,* by Annette Martin Ludeman, as late as 1910,
there was no Presbyterian church in Encinal. Mr. T. A. Coleman,
who owned the most extensive ranch in the area, donated a lot in
Encinal for the construction of a building. At a meeting of the
congregation on March 6, 1910, Oliver Pratt was among those
named as trustees of the church, and contributed the first one
hundred dollars toward the building fund.

In 1917, my mother, Josephine Davis Pratt, and her youngest
sister, Laura Rebecca, visited their half-brother for several months.
Mother has reported that while she was there, Oliver had living
with him a very young son, Oliver, Jr., as well as his nephew, Kit
Carson Pratt, son of Oliver's brother Henry Thompson Pratt, then
deceased. We know that, about 1915, Martha Carson Pratt, the
widow, moved to Encinal with her three small children, and lived in
a house in town owned by Oliver, while her youngest son, Kit
Carson, lived and worked on the ranch.

When mother arrived in Texas, she was not aware for some
time that Oliver had children. However, she has told us that when
they went riding on the ranch each day, the small boy was always
with them. On one occasion, she was stopped beside him on his
pony, as they looked at the vast herd of cattle grazing around them.
Uncle Oliver branded his cows with a large letter "P", but mother
noticed that some were different. She commented to the youngster
that all the brands did not appear to be the same, and he responded,
"Yes, they are different sizes; all the little "Ps" are mine." She soon
realized who this little fellow was, commonly known as Little Ol.

In 1980, my wife and I were in Encinal, and were directed to
the house where the family had lived. There, we met Mrs. Mamie
Brown, who lived there, and welcomed us warmly, as soon as I had
identified myself. She was then in her late 80s, had taken care of
Sue Anne Pratt and Martha during their latter years, and knew the

family well. She told us of an interesting feature of the house, dating from the very early years.

She had called workmen to fix a leak in the roof, and after a bit, they called her to take a look at what they had found. On the top of the house, under the roof, they had found a small room-like area, which could apparently have been entered from the attic. A section of the roof could then be opened back, and there was then a sheltered area at roof level for fighting off attacks of the Indians and outlaws.

Uncle Oliver died October 11, 1932 at Mercy Hospital in Laredo, and is buried at Encinal. The principal cause of death is listed as diabetes, with carbuncles as a contributing factor. The certificate is signed by his son, Oliver Pratt, Jr., but the lines relative to his parents are blank, with the comment, "don't know."

Oliver had three children, including an infant death, born to Margaret Bell Spindle, who was born July 2, 1872 at Carrizo Springs, Texas on the old Pena Ranch, and died May 31, 1963 of heart failure. She was a widow, and had at least two children from an earlier marriage: a daughter Marguerite Spindle, who married Breeding; and a son, Hargus Spindle. Eva Pratt, widow of Oliver, Jr., reportedly has a photograph of Oliver Pratt and Margaret Spindle, dated March 7, 1907. It is said to have been taken just a few days after the couple were married, perhaps at Laredo. The land records of La Salle County raise a few questions, however. On February 15, 1936, Oliver Pratt, Jr., conveyed property to Mrs. M. Spindle (his mother). From family verbal records, it is assumed that Oliver and Mrs. Spindle were not married. The children were:

1. Oliver, Jr., born June 9, 1908 at Encinal, Texas; died on or about December 27, 1967 of a heart attack. Married to Eva, lived in or near Laredo, Texas, and had one daughter:
    a. Elizabeth, married Oscar Rodriguez. Six children:
        (1) Olivia, born 1961
        (2) Esther, born 1963
        (3) Oscar, Jr., born 1965
        (4) Sammie, born 1967
        (5) Rebecca, born 1970
        (6) Elizabeth, born 1973
2. Helen Evelyn, born October 19, 1910, of whom more.

Left to right, front: Alma Woodland Pratt, Kit Carson Pratt,
Martha Loraine Carson Pratt, Oliver Pratt
Rear: Susie Pratt and Oliver Pratt, Jr.
c.1929 on porch of the home in Encinal, Texas (see page 130)

Helen Evelyn Pratt
1910-1957

This daughter of Oliver Pratt (1865) and Margaret Bell Spindle (1872), was born October 19, 1910 at Encinal, La Salle County, Texas, and died of breast and uterine cancer February 25, 1957 at home in Laredo, Texas. Married June 18, 1932 to Samuel Joseph Jordan, Jr., born September 20, 1908 in Encinal and died June 9, 1992 at Laredo. *La Salle County, South Texas Brush Country, 1856-1975*, by Annette Martin Ludeman, contains a number of photographs of buildings in Encinal. One of them is the home of the Sam Jordan family, said there to be the oldest home in Encinal, Texas. Seven children:

1. John Frederick, born August 22, 1938; married Ruth, and adopted four children from her first marriage.
2. Carolyn Alvina, born December 30, 1939 and married first September 19, 1957 to George Nash McLean, his adoptive name. His father was Rufus Burlus Satterlee from Houston, Texas, and his mother was Mary Miller. They were divorced February 27, 1961 after having a daughter. Carolyn married second November 21, 1962 to Henry Paul Scott, from whom she was divorced, after having a daughter. Her children were:
    a. Helen Elizabeth (McLean), born August 5, 1958; married June, 1979 to Winters Robert Alley at Chattanooga, and had one child. Divorced, and she married there second Robert Baker. Two sons, born Laredo, Texas:
        (1) Michele Brook (Alley), born June 16, 1981
        (2) Jesse Nash (Baker), born April 7, 1985
        (3) Eric Samuel (Baker), born June 26, 1986
    b. Evelyn Kathleen (Scott), born December 18, 1964
3. Samuel Joseph, III, born September 2, 1941; died March 23, 1992, and buried at Encinal, Texas. Married to Lotus Bowers, postmistress of Encinal. Five children, two of whom survive:
    a. Deborah, born October 22, 1963 in Blythe, California. Married Barry Ross; lived in Schertz, Texas
    b. Oliver Joseph married to Sandra, and had two sons:
        (1) Oliver Joseph, Jr.
        (2) Thomas

4. Richard Jerome, born December 15, 1942; married August, 1960 to Sharon Peterson, and had four children:
   a. Pamela
   b. Jeynne
   c. Shannon, a son; died in Paris, France on May 27, 1991
   d. Russell
5. James Robert, born April 21, 1945; married Judith Arce and had three children:
   a. Elizabeth
   b. John David
   c. Helen
6. Rosemary, born December 17, 1947; married John Contreras. In 1991 lived in Laredo, Texas; no children.
7. Anna Margaret, born January 31, 1949; married David Dodier December 18, 1975. In 1991, lived in Laredo, Texas.

Nancy America Pratt
1868-1888

This daughter of Isaac Thompson Pratt (1827) and Nancy Emeline Pritchett (1832) was born May 28, 1868 at Chatham Hill, Smyth County, Virginia, and died May 28, 1888. Married February 20, 1884 to Samuel J. Spence, born 1859, and died 1930, son of Jonathan and Ruth Spence. After the death of Nancy America, he married second Min Cypher, and later for a third marriage, Della Mae Stinson. He had one daughter, Pearl, from his second marriage and three sons from the third: Ottie, Harry L., and George. They were not, of course, descendants of the Pratt families, and will not be further discussed here. Nancy America had two daughters:
1. Birdie Gray, born April 13, 1885, of whom more.
2. Martha, born September 16, 1887 at Chatham Hill and died February, 1971. Married Tabor Crabtree and had at least two daughters:
   a. Lucille
   b. Edna

Birdie Gray Spence
1885-1939

This daughter of Samuel J. Spence (1859) and Nancy America Pratt Spence (1868), was born April 13, 1885 at Chatham Hill, Smyth County, Virginia, and died December 24, 1939. Married September 3, 1903 to William D. Cook, one of the four children of Henry H. and Martha L. Fox Cook. They had five children, all born at Chatham Hill in Smyth County:

1. Mattie Mae, born December 13, 1906, of whom more.
2. Henry Samuel, born June 14, 1905; died November 23, 1941; single.
3. Hobart Holmes, born June 20, 1909; died April 4, 1971. Married Virginia Edna (or Vergie) Gillespie, born May 25, 1915, and had children:
    a. Patsy Ann, born August 14, 1933; died c.1939
    b. Charles William, born November 20, 1935, and married Mary Christine Taylor.
    c. Mary Gray, born April 25, 1938; married Willis O'Neal Sanders.
    d. Hobart Holmes, Jr., born December 6, 1941, and married Nyoka Vesoline Talbert.
    e. Peggy Jean, born May 1, 1944; married Charles Brittain Taylor.
    f. James Lee, born September 22, 1945, and married Toby Lane Frye. Two children:
        (1) Catherine Lynn, born August 24, 1970
        (2) James Lee, Jr., born July 9, 1973
4. George Fred, born August 18, 1911; died July 1, 1963. Married August, 1939 to Jettie Dameron, born March 3, 1921, and had children:
    a. George Fred, Jr., born April 26, 1940, and married June 21, 1958 to Patsy Carter, born August 15, 1941. Two children:
        (1) Geoffrey Fred, born January 12, 1961; married May 3, 1985 to Deborah Musick, born January 26, 1964
        (2) Kimberley Lynette, born December 31, 1962

b. Henry Samuel, born July 11, 1942; married October 10, 1966 to Gail Scott, born February, 1948, and divorced. One son:
    (1) Scott, born January 16, 1970
c. Carol Anne, married David Woodrum; a son:
    (1) David, Jr.
d. Irene Neal, married Steele and had a daughter:
    (1) Tamara, married June 29, 1991 William Altizer.

5. Anne Beatrice, born October 29, 1914; married April 30, 1940 James Thomas Crabtree, born April, 1907, and had two daughters:
a. Birdie Jane, born April 7, 1941; married November 6, 1964 to Charles Howard Woodmore, born April 11, 1942. They had three children and divorced. Married second October 28, 1983 Allen Tooney Craighead, born May 22, 1928; no children. Her children were:
    (1) Tracie Lynn, born August 6, 1967; married April 15, 1988 to Timothy Wayne Selfe, born May 31, 1966, and had a son:
        (a) Conner Allen, born January 31, 1992
    (2) James Edward, born January 30, 1970
    (3) Christine Ann, born October 8, 1971
b. Betty Anne, born July 19, 1942; married September 18, 1965 to Kent Howe Hoge, born 1940. Two children:
    (1) Monty Crabtree, born July 20, 1967; married May 18, 1989 to Kelli Melissa Meldin, born August 14, 1969
    (2) Scott, born June 21, 1971

Mattie Mae Cook
1906-

This daughter of William D. Cook and Birdie Gray Spence Cook, was born December 13, 1906 and in 1992 was still living near Saltville, Virginia. Married September 27, 1930 to William Frederick Neal, born July 17, 1905; died February 13, 1986, son of William Oscar Neal and Daisy S. Andes Neal. Three sons:

1. William Cook, born July 6, 1931; married July 11, 1952 at Woodlawn, Virginia, to Betty Tate Taylor, born November 27, 1932, daughter of Charles Taylor and Mary Louise Campbell Taylor (1912). The ancestry of Betty Tate Taylor has been discussed in Chapter 12 of this study. She is a fourth generation descendant of Nicholas H. Pratt (1811); William Cook is a fourth generation descendant of Isaac Thompson Pratt (1827), brother of Nicholas H.; thus the couple were distant cousins through their Pratt ancestry. It appears that they are also distantly related through perhaps two other branches of their lineages. They had four children:
   a. Stephen Allen, born May 26, 1953 at Charleston, South Carolina; married April 20, 1985 Suzanne Marie Crouere from New Orleans and had children:
      (1) Jessica Tate, born April 16, 1987
      (2) Stephan Allen, Jr., born November 11, 1988
      (3) William Watson, born July 27, 1991
      (4) John Christian, born February 15, 1995
   b. Regina Anne, born May 7, 1955 at Marion, Virginia, and married April 8, 1978 to Charles Stanley Wimmer, born March 11, 1954. No children.
   c. Patricia Beth, born February 15, 1957 Pulaski, Virginia; married December 29, 1979 Cary Allen Ratliff, born August 25, 1954, and had children:
      (1) Taylor William, born September 7, 1985
      (2) Spencer Neal, born November 9, 1987
      (3) Abigail Christina, born September 21, 1989
   d. Nancy Carol, born September 10, 1958 at Roanoke, Virginia; married July 11, 1981 Nathan Smith White, IV, born July 4, 1955, and has a son:
      (1) Jacob Adamson, born October 25, 1990
2. James Frederick, born March 25, 1937; married September 15, 1962 Mary Anne Ivers, born January 2, 1936. She was first married to Richard A. Robbins; divorced; two children, adopted by James Frederick. They had two more children:
   a. Michael Windsor, born February 14, 1955, and married November 27, 1976 Deborah Kowa, born April 19, 1958, and had children:

        (1)   Christopher, born September 29, 1981

        (2)   Brandon, born July 19, 1983

        (3)   Amanda, born October 22, 1986

   b.   Jann Marie, born May 21, 1956, married March 6, 1982 Dr. Nick J. McLane, born June 26, 1956. Two daughters:

        (1)   Christina Lee, born July 17, 1986

        (2)   Kelli Anne, born May 25, 1990

   c.   Tammy Caroline, born October 18, 1967

   d.   Terri Lynn, born March 21, 1969

3.   David Michael, born April 21, 1948; married November, 1989 to Kathleen Waller.

Charles Edward Pratt
1873-1941

Charles Edward Pratt
1873-1941

This son of Isaac Thompson Pratt (1827) and Nancy Emeline Pritchett (1832) was born December 16, 1873 at Chatham Hill, in Smyth County, Virginia; died June 13, 1941; buried at Ridgedale Methodist Church in Rich Valley. Married May 5, 1897 to Jennie Webb, born July 30, 1879; died June 25, 1949; buried with her husband. She was daughter of Francis Marion Webb, born October 5, 1853 and died December 22, 1912; and his wife, Elizabeth Thurman McCready Webb, born April 15, 1860, and died February 8, 1936. Both are buried at Ridgedale, with numerous other family members. Charles Edward and Jennie had thirteen children:

Six of the nine sons of Charles Edward Pratt (1873)
Left to right: George 1903 ; Walter 1924; Frank 1899; Bill 1909;
Marion Thompson 1898 Front: Jack 1917

1. Marion Thompson, born February 6, 1898, of whom more
2. Frank, born October 5, 1899, of whom more
3. Annie Laura, born September 6, 1901; married September 17, 1922 to William James Orr, born August 18, 1891; died Feb-

145

ruary 11, 1970. Annie died July 12, 1985 in Florence, South Carolina. Both are buried at Ridgedale Cemetery in Smyth County, Virginia. Three children, born in Rich Valley:

a. Harold Edward, born August 10, 1923; died February 1, 1933; buried at Ridgedale

b. Dorothy Kate, born October 7, 1929 in Elizabethtown, Tennessee; married August 18, 1957 to Dr. Glen Gilbert Foster, born January 31, 1897 at Mt. Moriah, Missouri, and died September 28, 1986 at Galax, Virginia. Buried there at Felts Memorial Cemetery. They had two children:

    (1) David Gilbert, born June 30, 1959; married June 29, 1991 at Galax, Virginia, Debra Lynn Heavers Hart, born June 2, 1965. Both are professional musicians.

    (2) Ann Stuart, born February 1, 1961; she works as a vice/narcotics detective in the Sheriff's office of Stafford County, Virginia. She was married May 19, 1990 in Galax, Virginia, to Charles Everett Jett, born March 16, 1959, who is Captain of the Sheriff's office.

c. Barbara Jean, born February 7, 1936, and married James Thomas "Mickey" Foster (no relationship to Glen Foster), born August 21, 1933, and had two sons:

    (1) James Harrison, born November 17, 1957 in Galax, Virginia. Married first August 29, 1981 in Florence, South Carolina, to Jackie Green, born September 29, 1958. They had two children, and he was married second April 16, 1988 in Bel Aire, Maryland, to Kimberly McGee, born November 5, 1964. They also had two children, last listed:

        (a) James Ryan, born July 19, 1982 at Florence
        (b) Jack Keegan, born May 5, 1986 at Florence
        (c) Kylie Danielle, born December 28, 1988 at Russellville, Arkansas
        (d) Jonathan Kody, born July 13, 1990 at Russellville, Arkansas

    (2) Robert Orr, born August 22, 1960; single; lives in Effingham County, South Carolina

146

4. George Washington, born November 3, 1903; died July 31, 1954, single. Buried at Ridgedale cemetery.
5. Henry Oliver, born November 4, 1905, of whom more
6. Clarence Pritchett, born October 1, 1907; died February 28, 1926, single.
7. William Mann, born November 18, 1909, and died April 5, 1994; single.
8. Charles Edward, Jr., born December 5, 1911; died August 16, 1964. Married March 6, 1942 to Dolly Mae Hagy Glovier, who died October 15, 1974 in Greensboro, North Carolina. She had been previously married, with two children, raised by Charles Edward. One more child was born to their marriage:
   a. Nina Jane (Glovier); married Mathena
   b. Robert Blaine (Glovier)
   c. Libby Ann, born February 12, 1943 at English, West Virginia; married February 15, 1964 to Thomas Heflin Freeman. Divorced July, 1972 after two children:
      (1) Dennis Edward, born December 28, 1965 at Greensboro, North Carolina
      (2) Carol Lynn, born December 6, 1967 at Memphis, Tennessee
9. Agnes Gertrude, born May 12, 1914; of whom more
10. John Carson, born January 31, 1917; died December 8, 1989 at the hospital in Marion, Virginia. He owned and operated the farm originally owned by his father, having restored the old home place. Married November 10, 1945 Annie Evelyn Clear, born September 22, 1919, daughter of Harve Franklin Clear and Annie Hubble Clear. On one of my visits to their home, I was going to walk down to the small farm where grandfather Isaac Thompson Pratt had lived and raised his family. Since I do not walk very well, due to multiple by-passes in my legs, Jack gave me an old cane from the barn. He believes it to have been made by grandfather during the latter years of his life and, when I left, Jack gave me the cane as a family heirloom. They had one daughter:
    a. Pamela Joan, born July 18, 1955 at Chatham Hill, and married March 30, 1991 to Edward Rhudy Harmon.

11. Edith Mable, born December 6, 1918, and died November 24, 1993. Married December 13, 1941 to Isaac Henry Talbert, known as Tony. He was born February 14, 1912 and died July 4, 1979 after a long illness. Buried at Mt. Rose Cemetery, Glade Springs, Virginia. No children.

12. Mamie Olivene, born August 4, 1921; married December 13, 1941 to Walter R. Talbert, in a double wedding with her sister, who married his brother, Tony.

13. Walter James (or James Walter, known as "Slick"), born January 20, 1924 at Ridgedale; married July 30, 1950 to Effie Angeline Blevins, born August 4, 1931 at Seven Mile Ford, Virginia, daughter of Uriah Smith Blevins and Mary Collins Blevins. They live in the Atkins area, and had two children:

    a. Charles Walter, born April 23, 1951; married first to Ann and divorced. Married second September 3, 1982 to Shirley Marie Leonard, born December 11, 1953 at Marion, Virginia, a daughter of Ray and Thelma Bolt Leonard. He has raised registered Angus cattle since the age of twelve, and received the Bartenslager Award as distinguished Virginia cattleman for 1986; the Evergreen Soil and Water Conservation District Clean Water Award for 1994; and the 1994 Governor's Model Clean Water Farm Award. Shirley was nominated the first Teacher of the Year at Atkins Elementary; named in *Who's Who Among America's Teachers* in 1990 and 1995. They had two children:

        (1) Charles Jason, born July 6, 1983
        (2) Sara Elizabeth, born July 5, 1985

    b. Norma, born July 8, 1952, and married Charles Allen Teaters; children:

        (1) Charles Houston, born October 15, 1973
        (2) Jessica Lee, born March 19, 1979

Family of Marion Thompson Pratt c.1977
Left to right, front: Eleanor Pratt Armentrout; Twyla Jane Pratt Clark;
Linda Carol Pratt DiYorio; Nina Kate Buchanan Pratt
Rear: Stuart Thompson Pratt; Janet Laine Pratt;
Roberta Marion Pratt Griffin.

Marion Thompson Pratt
1898-1954

This son of Charles Edward Pratt (1873) was born February 6, 1898; died July 11, 1954; and is buried at Ridgedale Methodist Church cemetery. He was a farmer in the Cove, and ran a country store at Ridgedale. In 1943, he purchased the W. P. Buchanan farm near Chatham Hill, Smyth County, Virginia, where his family still lived in 1992. He was active in the Rich Valley Presbyterian Church, donating a steer for the building of the manse. Married twice; first to Sarah C. Brown, born August 22, 1898; died June 30, 1934; buried at Ridgedale. Married second August, 1935 Nina Kate Buchanan, born October 30, 1907. They had seven children, all born in Smyth County, Virginia:

1. Roberta Marion, born August 8, 1936; married Eugene McMurran Griffin of Woodlawn, Virginia, and had a son:
   a. Eugene McMurran, Jr., born August 8, 1958; married December 23, 1990 to Debra Horan.
2. Janet Laine, born October 11, 1938; single. Graduate nurse and has spent her life devoted to the profession. Masters degree in education from Virginia Tech. Teacher at Norfolk General Hospital; Community Hospital of Roanoke Valley, and Wytheville Community College.
3. Stuart Thompson, born October 24, 1940; married Dreama Spence of Blacksburg, Virginia, and had four children:
   a. James David, born July 23, 1969
   b. Timothy, a twin, born July 31, 1972
   c. Todd, a twin, born July 31, 1972
   d. Stephen, born November, 1976
4. Eleanor Pritchett, born September 9, 1944, and married Dr. William M. Armentrout of Tazewell, Virginia. Divorced, after one child:
   a. Carol Tipton, born September 1, 1968; married November 28, 1993 James Edward Matherley.
5. A stillbirth son, May 18, 1947
6. Linda Carol, born September 24, 1948; married June 20, 1970 to Dr. John Salvatore DiYorio of Charleston, South Carolina, born January 23, 1943. He was professsor of chemistry at

Wytheville Community College. Both have been active in church and civic activities; two children:
a.   John Christopher, born April 3, 1971; married November 14, 1993 to April Crouse, born December 17, 1974, and had a child:
(1)   Jonathan Gabriel, born April 15, 1993
b.   Ashley Diane, born March 5, 1977
7.   Twyla Jane, born September 17, 1952; married Charles Champ Clark, Jr. of Chilhowie, Virginia, a son of Charles Champ Clark and Mildred Virginia Bonham Clark. They had three children:
a.   Charles Champ, III, born September 13, 1980
b.   William Thompson, born May 4, 1982
c.   James Benjamin, born July 1, 1986

Frank Pratt
1899-1974

This son of Charles Edward Pratt (1873) was born October 5, 1899; died April 7, 1974; buried at Ridgedale Methodist Church in Smyth County, Virginia. Married December 24, 1927 to Blanche Beatrice Buchanan, born February 27, 1905; died October 7, 1963. Her parents were William Worth Buchanan, born March 5, 1880; died January 28, 1955; and Edna Lee Coulthard Buchanan, born January 13, 1879; died November 14, 1964. In the early years of their marriage, Frank worked for his father-in-law in sawmill camps in Smyth County, later moving to Cussin' Hollow, and about 1935, to Locust Cove. Frank and Blanche had five children:
1.   William Frank, born October 18, 1928; married October 15, 1949 to Lois Emogine Olinger (known as Peggy), born February 10, 1931, daughter of David and Mary Virginia Mitchell Olinger. They had children:
a.   Andrea Carole, born August 27, 1951; married May 19, 1973 Richard Herbert Mansell, born January 14, 1944. Carole furnished massive amounts of information for this study, for which we are grateful. She also sent along a copy of *The Pratt Family Cookbook*, containing favorite recipes of members of this branch of the family, which is

sure to become a collectible. She holds a DDS from the Medical College of Virginia, where she met her husband. Both are dentists, practicing together in Dublin, Virginia. Two children:

    (1)   Megan Pratt, born April 20, 1979

    (2)   William Matthew, born July 18, 1981

b.   Nancy Mason, born May 25, 1954; a graduate of Emory and Henry College, and holds a masters in community counseling. Married August 30, 1975 to David Allen Stevenson; divorced January 6, 1984

2.   Edna Virginia, born March 24, 1930; married September 2, 1948 William Franklin Lamie at Marion, born February 26, 1926, son of Raymond Etny Lamie (1884-1949), and his second wife, Virginia Tennessee Horton Lamie (1891-1976). William Franklin is an uncle of Lee Garfield Lamie, who married Mary Patsy Pratt, following. The children of this marriage were:

a.   Betty Kay, born November 17, 1949; married June 19, 1971 Charles Sydenstricker Armentrout, born April 5, 1948, and had two children:

    (1)   Charles Lewis, born December 5, 1975

    (2)   Ethan William, born December 4, 1977

b.   Raymond Franklin, born September 2, 1952, and married January 3, 1972 to Cynthia Diane Gates, born January 1, 1956. Divorced October 19, 1994, and had children:

    (1)   James Travis, born April 16, 1975

    (2)   Trenton Lee, born August 28, 1976

    (3)   Troy Etny, born October 15, 1977

c.   Carl Carson, born October 25, 1953; married July 12, 1974 Sally Lorraine Puckett, born June 29, 1956, and had children:

    (1)   James Wesley, born April 7, 1977

    (2)   Alicia Lorraine, born February 16, 1979

d.   Vicki Jean, born December 9, 1955 at Saltville, Virginia;; married June 7, 1974 Ronald Dean Call; divorced March 13, 1981, and moved to Houston, Texas. Married second June 12, 1982 to Carroll Lynn Gonzales, born November

10, 1950 at Houston. He had two children from a prior marriage, and they had a child, the third listed:

    (1)   Brandt, born 1971

    (2)   Stefanie, born 1972

    (3)   Justin Lynn, born January 29, 1987 who, at the age of eight, water-skis, and holds a green belt in karate.

e.   John Mantz, born February 2, 1957; married August 31, 1991 to Patricia Ann Morrell, born June 1, 1960, and had a child:

    (1)   Murphy Franklin, born November 7, 1994

f.   Mark Pratt, born August 18, 1958

3.   Mary Patsy, born October 30, 1931 at Chatham Hill, Smyth County, Virginia; married January 11, 1957 Lee Garfield Lamie at Marion, Virginia. He was born December 4, 1931; died August 28, 1976, son of Walter Early Lamie and Ruby Pauline Buchanan Lamie. Two children:

a.   Gary Lee, born July 17, 1958

b.   Pattie Jean, born February 13, 1960; married June 12, 1987 to Proffit, Charles H. Proffit, Jr., born October 21, 1956. He had two children from a prior marriage, and they have a son:

    (1)   Michelle

    (2)   Charles

    (3)   John Lucas, born January 5, 1995 at Bristol, Tennessee.

4.   Robert Preston, born December 13, 1933; married June 25, 1954 Carolyn Warner Taylor, born May 3, 1936 at Broad Ford, Virginia, the youngest of the eleven children of Harvey George Taylor and Ovella Henegar Taylor. Three children:

a.   Theresa Anne, born December 13, 1956; married August 28, 1976 to Jerry Dean Hubble, born February 20, 1954, and had children:

    (1)   Robert Nathan, born July 3, 1981

    (2)   David Owen, born January 12, 1984

b.   Brenda Joy, born March 4, 1960; married June 16, 1979 to Benjamin Rogers Lee, Jr., born November 21, 1956. She holds a BS in clothing and textiles, and enrolled in a masters program. Moved to Newport News, Virginia, in 1981; she was a security officer/hotel detective for Colonial Williamsburg. Moved to New Kent County 1990, where they currently live. He does aerospace research and development for Dynamic Engineering.

 c. Sheila Lynn, born February 6, 1965

5. Paul Denny, born October 9, 1935; married June 15, 1962 to Mary Ann Gilbert, born October 4, 1942. Three children:

 a. Deborah Jean, born June 10, 1963

 b. Gregory Allen, born June 15, 1965; married June 8, 1991 to Beth Anne Chisler, born May 23, 1971. He is a third grade teacher, currently living at Rural Retreat, Virginia.

 c. Dana Rae, born June 30, 1977

Henry Oliver and Hattie Mae Walden Pratt
Rosedale Farm, Lebanon, Virginia

Henry Oliver Pratt
1905-1972

This son of Charles Edward Pratt (1873) was born November 4, 1905; died March 13, 1972; and is buried at Russell Memorial Cemetery, Lebanon, in Russell County, Virginia. Married January 15, 1927 Hattie Mae Walden, born August 28, 1909; died December 28, 1971; buried with her husband. He was known by all simply as "H. O." and was a highly successful farmer and livestock dealer. Their home at Lebanon, known as the *Rosedale Farm*, is a magnificent example of the southern colonial plantation style architecture, complete with massive columns and the Monticello-type dome over the entry. My mother has told me that H. O. was a very shrewd, but honest, trader in stock, and that he symbolized his agreement on a deal by slapping his leg, with the comment, "Done!" That leg slap was widely known as being just as binding as a written contract. He was the father of ten children:

1. Harry Edward, born October 31, 1928 at Ridgedale, Virginia
2. Geraldine Josephine, born December 31, 1929, and married Herbert MacNeil.
3. Annie Lee, born March 2, 1931; married March 14, 1950 to Kenneth Warren Eyestone, born December 31, 1916 at Upper Sandusky, Ohio. Two children:
   a. Margaret Ann, born May 3, 1951
   b. Kenneth William, born June 29, 1953
4. Dott Clarence, born September 2, 1932 at Clifton, Virginia; married June 14, 1963 to Patsy Sue Butcher, born July 1, 1942 at Richlands, Tazewell County, Virginia, daughter of James Butcher and Mary Elizabeth Shortt Butcher. He is a teacher and has published several books and pamphlets of his original short stories and poetry. Two daughters:
   a. Jacqueline Ann, born January 4, 1965
   b. Samantha Adria, born April 19, 1969
5. Betty Sue, born October 31, 1933 at Belfast, Virginia; died 1994. Married to Herbert S. Hale. Two children:
   a. Lloyd Henry, born July 31, 1963
   b. Barbara Jane, born November 11, 1965

The Daughters of Henry Oliver Pratt
From left: Geraldine; Annie; Betty Sue; Jean; Peggy Ruth; Marion Paige

Sons of Henry Oliver Pratt
From left: Harry and Henry Carlton; Charles Arthur in painting.

6. Charlotte Jean, born May 1, 1935 at Belfast; married in 1958 to Sampson P. Leazer, who died of lung cancer October 16, 1990. One child:
   a. Laura Francine, married to Christopher Keith Murray of Atlanta, Georgia. Two daughters:
      (1) Melissa Elaine, born August 8, 1982
      (2) Allison Taylor, born April 27, 1984
7. Peggy Ruth, born November 12, 1936 at Belfast; married May 24, 1959 at Duluth, Georgia, to James Thomas McGee, born there July 24, 1927, son of Carl and Minnie Morton McGee. They had one son:
   a. James Thomas, Jr., born September 25, 1960 in Duluth and has one son:
      (1) Killian, born May 3, 1989 in Lawrenceville, Ga.
8. Marion Paige, born June 18, 1938 at Belfast; single.
9. Henry Carlton, known as "Foots", born May 30, 1939; married to Judge Susan Bundy, and had two children. In 1985, he was the owner of the family estate known as *Rosedale Farm*, as well as the Carriage House Motel in Lebanon, major stockyards and other investments.
10. Charles Arthur, born July 10, 1940 at Lebanon, and died September 26, 1972 at Richmond, Virginia; single.

Agnes Gertrude Pratt
1914-

This daughter of Charles Edward Pratt (1873) was born May 12, 1914; married May 30, 1931 to Robert Buchanan Carter, born May 27, 1911 in Smyth County, Virginia, son of James Wesley Carter and Cora Buchanan Carter. Eight children, born at Chatham Hill, in Smyth County:
1. Lois Christine, born March 17, 1932; married June 3, 1950 to Harley Thomas Keesee, born September 27, 1931 in Smyth County; died April 18, 1987 of lung cancer, and is buried at Ridgedale cemetery. Three children, the first born at Roanoke, and the last two at Nebo, Virginia:
   a. Howard Thomas, born September 21, 1952, and married 1990 to Kimberly Box; divorced, no children.

157

b. Judy Beth, born July 29, 1955; married Robert Atkins, Jr. from Ceres, Virginia, and had two children:
   (1) David Brian, born c.1977
   (2) James Thomas, born c.1979
c. Daniel Richard, born September 26, 1956; married to Rebecca Breedlove from Pulaski, Virginia; one child:
   (1) Michelle Dawn, born 1989
2. Bettie Sue, born September 10, 1933; married August 4, 1950 to Elbert M. Tibbs, born November 6, 1930. Three children:
   a. Gary Wayne, born July 17, 1953 in Kansas City, Kansas; died April 11, 1992 of pneumonia. Married Janet Harmon. Two children:
      (1) Dennis
      (2) Missy; married Danny Delp, and has a son:
         (a) Daniel Wayne
   b. Sharon Kay, born April 26, 1957; married John Olinger. An adopted daughter:
      (1) Sonya Joyce; married Randall Evans, and had two daughters:
         (a) Lisa
         (b) Jennifer
   c. Joyce Elaine, born January 20, 1960; died December 2, 1991 of breast cancer. Married to Ronald Evans.
3. Daisy Ruth, born June 9, 1935; married November 7, 1953 to Wesley Hart, and had children:
   a. Rita
   b. Michael
   c. Ronald
4. Donald Hugh, born February 11, 1937, and married May 15, 1962 to Linda Faye Lott, and had children:
   a. Beverly
   b. William
   c. Steve
5. Raymond Lee, born July 3, 1942; married first to Mary Ann Boothe. Divorced, and married second April 16, 1977 to Carol Hiersoux. He had children:
   a. Tina
   b. Raymond Scott

    c. Toni
    d. Christopher
6. Janet Faye, born September 29, 1943; married June 27, 1962
   Larry Malcolm Buchanan, born in Smyth County, a son of
   Samuel Lee Buchanan and Mae McGhee Buchanan. They had
   one adoptive child:
    a. Jonathan
7. Robert Buchanan, Jr., born November 28, 1945, and married
   November 19, 1969 to Peggy Stone. Two children:
    a. Wayne
    b. Vicky
8. Samuel Joe, born April 5, 1948, and married November 3,
   1976 to Margaret Ann Kirby. Two children:
    a. Kevin Keith
    b. Timothy Joe

Harrison Campbell Pratt
1876-1944

This son of Isaac Thompson Pratt (1827) and Nancy Emeline
Pritchett (1832) was born April 14, 1876; died January 12, 1944.
Married Minnie M. Asbury, born 1880 and died 1967, daughter of
George W. Asbury (born c.1836) and Rebecca E. Asbury (born
c.1837). Harrison Campbell and Minnie are buried at the Ridgedale
Methodist Church cemetery; they had seven children:
1. Margaret Virginia, born February 19, 1899 at Chatham Hill,
   in Smyth County, Virginia. Married Payton Howard Gregory,
   born August 16, 1895; died April 22, 1954. Both are buried at
   Ridgedale cemetery. Four children, the first born at Marion, in
   Smyth County, Virginia; the last three born at Thacker, West
   Virginia:
    a. Buford Lynwood, born October 13, 1919; died December
       13, 1974. Married February, 1946 Lois Moses
    b. Lloyd Haskell, born March 7, 1923; married first Febru-
       ary 12, 1946 at Pikeville, Kentucky, Ruth Graham, and
       second on June 12, 1976 to Virginia Lee Reed. Three
       children from first marriage, all born at Bluefield, West
       Virginia:

      (1)   Winston Haskell, born October 1, 1947; married Jackie Clark.

      (2)   William Howard, born February 15, 1950; married Brenda Perry.

      (3)   Donna Lynn, born April 22, 1954; married Robert Ershine.

  c.   Basil Carson, born April 16, 1927; died September 22, 1947. Buried at Ridgedale cemetery.

  d.   Kenneth Kera, born June 10, 1930; died May 25, 1976

James Washington Pratt & Beatrice Gilley Pratt

2.   James Washington, born June 3, 1901 at Bondtown, Virginia; died January 15, 1965 and buried at Ridgedale cemetery with other family members. Married c.1925 in Bristol, Virginia to

Beatrice Gilley, born November 10, 1905; died July 27, 1982, and is buried in West Virginia. Five children:

a. Nancy Ann, born August 22, 1935 in Davy, West Virginia; died August 21, 1979 in Portsmouth, Virginia. Married there in 1954 to David Rexford Smith, who died in 1986. Three children, born in Portsmouth and, in 1992, all living there:
    (1) David Rexford, Jr.; married to Glenda Elaine Faulkner, and had a daughter:
        (a) Kelly Jorden
    (2) Debra Ann; married Vernon Bowers; two children:
        (a) Angelina Marie
        (b) Amber Leigh Nancy Ann
    (3) Robert William; married and had a son:
        (a) Robert William, Jr.

b. Shirley Jean, born April 6, 1936 in Wyoming, West Virginia; married in 1953 Walter Junior Toler, and had two children:
    (1) Kenneth James, born February 10, 1956; married Rita Bailey. No children.
    (2) Veanna Lynn, married Richard Gardner; divorced, after one child. Married second James Roberts and had a second daughter:
        (a) Tammy Lynn, born February 17, 1974
        (b) Amy Renae, born November 1, 1977

c. Frederick Noel, born July 23, 1937 at Wyoming, West Virginia; married 1966 to Amelia Marara. They lived in San Diego, California (in 1992), where Fred was a retired Navy Chief after twenty-three years of service. One son:
    (1) Frederick Noel, Jr., born July 21, 1967

d. Betty Ruth, born September 13, 1940 in Baileysville, West Virginia; married June 9, 1961 Kenneth R. Larson in Rosemead, California. He was a high school teacher, and she an Administrative Assistant in Santa Barbara, California. Two sons:
    (1) Kenneth James, born May 2, 1967, and married January 18, 1992 to Gretchen Schmidt

      (2)   Robert Paul, born January 20, 1970; married June 6, 1992 to Carolyn Ray.

e.   Harrison Campbell, born March 16, 1943 and died April, 1968; single.

Kenneth Larson; Betty Pratt Larson; Sons Kenneth James & Robert Paul

3.   Edna, born January, 1904 at Chatham Hill, Virginia; married to Neal Fox.

4.   Martha, born March, 1907 in Warrensburg, Missouri; died October 14, 1975. Her parents apparently visited her father's brother, Henry Thompson Pratt (1861) in Missouri, and while there, Martha was born, and presumably named for her aunt, Martha Loraine Carson Pratt (1866). Married three times: Ray McClure; Frank Hammond; and William Fisher.

5.   Oliver, born July 7, 1912 at Chatham Hill; died December 23, 1958 at Marion, Virginia. Married Mary Petty.

6.   Vivian, born 1913 at Chatham Hill; married first Roy Grimes and second William Fisher. Daughter from first marriage:
    a.   Dianne, married to Wittek.

7.   Donald Ray, born August 25, 1921 at Marion, Virginia; and married October 13, 1942 to Mabel Evelyn Bise, born c.1921, daughter of John Walter and Georgia Burgess Bise. One son:

a. Donald Gary, who had twin sons from a first marriage, and married second December 20, 1980 at Richmond to Virginia Diane Miles Doucet, daughter of John Henry Miles, Jr.; her second marriage also.

Harrison Campbell Pratt
1876-1944

CHAPTER 14

The Pritchett Families

The first wife of Isaac Thompson Pratt (1827), and the mother of his first eleven children, was Nancy Emeline Pritchett, born May 19, 1832, daughter of John Anderson Pritchett (1794) and Nancy Hilton Albert Johnston (1790). The Pritchetts were found early in the mountains of southwest Virginia, and as will be discussed, many of them joined the Mormon movement, and made their way west, settling with large families in Utah and nearby areas.

The earliest member of the family we have found in Virginia records was one James William Pritchett, reportedly born c.1740 and married to Elizabeth. They were the parents of, at least, Samuel Pritchett, who will be the head of the first family reported following. It should first be noted that the Pritchett name is found in various records as Prichard, Pritchard, Pretchett and Pritchet, which is not uncommon in early records of America. In those early days, many of our ancestors could not read nor write, and names were recorded as best they could be understood by the clerk making the record.

Another important factor in the lives of the Pritchett families is that during the 1800s, elders of the Church of Jesus Christ of Latter Day Saints apparently travelled widely through the mountains of southwest Virginia. Numerous members of the Pritchett family; and those of the Lowder, Heninger, Painter, Claypool, Thompson, Clark and other families; joined the Mormon movement, and large numbers of them moved westward, where they had large families. Many of their descendants are found in the Mormon church records and large numbers of them are currently living in Utah, Idaho, and other western states with substantial Mormon populations. Mormon ancestral file records contain much more extensive records on some of these families beyond what is presented here.

Samuel Pritchett
c.1761-

This son of James William Pritchett (1740) and wife Elizabeth was probably not their only child, and was born between 1761 and 1768 in Shenandoah County, Virginia, in an area that later became part of Page County, and died in Rockbridge County, Virginia. He was married November 20, 1793 in Culpeper County to Rebecca Anderson, born c.1776, perhaps in Scotland; died December 27, 1858 in Rockbridge County, Virginia; daughter of John and Mary Anderson. Samuel and Rebecca were parents of a number of children, all reported in the records mentioned as being born in Smyth County, Virginia, although it was not created until 1832. The Mormon records are apparently indexed to current counties. The children were:

1. Eddy Campbell, born c.1792; married 1814 Martha Filmett.
2. John Anderson, born August 4, 1794, of whom more
3. William DeCalb, born c.1798; married c.1820 Sarah Rouse
4. David, born c.1800; died 1817
5. Eunice, born c.1804; married to Quigley.
6. Napoleon Bonaparte, born c.1806
7. James Mitchell, born June 1, 1817, of whom more
8. Polly, born c.1820, and probably married January 21, 1834 to William Bise.

John Anderson Pritchett
1794-1875

This son of Samuel Pritchett (1761) and Rebecca Anderson Pritchett (1776) was born August 4, 1794 in an area that in 1832 became part of Smyth County, Virginia; and died there November 16, 1875. Married in 1816 to Nancy Hilton Albert Johnston, born December 25, 1790 in Pennsylvania, daughter of William Johnston and Nancy Scarr Johnston. He was reportedly married second in August, 1860 to Martha Jane DeBord, born c.1830 in Smyth County. Mormon records suggest that he may have been married a third time to Nancy Jane DeBord, born May 17, 1834. His children, the first born in Tazewell County, Virginia, and the rest in

165

Smyth County, included nine from the first marriage, and four from the marriage to Nancy Jane DeBord, the last two daughters (twins) being born when John Anderson was about 71 years of age, although his wife was only about 31 at the time. That is very close to the age of my grandfather Isaac Thompson Pratt when his eighteenth child was born. The children of John Anderson Pritchett were:

1. Eliza Ann, born August 27, 1817; married June 7, 1844 to Coleman Joplin (or Joplen).

2. Susanna Jane, born November 12, 1818; marriage bond dated July 10, 1840 with Jackson Hambrick (or Hamrich), born January 8, 1815 at Franklin, Virginia. Four children, born at Chatham Hill:

    a. Mary Virginia, born May 10, 1842; died July 25, 1926 at Fairview, Sanpete County, Utah. She was first married to Samuel Williams and may have had children. Married second her cousin, John Anderson Pritchett, born September 23, 1840 Smyth County; died October 20, 1920 at Fairview, son of James Mitchell Pritchett (1817), and had a rather large family, discussed in the section devoted to her husband, which see.

    b. Thaddeus Clay, born October 4, 1844, of whom more

    c. Martha Ann, born May 25, 1846; died September 18, 1901 at Ontario, Oregon. Married January 5, 1862 to Alexander Darr, born June 5, 1838 in Russell County, Virginia; died February 26, 1899 at Ontario, Oregon; and had seven children. Married second April 18, 1900 to James Edward Long. Children born to marriage to Darr:

        (1) Eliza Penelope, born March 9, 1865 at Springfield, Missouri; died July 23, 1929. Married October 19, 1884 at Payette, in Ada County, Idaho, to George Washington Long, born February 1, 1863 in Browning, Missouri. At least a son:

            (a) Son, married Jennie Isabelle King, born January 16, 1900 at Wallace, Idaho.

        (2) George, born c.1867; married Betty

        (3) Mary Susan, born December 14, 1868; died May 12, 1951. Married Leonard M. Morton, born 1859 in Kansas.

166

(4)   May, born c.1870; married John Fresh
(5)   Annette, born c.1872; married Fresh.
(6)   Alonzo, born c.1874; married Morton.
(7)   James, born c.1876
d.   Catherine, born c.1860; apparently died young.

3.   Mary Ann, born October 31, 1821; died October 5, 1879 at Mt. Pleasant, Sanpete County, Utah. Married April 20, 1856 to Alexander Jackson Brooks, born April 2, 1813 at Burkes Garden, Tazewell County, Virginia; died October 3, 1864 at Abingdon, Virginia; son of Thomas Brooks and Catherine Clancy Brooks. They had three children:

a.   Nancy Eliza Snow, or Nancy Jane, born October 1, 1857, of whom more.
b.   Susan Sarah, born April 18, 1859, of whom more.
c.   Mary Ann Barbara, born June 20, 1862 at Chatham Hill, Smyth County, Virginia; died April 12, 1947. Married there February 9, 1880 to Thaddeus Clay Hambrick, born October 4, 1844 at Chatham Hill, son of Jackson Hambrick (1815) and Susanna Jane Pritchett Hambrick (1818). She was his second wife, and their children will be discussed under his name listing.

4.   William DeCalb, born March 3, 1824, and died December 29, 1885 at Ogden, in Weber County, Utah. Bond dated September 22, 1849 for marriage to Barbara Ellen Fulcher, born March 11, 1828 at Marion, Smyth County; died April 12, 1884 at Harrisville, Weber County, Utah; a daughter of Douglas Jackson Fulcher (1791) and Nancy Atwell Fulcher. They had as many as ten children, the first eight born in Smyth County, Virginia (obviously some of the birth dates do not work; that is how they were recorded where I found them) and the last two in Utah:

a.   Susan Calpernia, born January 7, 1851, of whom more.
b.   John Douglas, born November 12, 1853, of whom more.
c.   Barbara, born November 9, 1854; died June 21, 1938.
d.   Nancy Elizabeth, born January 22, 1856; died May 30, 1924 at Sheridan, Montana. Married May 3, 1876 to Thomas Loy Lee, born June 17, 1846 at Bullit, Ken-

tucky; died April 19, 1923 at Sheridan, Montana; son of R. N. Lee and Nancy Ann Villars Lee. Five children;

(1) Loy Homer, born April 16, 1877 at Ogden, Utah; died December 13, 1957. Married December 25, 1898 to Susanna Frances Long.

(2) Howard Closson, born December 2, 1878 at Ogden; died August 31, 1954. Married September 18, 1912 to Martha Carrolin Hodge.

(3) Rector Lawrence, born February 11, 1881 at Harrisville, Utah; died August 20, 1970 Los Angeles, California. Married June 15, 1903 at Salt Lake City to Betsy Robbins, born January 6, 1885 at Santaquin, Utah; died August 8, 1954 at Salt Lake City; daughter of William Carter Robbins and Betsy Taylor Robbins. Married second on May 22, 1956 to Margaret Starbuck. He had children from his first marriage:

(a) Rector Leonard, born March 11, 1904 at Midvale, Utah; died May 15, 1907

(b) Fredric Arthur, born May 10, 1907 Midvale and died September 12, 1907

(c) Harry James, born April 14, 1908 at Provo, Utah, and died September 25, 1908

(d) Thomas William; married Ada Schaerrer

(e) Lawrence Howard

(4) Viola Desseretta, born October 24, 1882 Ontario, in Malheur County, Oregon; died May 8, 1958. Married March 18, 1903 Charles Green Bennett.

(5) Estella, born October 11, 1887 Lima, Beaverhead County, Montana; died at age two.

e. Margaret Adeline, born August 28, 1860; died April 16, 1918 at Idaho Falls, Idaho. Married December 27, 1877 at Salt Lake City, Utah, to David Hastings Hiatt, born September 17, 1855 in Surry County, North Carolina. They had five children; first three born in Weber County, Utah; the last two at Coltman, Idaho:

(1) John William, born October 12, 1878

     (2)   Clarence Rodolphus, born March 27, 1881, and married Edith Mae Jones.

     (3)   Sara Frances, born June 17, 1888; married twice: Reuben George Boam, and Henry Fearon.

     (4)   Lizzie Velettie, born October 20, 1893; died June 27, 1974 at Idaho Falls, Idaho. Married November 22, 1911 at Coltman to John Edwin Pritchett, born April 22, 1881, which see.

     (5)   Geneva Deseret, born May 29, 1897

f.   Samuel Spottswood, born August 28, 1862; died May 30, 1923.

g.   Stonewall Jackson, born February 8, 1862

h.   Mary Virginia Desserete, born January 30, 1864

i.   Katherine Emaline, born August 15, 1867; died February 23, 1874. Married Frank Vines.

j.   William Frank, born February 13, 1870

5.   Samuel Napoleon Bonaparte, born January 18, 1827, of whom more.

6.   Sarah Bryant, born March 21, 1829, of whom more.

7.   William, born c.1830

8.   Barbara, born c.1830

9.   Nancy Emeline, born May 19, 1832; and married to Isaac Thompson Pratt (1827), of whom more in Chapter 13

10.   Kitty Emeline Alice, born June 1, 1860; died October 9, 1911. Married May 3, 1877 to John Goff.

11.   Rebecca Rachel, born December 27, 1861 (or December 29, 1863); died March 4, 1923. Married April 13, 1888 to Samuel Porter.

12.   Fannie Elizabeth, a twin, born February 8, 1865; died August 30, 1911. Married January 1, 1884 to William Patrick.

13.   Virginia Clementine, a twin, born February 8, 1865; married to James Nelson.

Thaddeus Clay Hambrick
1844-

This son of Jackson Hambrick (1815) and Susanna Jane Pritchett Hambrick (1818), was born October 4, 1844 at Chatham

Hill, Smyth County, Virginia; died February 24, 1904 at Castle Dale, Emery County, Utah. Married c.1868 Harriet Harris, born c.1841 Browning, Lynn County, Missouri; three children. Married second February 9, 1880 to his cousin, Mary Ann Barbara Brooks, born June 20, 1862 at Chatham Hill, Virginia, daughter of Alexander Jackson Brooks (1813) and Mary Ann Pritchett Brooks (1821), and had the last twelve children listed:

1. John, born May 9, 1868 at Browning, Lynn County, Missouri; died September 9, 1869.
2. Lucetta, born December 5, 1869 at Browning; died December 27, 1958 at Salt Lake City, Utah. Married October 31, 1890 at Manti, Sanpete County, Utah, to Ezekiel Thomas Cheney, born June 15, 1872 at Fairview, Sanpete County, Utah; died there July 3, 1922; son of Elam Cheney and Martha Taylor Cheney. They had children, born there. Married second November 20, 1929 to Andrew Christensen. Her children from the first marriage, born at Fairview, included:
   a. William Thadd, born January 20, 1892; died that day
   b. Aaron Linden, born February 4, 1893; died September 28, 1970 at Provo, Utah. Married January 7, 1914 to Valera Stewart at Manti, Utah; born April 5, 1893 at Milburn, Utah.
   c. Clyde Leon, born July 30, 1895; died January 13, 1968; married June 5, 1915 to Iva Pearl Crowdis.
   d. Mervin Ezekiel born November 27, 1897. died December 29, 1898.
   e. Harriet Glenda, born April 9, 1901; died May 14, 1907
   f. Thaddeus Faugne, born March 5, 1905; lived nine days
   g. Monta Kreal.
   h. Harris Bennett.
   i. Crystal Pearl, born June 26, 1914; died March 15, 1961. Married May 14, 1930 Oscar Ivie Shepherd, born July 18, 1910; married second Earl Wineford Stevens.
3. Emily, born c.1870
4. Mary Susan, born November 29, 1880 Mt. Pleasant, Sanpete County, Utah, as were the next four children; died December 18, 1922. Married October 13, 1899 to Floren Peterson, born

December 8, 1876 at South Cottonwood, Salt Lake County, Utah.

5. Alice Maud, born April 15, 1882; married June 30, 1902 to Charles A. Swasey.

6. William Thaddeus, born December 9, 1883; died March 11, 1954. Married to Alice Sargent.

7. Alexander Jackson, born December 1, 1885, and died October 26, 1926.

8. Margaret Myrtle, born November 29, 1887; married July 23, 1907 Charley Peter Olsen, born February 19, 1882 at Castle Dale, Emery County, Utah.

9. Winnie Jasmine, born March 5, 1890 at Castle Dale, Utah, as were the rest of these children; married March 18, 1914 to Robert Jarrett Ockey, born May 12, 1890 at Nephi, in Juab County, Utah.

10. John David, born May 18, 1892; died May 26, 1945. Married October 9, 1919 to Ellen Robertson.

11. Clarence Franklin, born May 28, 1894; died May 12, 1903

12. Lillian Virginia, born May 2, 1897; died same day

13. Eugene Earl, born May 3, 1898; died April 7, 1901

14. Douglas Lee, born July 19, 1900; died November 3, 1964

15. A daughter, married Leonard Charles Jensen, born September 26, 1897 at Orangeville, Emery County, Utah.

Nancy Jane Brooks
1857-1940

This daughter of Alexander Jackson Brooks and Mary Ann Pritchett Brooks, was born October 1, 1857 and died March 5, 1940 at Mt. Pleasant, Sanpete County, Utah. In Mormon records, her name is listed variously as Nancy Eliza Snow or Nancy Jane Brooks, and we are not now sure of the proper name. Married to Joseph Frend, or Joseph Friend, or Frank Burton (again, various listings found in the Mormon records), born June 2, 1849 at Warmfield, Yorkshire, England, son of Joseph Burton and Eliza Cusworth Burton. Sixteen children listed under the Burton surname in those records, born at Mt. Pleasant, Sanpete County, Utah:

171

1. Joseph Alexander, born March 11, 1875; died September 6, 1875
2. John Arthur, born July 13, 1876; died May 14, 1942. Married May 27, 1902 to Anna Maybell Lundgren.
3. William Leonidas, born March 2, 1878; died January 20, 1919 at Storrs, Utah. Married October 10, 1906 at Salt Lake City to Marian Belle Allred, born May 8, 1883 at Mt. Pleasant; died January 17, 1956, daughter of Milford Alexander Allred and Inger Elizabeth Johnson Allred. Seven children:
   a. Virginia Belle, born July 18, 1907 at Salt Lake City; died October 17, 1924
   b. Milford Leonidas.
   c. Joseph William, born September 30, 1911; died young
   d. Mable Elizabeth; married Albert Emerson McPhee, born December 17, 1908 at Laramie, Wyoming
   e. Viola
   f. Dorothy; married Ralph Jean Chamberlain.
   g. Wilbert Larue, born February 21, 1919 at Storrs, Carbon County, Utah; died as an infant
4. Mary Ann, born January 5, 1880; died September 30, 1937. Married March 15, 1900 at Mt. Pleasant, Utah, to John Frederick Larsen, born there September 18, 1875; died March 19, 1940, son of Christian and Sophia Fredricksson Stromberg Larsen. They had children:
   a. Vernon Frederick; married Susan Merlene Whitaker.
   b. Leo Christian; married Relia Shaw.
   c. Burton; married
5. James Cusworth, born January 8, 1882; died October 9, 1966 at Salt Lake City, Utah. Married July 20, 1908 at Price, Utah, Ruvina Almira Allred, born September 30, 1890 at Fairview; died June 18, 1980 at Austin, Texas, daughter of John Martin Allred and Lula Almira Mower Allred. They had children:
   a. Ethel
   b. Lula
   c. Clarence James, born March 6, 1912 at Kenilworth, in Carbon County, Utah; died February 10, 1940
   d. Clyde Brooks
   e. Robert R.

  f. Max Leroy

  g. Grant Harold

  h. Vivian

  i. Helen Ruth

  j. Donald Bruce

6. Eliza, born May 1, 1884; died September 20, 1968. Married March 20, 1912 to John Christian Christensen, born March 26, 1883 at Fairview, Sanpete County, Utah

7. Martha Grace, born July 13, 1886; died November 17, 1960 at Mt. Pleasant. Married May 20, 1908 at Manti, Utah, to Moroni Johansen, born June 19, 1876 Mt. Pleasant, Sanpete County, Utah; died there March 29, 1959. They had children, born in Sanpete County:

  a. Ray Arvil, born July 25, 1909; died November 8, 1959 at Kenilworth, Utah. Married to Lydia Louise Otten.

  b. Hugh Noyle, born September 16, 1911; died December 22, 1944.

  c. Blanche Nancy

  d. Earl Jay, born July 15, 1916; died December 21, 1979 at Ogden, Utah. Married to Olive Bernice Christensen.

  e. Pearl May; married Frayne Wilford Christensen.

  f. Vea, born October 19, 1918; died October 26, 1918

  g. Florence Sena, born February 15, 1920; lived six days.

  h. Neal, born July 3, 1922; died July 12, 1922

  i. Nola Ruth, born July 4, 1928; lived four days

  j. Robert Kay, born December 22, 1930; lived five days

8. Susan Virginia, born December 17, 1888; died May 18, 1979. Married October 12, 1912 to Edward Stephen Kimer.

9. Stillbirth twin, January 23, 1891

10. Tea, a twin, born January 23, 1891

11. Nancy Josephine, born January 25, 1892; died at two days old

12. Henry Brooks, born April 24, 1893; died October 13, 1960. Married Mrs. Arffa Miller

13. Clarence Friend, born July 13, 1895; died February 4, 1896

14. Wilford Coleman, born December 16, 1896; died May 17, 1956. Married Coila Rosena Otten.

15. Sarah Alice, a twin, born March 27, 1900; died April 6, 1900

16. Silva Elis, a twin, born March 27, 1900; died May 25, 1900

Susan Sarah Brooks
1859-1881

This daughter of Alexander Jackson Brooks and Mary Ann Pritchett Brooks, was born April 18, 1859 at Chatham Hill, Virginia; died March 4, 1881 at Mt. Pleasant, Utah. Married Thomas Eldridge Fuller, Jr., born May 10, 1847 at Florence, Nevada; died March 20, 1896 at Mt. Pleasant; son of Thomas Eldridge Fuller and Sarah Elizabeth McArthur Fuller. He was married second April 1, 1885 to Mary Elizabeth Hudson, and third to Rosanna Hudson. Children, born to Susan Sarah, his first marriage, at Mt. Pleasant, in Sanpete County, Utah, included:

1. Thomas Eldridge, born March 7, 1875; died August 1, 1955.
2. Fanny Adell, born December 12, 1876; died November 23, 1950 at Jackson, Wyoming. Married May 6, 1893 to Alexander Nephi Robertson, born September 7, 1865 at Castle Dale, Utah; died November 28, 1934 at Jackson, Wyoming; son of John Robertson and Elizabeth McIndoe Robertson. They had children, born at Castle Dale, Utah:
   a. Dell; married Leora Maude Kitchen
   b. Ellen, born February 17, 1894; died August 24, 1972; married June 2, 1912 to Frederick Clark.
   c. Susan Elizabeth, born May 8, 1896, and married November 16, 1915 to Roy Lamb.
   d. Eldridge
   e. George Isaac, born August 11, 1901; died July 21, 1961. Married.
   f. Alexander
   g. Marion Thomas
   h. Dell Brooks
   i. Crystal; married Robert Alfred Nethercott.
3. Alexander, born October 17, 1877
4. Mary Elizabeth, a twin, born June 1, 1878
5. Susan Sarah, a twin, born June 1, 1878; died young

Susan Calpernia Pritchett
1851-1903

This daughter of William DeCalb Pritchett (1824) and Barbara Ellen Fulcher Pritchett (1828), was born January 7, 1851 at Marion, Smyth County, Virginia, and died June 9, 1903 at Ogden, Weber County, Utah. Married November 27, 1871 at Salt Lake City, Utah, to Seth Painter, born January 4, 1871 at Blackwood, Monmouth, Wales; died September 14, 1911 at Farr West, Weber County, Utah, a son of Thomas Painter and Martha Jane Williams Painter. Ten children, born in Weber County, Utah:

1. Martha Jane, born November 12, 1864; died April 23, 1940; married August 23, 1913 to Frank Sherwood. Another report shows this daughter born August 7, 1874; died October 23, 1940; married August 23, 1893 to Frank Sherwood.
2. John Seth, born October 30, 1872; died April 11, 1950; married October 1, 1913 at Ogden, Utah, to Godelia Andrea Folkman, born April 7, 1881 at Plain City, Weber County, Utah; died April 12, 1950 at Burley, Idaho; daughter of Christopher Olsen Folkman and Caroline Anderson Folkman. Four children:
   a. Susan Alice
   b. John Seth, Jr.
   c. Sylvia Bernice
   d. Louise
3. Barbara Ellen, born September 16, 1878; died August 18, 1967; married February 25, 1896 to Charles H. Murdock.
4. Thomas Jackson, born June 7, 1881; died July 12, 1923; and married January 15, 1900 to May Pritchett.
5. Jessie Estella, born February 15, 1885; died May 25, 1947 at Burley, Idaho. Married January 7, 1902 at Ogden, Utah, to Levi Hamilton Draney, born October 19, 1882 at Plain City, Weber County, Utah; dide April 20, 1952 at Burley, Idaho; and had children, born in Weber County, Utah:
   a. Levi Harold, born January 18, 1904; died July 21, 1971
   b. Hazel Maybell, born March 31, 1906; died February 29, 1972 at Mesa, Arizona; married to Charles Earl Stanger.

c. Jessie Gay; married to Carlos Smith Moffett, born September 17, 1904 at American Fork, Utah.

d. Albert Floyd, born October 19, 1912; died December 15, 1967; married Floy Manning.

e. Sherman Park.

f. Afton Delora; married Earl Dean Lyons.

g. Jack Leroy, born April 9, 1920 at Burley, Idaho; died June 26, 1968 at Warden, Grant County, Washington; married Elda Jane Fowles.

h. Leonard Lee.

i. Donna Dean.

6. William Wyatt, born August 19, 1886; died April 18, 1960 at Ogden, Utah. Married December 22, 1909 at Salt Lake City to Elizabeth Mae Holdren, born January 12, 1894 at Thane, Lincoln County, Wyoming; died May 20, 1955 Ogden, Utah; and had children:

a. Abbie Elaine; married William Silas Bonham.

b. Helen Ella; married Jasper Kenneth Bonham.

c. Bertha Orlene

d. Wyatt Lee; married Cleo Holmes.

e. Robert Byron

7. James Francis, born October 9, 1888; died June 16, 1958 at Farr West, Utah. Married January 8, 1914 at Paris, Bear Lake County, Utah, to Leona Caldwell, born January 27, 1894 at Samaria, Idaho; died September 1, 1947 at Farr West; daughter of Robert William Caldwell and Margaret Williams Caldwell; and had children. Married second November 24, 1948 to Verna Drake (or Hartley). Children from the first marriage included:

a. James Leslie, born November 15, 1914 at Paris, in Bear Lake County, Idaho; died August 15, 1975 at Syracuse, Davis County, Utah; married Donna Darlene Johnson.

b. Child, born April 6, 1916 at Paris, Idaho; infant death

c. James Francis, Jr.

d. Cleo; married Myron John Simpson.

e. William Drew; married Eloise Robinson

f. Virgil Laurence

g. Darrel Oliver, born March 25, 1926; died September 4, 1960.
h. Clarence Hyrum
i. Belva Rae
8. Sarah Elizabeth, born May 27, 1890; died October 7, 1890
9. Susan May, born January 15, 1893; died March 14, 1973 at Ogden, Utah. Married July 23, 1913 at Logan, Utah, to Ivan George Carver, born March 12, 1893 at Plain City, in Weber County, Utah; died August 28, 1951 at Ogden. Children:
a. Willard Ivan
b. Irma May, born March 7, 1918; died November 21, 1935
c. Florence Idell
d. Charles Douglas; married Donna Rae Baker.
e. Harold Murray; married Donna Pearl Allen.
f. Marvin George
10. Kittie Idell, born May 25, 1894; died September 20, 1963 at Idaho Falls, Idaho. Married July 23, 1913 in Idaho to William Leslie Taylor, born May 28, 1893 at Mapleton, Franklin County, Idaho, and had children. Married second February 16, 1944 George Washington Zuver. Children from first marriage:
a. Ada Vilate
b. Lola Evelyn, born May 17, 1917 at View, Idaho

John Douglas Pritchett
1853-1935

This son of William DeCalb Pritchett (1824) and Barbara Ellen Fulcher Pritchett (1828), was born November 12, 1853, and died August 3, 1935 at Salmon, Idaho. Married December 31, 1874 to Elizabeth Eames, born March 11, 1858 at Herfordshire, England; died March 27, 1947 at Idaho Falls, Idaho; daughter of John Eames and Hannah Jenkins Eames. Seven children, first four born in Weber County, Utah, and the last three in Jefferson County, Montana:
1. Roy Douglas, born June 26, 1877 at Plain City, Utah; died May 1, 1957; married in 1910 to Georgie Brady.
2. George, born January 22, 1879 at Farr West, Utah; died February, 1943; married to Marian Finnerty.

3. John Edwin, born April 22, 1881 at Plain City; died August 8, 1942 at Arlington, Snohomish County, Washington. Married November 22, 1911 to Lizzie Velettie Hiatt, born October 20, 1893 at Coltman, Idaho; died June 27, 1974 at Idaho Falls, Idaho; daughter of David Hastings Hiatt (1855) and Margaret Adeline Pritchett Hiatt (1860). Eight children:
   a. Margaret Elizabeth
   b. George Edwin, born November 12, 1914 at Grant, Idaho; died December 25, 1914.
   c. Jessie Adaline, born December 18, 1915 at Twin Bridges, Montana; died September 14, 1968
   d. Vivian Velettie
   e. William Howard
   f. John David
   g. Robert Wesley
   h. Frances Gertrude; married Ralph Verl Balls, born April 22, 1931 at Hyde Park, Utah
4. Mary Elizabeth, born December 16, 1883 at Plain City, Utah; died March 26, 1960; married January 10, 1900 to Thomas Painter.
5. Gertrude Alice, born March 2, 1885 at Comet, Montana, and married to William Thomas.
6. Glenn Albert, born May 13, 1888 at Boulder, Montana; died August 24, 1966 at Salt Lake City; and married March 6, 1910 to Annie Jane Mundy, born June 26, 1889 at Cornwall, England; died March 10, 1947 at American Falls, Idaho; daughter of James and Jane Rule Mundy. Nine children, five of whom were:
   a. John Albert
   b. Marjorie Elinore
   c. Donald Keith, born September 4, 1918, and died April 18, 1919
   d. Catherine Annie, born September 2, 1919; died same day
   e. Lowell Robert, born May 26, 1924; died July 20, 1944
7. Barbara Ellen, born June 22, 1890 at Boulder, Montana; died young.

Samuel Napoleon Bonaparte Pritchett
1827-1870

This son of John Anderson Pritchett (1794) and Nancy Hilton Albert Johnston Pritchett (1790), was born January 18, 1827 at Chatham Hill, Smyth County, Virginia, and died October 22, 1870 at Fairview, Utah. Married first under marriage bond dated December 21, 1850 to Mary Elizabeth McEntire (or McIntire), born February 2, 1837 in Person County, North Carolina; and second to Mary Jane Gillespie, born July 1, 1840 at Chatham Hill in Smyth County, Virginia; died August 2, 1903 at Fairview, Utah. She was a daughter of John and Nancy Thomas Gillespie. At least six children, the last four listed here born to the second wedding:

1. Kittie Evelyn, born December 12, 1851, of whom more.
2. Eunice, born August 10, 1854 at Marion, Virginia
3. John William, born August 8, 1860, of whom more.
4. Napoleon Bonaparte, born March 19, 1863, of whom more.
5. Simon Philemon, born August 10, 1865 at Fairview, Utah; died November 24, 1934. Married Ida McDonald.
6. Elizabeth Arminta, born July 6, 1868 at Fairview, Utah; died June 6, 1946. Married July 13, 1891 Joseph Osborn, born October 21, 1864 at Union, Salt Lake County, Utah.

Kittie Evelyn Pritchett
1851-

This daughter of Samuel Napoleon Bonaparte Pritchett (1827) and Mary Elizabeth McEntire (1837), was born December 12, 1851 at Marion, Smyth County, Virginia; married Harvey Dixon, born September 12, 1844 at Augusta, Illinois; nine children:

1. Mary Elizabeth, born May 12, 1871 at Harrisville, Utah
2. Alice Eveline, born May 11, 1872 at Harrisville; married Hyrum Bracken Lee, born May 18, 1865 at Tooele, Utah, and had fourteen children:
    a. Alice Evelyn, born December 2, 1890 at Afton, in Lincoln County, Wyoming; married Madison Cecil Kent, born January 8, 1890 at Minden, Nebraska

179

b. Essie Idella, born September 27, 1892 at Freedom, Wyoming; married William Thomas Borup, born March 2, 1888 at Goshen, Utah

c. Hyrum Dixon, born June 15, 1894 at Freedom, Uinta County, Wyoming; married Florence Miranda Adams, born August 27, 1896 at Teasedale, Utah.

d. Isaac Harvey, born August 4, 1896 at Freedom, married Hazel White and second Aletta Magee.

e. Mary Juanita, born October 22, 1898 at Afton, Wyoming

f. Roy Dixon, born March 15, 1901 at Manard, in Blaine County, Idaho

g. Stillbirth daughter, September 3, 1903 at Ogden

h. Edna May, born July 20, 1904 at Manard, Idaho

i. Metta Fern

j. Harold Dixon, born December 9, 1908 at Manard, Idaho; married Dora Packham.

k. Clyde Dixon, born January 11, 1911 at Manard, Idaho

l. Cecil Dixon, born October 17, 1913 at Manard

m. Russell

n. Stillbirth son, August 15, 1917 at Manard, Idaho

3. Harvey, Jr., born August 16, 1874 at Clifton, Idaho; married Emily Sarah Grow, born November 20, 1875 Huntsville, Utah. They had fourteen children. He married second to Hermina Walser Teuscher, born c.1876. Children from the first marriage were:

a. Girl, born October 30, 1893 at Farr West, Utah

b. Charles Harvey, born on November 8, 1894 at Afton, Wyoming

c. Riley Grow, born February 10, 1896 at Afton; married twice: first to Kristie Elizabeth Huttiball; and second to Ilene Verness Wood.

d. Emma Fern, born June 2, 1898 at Afton, Wyoming

e. Samuel Wilkinson, born November 7, 1901 at Hagerman, Wyoming. Married Lela Mae Hall, born December 14, 1906 at Afton

f. James Frederick, born May 4, 1904 at Fair Grove, Idaho.

g. Elwood Grow; married Hermiena Staker.

h. Kittie Virginia, born October 18, 1908 at Manard, Idaho; married Allyn Boyd Jackson.
i. Myrtle Vivian
j. Harold Grow
k. Beulah
l. Grace
m. Wanda
n. Elsie Katherine

4. Kittie Calpurnia, born January 17, 1877 at Clifton, Idaho and married to Arthur Fielding Burton, born June 30, 1873 at Ogden, Utah. Eleven children, probably all born at Afton, Lincoln County, Wyoming:
a. Mable, born July 7, 1896; married Byron Rees
b. Arthur Dixon, born November 28, 1897; married Ellen Kathleen Powell.
c. Calpurnia, born August 29, 1900; married Lyman Wilford Fluckiger.
d. Helen; married Parley Junius Bennion
e. Elsa Mae, born September 16, 1904; married to Kenneth Barlow Holbrook
f. Bernice; married Lamar Lindsay Holmes.
g. Eva; married John Cahoon Franz.
h. Ruth
i. Alta; married David Herbert Dalton
j. Reese Dixon
k. Gail Dixon; married Eileen Warner

5. John Frederick, born May 25, 1879 at Clifton, Idaho; married Martha Laurrennia Wells, born November 6, 1885 at Oakley, Idaho. Seven children:
a. Harvey Wells, born July 24, 1907 at Oakley, Idaho and married to Persis Alice Tinker.
b. Arta May
c. John Pritchett; married Elizabeth Anderson, born October 10, 1915 at Cleveland, Idaho
d. Vilas Hale, born February 3, 1913; married to Maurine Carolina Adams.
e. Forest B.; married Mildred Ladean Parry, born April 15, 1919 at Malad, Idaho

f.   Virge Joseph; married Marjorie Mae Anderson

g.   Ora Hartness; married Archie Dick Miller

6.   Sarah Lucinda, born August 24, 1882 Clifton, Oneida County, Idaho; married Carl Augustus Roberts, born May 30, 1878 at Salt Lake City. Eleven children, perhaps all born at Afton, Uinta County, Wyoming, nine of whom were:

    a.   Melford Augustus, born March 31, 1901; married Lois Delila Campbell.

    b.   Carl Dixon, born June 21, 1903

    c.   Fred Dixon, born January 22, 1906

    d.   Wilford Dixon; married Nora Low.

    e.   Kenneth Dixon

    f.   Thomas Dixon, born April 18, 1913

    g.   Atha; married Don S. Nield

    h.   Willa

    i.   Byron Dixon, born May 19, 1920, and married to Marise Holbrook

7.   Samuel Wilkinson, born February 19, 1885 at Clifton, in Oneida County, Idaho

8.   Asael Harold, born August 3, 1888 Afton, Wyoming; married Ethel Christina Jenkins, born November 26, 1893 Rockcreek, Blaine County, Idaho. Seven children perhaps all born Idaho:

    a.   Aloa; married Joseph Morris Richards.

    b.   Anatha, born December 30, 1917; married to Paul Saylor Perry.

    c.   Nordessa; married Murry D. Coates

    d.   Asael Jenkins

    e.   Lowell Don

    f.   Gloria Ethlyn

    g.   Kenwood LeDair

9.   Elsie Mae, born June 12, 1891 at Afton, Wyoming

John William Pritchett
1860-1943

This son of Samuel Napoleon Bonaparte Pritchett (1827) and Mary Jane Gillespie Pritchett (1840), was born August 8, 1860 in Lynn County, Missouri; died January 6, 1943. Married December

17, 1881 Martha Ann Tidwell, born December 22, 1863 at Mount Pleasant, Sanpete County, Utah, and had five children. Married second to Sarah Emily Rawson; five more children, all ten born at Fairview, Sanpete County, Utah. May also have married Amanda Sanderson Jones, with no children reported. The ten children were:

1. Kittie Eveline, born October 12, 1882; married Henry Richard Mills, born June 17, 1884 at Cholo, Arizona. Children:
   a. Cora Martha
   b. Frank Lamonte, born September 25, 1907 at Fairview and married Mary Ora Clement
   c. Richard Ray
   d. Bert Lee
2. Sarah Emma, born August 27, 1884; married Charles Martin Rigby, born July 20, 1870 at St. Johns, Utah. Seven children:
   a. William Neldon, married Helen Irene Rodgers
   b. Leo Deloy, married Ina Luella Bohne
   c. Martha Fanny, and married Laurel Daniel Nelson, born February 25, 1908 at Manila, Utah.
   d. Lloyd Lamar, born July 2, 1911
   e. Charles Lyle, born August 23, 1913
   f. Verla Mae; married Marvin Leroy Coates
   g. Emma Arzella, married Maurice Smith
3. Mary Elizabeth, born August 10, 1886; married James Lewis Jensen, born April 27, 1886 at Fairview, Utah. A daughter:
   a. Norma Lois
4. Martha Ellen, born July 7, 1888; married John Henry Spencer, born December 7, 1882 at Payson, Utah. Eight children:
   a. Francis Harold, born January 7, 1909 at Fairview, Utah; married Alice Clayson, born March 22, 1907 at Payson
   b. Beatrice Ione; married Arthur George Stade.
   c. Donna Fern; married Clyde Ellison Snow.
   d. Sterling Leon; married Maxine Stark
   e. Clarence, born January 31, 1921 at Spring Dale, Idaho
   f. Lewis Earl
   g. John Douglas
   h. Virginia Lee; married Glen Alden Perry, born March 10, 1924 at Payson, Utah

5. Maggie Ann, born September 8, 1890; married Nels Hansen, born April 8, 1881 at Fairview, Utah. Eight children:
    a. William Lamonte, born May 16, 1909 Caldwell, Alberta, Canada; married Inez Lapriel Mower, born August 13, 1909 at Fairview, Utah.
    b. Bertha Maggie
    c. Vennes May
    d. Mary Ellen
    e. James Lee
    f. Martha Elaine
    g. Wilford Nels; married Vada Louise Johnson.
    h. Ann, born March 27, 1935 at Council, Adams County, Idaho; married Joel Walter Hiatt
6. Leora, born March 31, 1895
7. John Colman, born November 24, 1896; married Iretta Arvina Monson, born July 6, 1912 at Mt. Pleasant, Utah; and married second Ruby Lois Gray, born August 5, 1907 at St. Anthony, Idaho.
8. Alta Jane, born September 20, 1898; married Henry Erastus Larsen, born July 11, 1879 at Ephraim, Utah. Six children:
    a. Maria Theresa
    b. John Darrell; married Lenna Clariece Johnson
    c. Estella; married John Delbert Seely, born February 28, 1917 at Mt. Pleasant, Utah
    d. Ila Winona
    e. Boyd Neureen
    f. Alta Alura; married Russel Frank Hunt.
9. William Napoleon, born November 29, 1901
10. Emily Elizabeth, born June 21, 1907

Napoleon Bonaparte Pritchett
1863-1931

This son of Samuel Napoleon Bonaparte Pritchett (1827) and Mary Jane Gillespie Pritchett (1840), was born March 19, 1863 in Lynn County, Missouri, and died February 6, 1931. Married November 16, 1887 to Olive Loretta Sanders, born October 19, 1870 at Fairview, Sanpete County, Utah; daughter of John Frank

Sanders and Mary Irene Clement Sanders. After her husband's death, Olive was married second November 29, 1933 to Oscar Norman, and third August 10, 1937 to Wells Hales. Napoleon Bonaparte was father of eleven children, born at Fairview:

1. Mary Loretta, born January 19, 1889; married November 18, 1908 to Lawrence Theophilus Epperson, born September 22, 1884 at Midway, Utah. Nine children:
   a. Ruby Loretta; married Irwin Bruce McQuarrie
   b. Earleen
   c. Beatrice Virginia
   d. Lawrence Leon
   e. Vaughn Elmo; married to Margaret Ann Stewart Hewlett.
   f. Elvert Pritchett
   g. Lillian Marylene
   h. Sidney Leroy, born December 16, 1924 at Provo
   i. Gerald Jean
2. Roland Napoleon, born February 7, 1891; died June 2, 1945; married July 16, 1919 to Anna Lillian Raymond and had at least four children.
3. Hazel Burdella, born February 9, 1893; married June 7, 1916 to Amasa Merritt Terry, born May 4, 1894.
4. John Frank, born August 1, 1895; married September 1, 1926 to Olive Monson, born c.1895.
5. Thomas Levern, born May 13, 1898; died February 6, 1930; married December 19, 1924 to Lola Lucy Clyde, born July 23, 1904 at Mt. Pleasant, Utah. Two children:
   a. Clyde Lee; married Alice Joyce Mickelson
   b. Enid Marie; married Roland Dorius Adams, born April 6, 1927 at Ephraim, Utah.
6. Gerald Darius, born October 1, 1900; died June 28, 1916
7. Beatrice Joyce, born January 13, 1903; married January 2, 1924 to Gunnar Budvorson, born March 24, 1902 at Winter Quarters, Utah, and had children:
   a. Vivian Beatrice; married Billy Junior Wilhite
   b. Richard Ned; married Mary Lou Wilhite
   c. Glen Lee
8. Thelma Lillian, born February 8, 1906; married June 7, 1928 to Milton Hales Woodward. Six children:

a. Zola Maurine; married Peter Moroni Johansen
b. Carma June
c. Patricia Lillian
d. Thomas Milton
e. Donald Eugene
f. Wayne Russell, born October 13, 1946 at Salt Lake City
9. Melrose Jed, born June 24, 1907; married February 15, 1928 to Lois Watson.
10. Sanders Kenneth, born January 11, 1911; married December 6, 1933 to Ruby Sanderson. Three children:
a. Dee Kenneth
b. Judy Shirlene
c. Joyce Ruby
11. June Elmo, born June 1, 1913; married October 9, 1937 to Ruth Diane Almquist.

Sarah Bryant Pritchett
1829-

This daughter of John Anderson Pritchett (1794) and Nancy Hilton Albert Johnston (1790), was born March 21, 1829 in Smyth County, Virginia. Married to William Frederick McEntire, born October 31, 1834 at Jeffersonville, Halifax County, Virginia. They had children:

1. James Beverly, born January 25, 1857 at Chatham Hill, and married Lucy Davis Wallace, born August 4, 1855 at Salt Lake City, Utah. They had a stillbirth child c.1882 at Ogden, and seven others:
   a. Maude Marion, born December 18, 1883 at Ogden, and married Sidney Albert Whitehead
   b. William Wallace, born August 18, 1885 at Harrisville, Weber County. Married Dora Halvorsen.
   c. James Heber, born June 2, 1887 at Harrisville
   d. Martha, born May 7, 1889 at Ogden
   e. Arthur Beverly, born November 5, 1890 at Harrisville, and married Naomi Cabble, born December 10, 1895 at Rexburg, Fremont County, Idaho

f. Ray, born August 20, 1892 at Farr West, Utah; married Caroline Wright

g. Eli Bryant, born January 18, 1895 at Grant, Idaho, and married Gazella Wagoner.

2. William Napoleon, born May 4, 1859, of whom more.

3. John Thomas, born January 6, 1862; married to Louisa Maria Josephine Witten, born September 23, 1861 at Burkes Garden, Tazewell County, Virginia. Nine children, born in Weber County, Utah:

a. John Earl, born August 2, 1885; married Lulu Murphy.

b. Cora Josephine, born December 20, 1886; married to George Sherwood Wardle.

c. Ira Wells, born September 15, 1888; married Ida Marion Davis, born August 4, 1890 at Willard, Utah

d. Marshall Andersen, born May 6, 1890; married to Amy Taylor, born May 28, 1891 in Weber County, Utah. Six children:

    (1) Eldon Taylor; married Zelda Skidmore

    (2) Mabel

    (3) Leah Maurine

    (4) Virginia

    (5) Marshall Allen

    (6) Betty Jean

e. Adrian Wilkensen, born December 26, 1891; married to Eva Sorenson, born March 25, 1892 at Ogden, Utah

f. Howard Witten, born April 9, 1896, and married Bessie Eva Woodward.

g. William Maynard; married Ester Rock.

h. Gladys Maud

i. Nina Virginia

4. Eli Colman, born April 12, 1864, married Elizabeth Jane Taylor, born December 4, 1865 Ogden, Weber County, Utah. Five children:

a. Raymond Eli, born April 10, 1889 at Harrisville, Weber County, Utah; married Sarah Ann Zollinger, born June 13, 1887 Rexburg, Fremont County, Idaho. Six children:

    (1) Afton; married Delbert Orville Welker

    (2) Elma; married Robert Alexander Erikson

   (3) Nolen Raymond, married Ada Lucille Machen

   (4) Marjorie; married William Claude Smith

   (5) Reed Zollinger

   (6) Marilyn; married Max Curtis

 b. Merdell William, born April 6, 1893 Grant, Idaho

 c. Myron Pleasant, born June 7, 1895 Grant; married Jennie Myrle Pingree, born March 4, 1896 Ogden, Utah.

 d. Emma Jane, born January 9, 1897 at Grant, Idaho

 e. Mildred Armine, born August 7, 1905 at Rexburg, Idaho

5. Nancy Elizabeth, born May 14, 1867, of whom more.

6. Ada Grace, born May 17, 1870 at Harrisville, Weber County, Utah; married David Riley Taylor, born there March 9, 1869, and had eleven children, the last being a stillbirth:

 a. Riley John, born January 10, 1892 at Harrisville; married to Pearl Elizabeth Cabble, born July 8, 1891 at Rexburg, Idaho. Three children:

   (1) Blaine Cabble

   (2) Megnild Gunda

   (3) Ray Cabble, born June 8, 1924 at Idaho Falls, Idaho

 b. William Pleasant, born February 2, 1894 at Grant, Idaho, and married to Florence Alpha Sargent.

 c. Florence Emily, born February 5, 1896 at Grant; married to Elmer Eckersley Rigby, born July 15, 1884 at Newton, Utah. They had a son:

   (1) Max E.; married Evelyn Walkingshaw

 d. Eli Marshall; married Bessie Groom.

 e. James Edwin, born November 4, 1900 at Grant, Idaho

 f. Golden Ray, born January 1, 1903 at Coltman, Idaho; married to Vera Laird, born November 4, 1906 at Salt Lake City, Utah and had children:

   (1) Shirley Jean; married Buddy Glen Larkins

   (2) Karen; married Roger Linn Sandall

 g. Arthur Leland, born November 9, 1904 Coltman, Idaho; married to Irmgard Herta Frieda Prusse. Children:

   (1) Ada Caroline

   (2) David Henry

 h. Loy Warren

i. Ralph Meredith
j. Dee Jay, born August 19, 1913 at Coltman, Idaho.
7. Henry Thompson, born May 6, 1875, of whom more.

William Napoleon McEntire
1859-

This son of William Frederick McEntire (1834) and Sarah Bryant Pritchett (1829), was born May 4, 1859 at Chatham Hill in Smyth County, Virginia. Married to Olive Ann Rawson, born September 11, 1862 at Ogden, Weber County, Utah; nine children, born in Weber County:

1. William Rawson, born November 26, 1884; married Rosene Maria Woodfield, born July 6, 1887 at North Ogden, Utah and had seven children, including:
   a. Virginia Mae; who married James Ritter Stallings, born August 7, 1905 at Eden, Utah
   b. Laura; married John Burns Hawkes
   c. William Rawson, Jr.; married Dauna Hardy, born December 6, 1916 at Blanding, Utah
   d. Helen Mary; married Arnold Ianthus Slater
   e. Jay Woodfield; married Doris Lucile Rose
   f. Don Woodfield; married Larae Porter
2. William Frederick, born November 26, 1884; married to Elizabeth Wells.
3. Cora Edna, born September 28, 1886; married Jens Alma Anderson, and had a son:
   a. Ivan Alma; married Helen Poulter
4. James Arthur, born October 29, 1888; married Sarah Orton, born January 4, 1889 at North Ogden, Utah. Ten children:
   a. Melba, born March 6, 1912 at Farr West, Weber County, Utah; married Allen Ammon Taylor, born August 30, 1906 at Bountiful, Utah
   b. William James, born October 15, 1913 in Weber County; married Marie Graham, born November 23, 1920 at Bountiful
   c. Lula, born August 25, 1915 at Farr West, Weber County

d. Ray Orton; married to Ila Whitesides, born December 5, 1917 at Layton, Davis County, Utah
e. Karl Orton, born June 11, 1920 at Clearfield, Utah
f. Marie; married Eldon Emmett Sill
g. Mauna Loa
h. Ruth
i. Vernon Napoleon, born October 20, 1928 at Ogden
j. Larene; married Russell Fred Nielsen
5. Olive Athalia, born July 14, 1890; married Adam Freckleton.
6. Sarah Eliza, born November 14, 1893; married Alonzo Wheeler, born October 2, 1892 at Plain City, Weber County, Utah, and second Benjamin F. Hawkins.
7. Horace Alexander, born August 9, 1895; married to Ethel Hammon, born March 16, 1896 at Roy, Weber County, Utah, and had eight children, born in Weber County:
   a. Robert Lyonal
   b. Bernice; married William Stanley Dunford, Jr.
   c. Donald Byron
   d. Kenneth Warren, born July 1, 1926 at Ogden, Utah
   e. Darlene
   f. Glen Hammon
   g. Diann
   h. Janice
8. Frank Wellington, born July 8, 1901
9. Ethel May

Nancy Elizabeth McEntire
1867-

This daughter of William Frederick McEntire (1834) and Sarah Bryant Pritchett (1829), was born May 14, 1867 at Chatham Hill, Smyth County, Virginia. Married to Joseph Lake Taylor, born August 1, 1864 at Harrisville, Weber County, Utah. They had twelve children, the first two born at Harrisville, and the remainder in Jefferson County, Idaho:
1. Lorin Ray, born December 16, 1887; married several times: Susan Clarissa Curtis, born June 21, 1888 at Newton, Utah;

second to Mae Clark; third to Velma Barney; and fourth to Lavon Hardcastle Killian.

2. Ira Joseph, born April 17, 1889; married Hilda Thornton
3. Orial Bryant, born November 19, 1890, and married Joseph Norman Brown, born July 23, 1889 at Harrisville, Utah. Six children, probably all born in Idaho:
   a. Afton
   b. Edna, born February 25, 1917; married Douglas Nelson
   c. Arduth; married Wilson Call Chandler
   d. Glen, a twin, born May 14, 1921
   e. Gale Taylor, a twin, born May 14, 1921
   f. Bonnie Mae
4. Grace Ethel, born October 14, 1892; married Thomas Leslie Clement, born September 27, 1892 Plain City, Weber County, Utah. They had seven children, perhaps all born in Jefferson County, Idaho:
   a. Leslie, born December 4, 1914
   b. Hollis Demont
   c. Gale Wilford; married Ellen Cherry
   d. Ray Lynn, a twin, born April 30, 1920
   e. Rhea, a twin, born April 30, 1920
   f. Thomas Ross; married Crissie Louise Weaver
   g. Nyla Grace
5. Delbert Guy, born April 24, 1894, and married Eva Viola Clement, born November 30, 1899 at Moreland, Idaho. They had six children:
   a. Joseph Levi
   b. Delbert Ray; married Thelda Hall Burns.
   c. Nola Mae
   d. Colleen; married Newel Jacobs Neibaur.
   e. Robert Milton
   f. Gerald Lynn; married Gae Bernice Connell.
6. Darwin Fredrick, born April 21, 1896; married to Edith May King, and had two children:
   a. Winston Grant
   b. Lois
7. Lawrence Ivan, born April 26, 1898; married Lucy Elvira Call
8. Dorthulia; married William Thomas Davidson McAlister

9. Lavaughn Leo; married Alice Louise Severson
10. Harold Pleasant, born February 10, 1905
11. Wells Demont, born April 29, 1906; married Thelma Grow, born September 29, 1906 at Grant, Idaho
12. Marion Earl; married Nellie Byram and had children:
    a. Mac Byram; married Leonora Mae Sauer
    b. Deloris Elizabeth; married Lynn Ogden Thueson
    c. Orial; married Lyle Jay Cottle
    d. Geraldine

Henry Thompson McEntire
1875-

This son of William Frederick McEntire (1834) and Sarah Bryant Pritchett (1829), was born May 6, 1875 at Ogden, Weber County, Utah. Married Rebecca Hegsted, born May 20, 1878 at Harrisville, Utah. Seven children, perhaps born in Weber County, Utah. The town is reported as Farr West, but I do not find that name in my atlas, or the Zip Code directory. Children were:

1. Leland Glenmore, born July 12, 1899; married Ivy Cassenda Slater, born December 15, 1899 at Slaterville, Weber County, Utah. Married second Norma Shaw.
2. Eli Albert; married Illa Artell McBride, born October 3, 1902 at Hyrum, Cache County, Utah. Three children:
    a. Lowell Albert
    b. Elaine; married Ernest Harold Alexander, a twin.
    c. Della Larae
3. Milton Vern, born December 20, 1903
4. Wesley Dee; married Almira Rynearson or Wright.
5. Lucille
6. Ross Henry
7. Gilbert Hegsted; married Clora Louise Daniels Brown

James Mitchell Pritchett
1817-1902

This son of Samuel Pritchett (1761) and Rebecca Anderson Pritchett (1776) was born June 1, 1817 in an area that was, in

1832, to become part of Smyth County, Virginia; and died January 20, 1902 in Fairview, Sanpete County, Utah. He signed a marriage contract January 3, 1837, and was married in Smyth County, Virginia, September 15, 1837 to Nancy Ann Fulcher, born July 4, 1819 in Persons County, North Carolina, a daughter of Douglas Jackson Fulcher (1791) and Nancy Atwell Fulcher. They were parents of at least nine children, all born in Smyth County:

1. William David, born July 28, 1837; died February 22, 1887 at Fairview, Sanpete County, Utah. Married November 13, 1856 to Margaret Letner Heninger, born c.1839 at Burks Garden, Tazewell County, Virginia; died November 2, 1880 at Harrisville, Weber County, Utah; daughter of Phillip Heninger and Elizabeth Ann Workman Heninger. The family apparently moved to Utah between 1864 and 1869, probably in company with other family members, many of whom joined the Mormon Church. The first four children were born in either Smyth or Tazewell Counties, Virginia; the last four at Harrisville:

    a. Mary Elizabeth, born November 15, 1858; died June 1, 1910 at Farr West, Weber County, Utah. Married July 4, 1875 to Hans Christian Westergard.

    b. Louisa, born February 19, 1860; died April 3, 1879; and married to James Shipe (or Shupe).

    c. Hannah, born c.1862; died March 23, 1878

    d. Cynthia, born c.1864, reportedly during the crossing of the plains on the way west.

    e. Axie Sarah, born June 2, 1869; died June 10, 1924. Married February 2, 1887 to Reuben Loran Short.

    f. David Harold, born July 26, 1871; died January 24, 1872

    g. William John, born December 8, 1873, and died March 28, 1874

    h. Grant, born c.1874; died c.1875

2. Leonidas Alfred, born December 14, 1838; died June 9, 1888 at Eden, Weber County, Utah; married June 18, 1861 Burkes Garden, Tazewell County, Virginia, Elizabeth Ann Heninger, born there May 6, 1833; died May 13, 1896 in Eden, Weber County, Utah; daughter of Phillip Heninger and Elizabeth Ann Workman Heninger. Nine children:

a. Catherine Letitia, born May 12, 1865 at Portsmouth, in Scioto County, Ohio; died December 5, 1918. Married December 18, 1884 to William Pollock Chambers.

b. Elizabeth Ann, born February 19, 1869 at Harrisville, in Weber County, Utah; died March 8, 1930. Married November 17, 1889 to Parley Pratt Carver.

c. Mary Ann, born February 22, 1871 at Harrisville; died April 12, 1871

d. Rosa Ellen, born February 22, 1872 at Harrisville; died December 6, 1942; Married August 2, 1892 to William Lindsay.

e. William James, born November, 1873 in Ogden, Weber County, Utah; died March 28, 1874

f. Leonidas Alfred, Jr., born December 17, 1874 at Riverdale, Weber County, Utah; died October 11, 1929. Married July 2, 1896 to Frances Katherine Heninger, born July 21, 1873 at Burkes Garden, Tazewell County, Virginia; died December 21, 1952 at Ogden, Utah. She was the daughter of Reese Thompson Heninger and Frances Jane Louthan Heninger. Seven children, all born Weber County, Utah, the first at Ogden, the rest at Eden:

    (1) Archibald Alfred, born January 25, 1897; married to Rhoda Plair

    (2) Neta Frances, born September 10, 1898; married to Lawrence Houston.

    (3) Elizabeth Electa, born July 26, 1900; married to Raymond Compton.

    (4) Rozella Mae, born February 28, 1903; died November 21, 1946. Married September 22, 1922 to Melvin Leonidas Mecham.

    (5) Pearl Ann, born March 6, 1905; married September 5, 1924 to Louis Henry Norman.

    (6) Clarice, born 1908; died at three weeks

    (7) Reece, born October 24, 1910; died at one month

g. Nancy May, born May 9, 1876 at Ogden, Utah; died June 2, 1939. Married October 25, 1893 to Wilmer Ferrin.

h.   Margaret Christian, born March 1, 1878 at Eden, Weber County, Utah; died November 4, 1963. Married October 12, 1898 to George Arthur Fuller.

i.   Matilda Parkerette, born January 16, 1880 at Eden, in Weber County, Utah; died March 28, 1959. Married May 7, 1897 to Charles Alfred Wood.

3.   John Anderson, born September 23, 1840; died October 20, 1920 at Fairview, Sanpete County, Utah. Married c.1861 to his cousin, Mary Virginia Hambrick, born May 10, 1842 in Smyth County; died July 25, 1926 at Fairview; daughter of Jackson Hambrick (1815) and Susanna Jane Pritchett Hambrick (1818). She had first been married to Samuel Williams, and had eight children from this second marriage, all born at Fairview, Sanpete County, Utah:

a.   Thaddeus Wasatch, born December 20, 1867; and died January 17, 1929. Married January 26, 1888 to Eleanor Ann Jones, born September 26, 1862 at Provo, Utah, and had children born at Fairview, Utah:

(1)   Iva Pearl, born January 7, 1889; married Archibald Christensen, born June 28, 1886 at Fairview.

(2)   Ernest Edwin, born April 23, 1892; married to Hannah (or Helen) Zelma Larsen, born August 18, 1896 at Spanish Fork, Utah; married second to Janey Exeter.

(3)   Leon Gay, born July 19, 1895; married first Mary Blair Holdaway, born September 6, 1897; second Edith Nerdin.

(4)   Lydia Margaret, born c.1896; married Bernard Englebert Christensen, born September 30, 1893 at Fairview, Utah.

(5)   Franklin Carl, born June 14, 1901

b.   Clarence Linden, born January 9, 1870; died March 10, 1961 at La Canada, California. Married first December 24, 1890 at Manti Temple, Utah, to Sarah Ann Petersen, born November 9, 1870 at South Cottonwood, Utah; second Jennie Dolores Kenneburg. Two children, born at Fairview, Utah:

(1)   James Linden, born June 7, 1893; married Mildred Spencer, born November 20, 1898 at Lake Shore, Utah; married second Tillie Remmick.

(2)   William Alexander, born August 6, 1895; married four times: Josephine Olsen, born March 27, 1893 at Salt Lake City; Ethel Virginia Knowles; Jessie Ann Burdett Standford; and Hazel Richmond Holberton.

c.   India Marie, born May 2, 1872; and died September 14, 1945. Married February 25, 1892 to James Jonathan Peterson, born November 11, 1868 at South Cottonwood, Utah.

d.   Aneliza Florence, born September 16, 1874; died August 28, 1892.

e.   John Edgar, born July 19, 1877; died October 24, 1879

f.   Grace Martha, born March 12, 1880, and died March 28, 1882

g.   John Jackson, born September 29, 1883

h.   Grace Pearl, born January 5, 1887, and died October 31, 1916. Married August 31, 1904 to Roy McArthur, born September 25, 1877 at Mt. Pleasant, in Sanpete County, Utah.

4.   Nancy Emeline, born July 1, 1843; married c.1864 John Floyd Young.

5.   Thomas Mitchell, born May 1, 1845; died September 11, 1932 at Hurricane, Washington County, Utah. Married first to Lavinia Heninger, probably a daughter of Phillip Heninger and Elizabeth Ann Workman Heninger. Married second June 30, 1890 to Ida Rebecca Huntsman, born November 13, 1873 at Fillmore, Millard County, Utah; died April 3, 1896 at Teasdale, Wayne County, Utah, daughter of Isaiah Huntsman and Rebecca Ames Huntsman. There were four children born to the second marriage, all at Teasdale:

a.   Ellis, born February 3, 1891; died June 6, 1953; married July 10, 1912 to Birdie M. Brown.

b.   James Mitchell, born July 30, 1893; died 1902

c.   Lester, a twin, born April 30, 1895; died May 13, 1895

d.   Leonard, a twin, born April 30, 1895; died same day.

6. Levi Franklin, born October 8, 1847, and died September 25, 1885. Married Sarah Ellen Thompson.

7. James DeCalb, born July 1, 1849; married c.1871 Katherine James. At least two sons:

    a. John Lester, born December 1, 1883 at Trescota, Elko County, Nevada; died November, 1918 at Phoenix, Arizona. Married May 4, 1911 Edna Adele Robinson, born January 27, 1883 at Scribener, Nebraska; died April 20, 1953 at Phoenix. Two children, born at Phoenix:

        (1) James Lawrence, born March 21, 1912; married January 27, 1940 Virginia May Vaughn.

        (2) Virginia Lee, born September 2, 1914; married October, 1944 to Edward Fetterer.

    b. William Ferris, born in Utah c.1906; died October 5, 1951 at Tuscarota, Nevada; married Alma Joan Chumbley, born c.1910 at Winters, Texas. Eight children, the first two and the last born at Long Beach, California; the third at Mesa, Arizona; the fourth through the seventh at Phoenix, Arizona:

        (1) Edward Barret, born August 24, 1932; married Alice Marie Colewall.

        (2) Charles William, born October 13, 1934

        (3) Walter Buford, born April 23, 1935

        (4) James Coit, born December 22, 1939

        (5) Fred Herman, born July 2, 1940

        (6) Kenneth Ernest, born October 23, 1942

        (7) Lynn Wiley, born February 21, 1945

        (8) Mark Harold, born August 1, 1948

8. Rebecca Emily, born October 23, 1851, and died October 13, 1930. Married March 23, 1867 to David Walker Sanders, and second to Lindsay Anderson Brady.

9. Douglas Jackson, born December 10, 1858; died c.1861

CHAPTER 15

The Second Family of Isaac Thompson Pratt
1827-1909

This son of Oliver Pratt (1784) and Mary Fulks Pratt, was born August 5, 1827 in an area later to become Smyth County, when it was formed in 1832, and died there June 16, 1909. Married July 15, 1885 in Smyth County to Nancy Jane Lowder, born April 8, 1858 in Tazewell County, Virginia; died February 12, 1917 at Marion, Virginia; daughter of George Washington Lowder (1830). Nancy Jane was his second wife; he was first married to Nancy Emeline Pritchett, who died in 1883, leaving him a widower with eleven children, the youngest being just seven years of age. Isaac Thompson is buried in the cemetery of the Ridgedale Methodist Church in Smyth County, Virginia, under a tall obelisk, between the final resting places of his two wives.

Nancy Jane was an older sister of Annie Liza Lowder (1861) who had married Isaac Thompson's eldest son, John Geddings Pratt (1851); the two sisters having married father and son. At the time of their marriage, Nancy Jane was 27 years of age, her husband was 58, with eleven children, the two youngest still living at home.

His will, dated June 1, 1900, is recorded in Will Book 8, page 339 in the records of Smyth County, and reads in part as follows:

To my beloved wife, Nannie Jane, the land and appurtenances situated thereon, known and described as a part of the Cox farm lying and being on the waters of the North Fork of Holston River, in the County of Smyth and State of Virginia, together with all the personal property I may die siezed; and after her death to be divided equally between my heirs by my wife Nannie Jane, and to my heirs by my first wife, Nancy Emeline, I given and bequeath to each the sum of one dollar. And I do hereby give as a reason for not giving to all equally is that I have already done more for the heirs by my first wife than I can in the course of Nature do for my younger children.

The will was witnessed by G. W. Pratt and W. H. Pratt of Ellendale, and entered for record August 4, 1909.

Mother has told me numerous stories of her father, and of the way they lived on the small farm. When mother was almost eighty years old, we encouraged her to write down some of her memories. That effort evolved into a detailed and entertaining autobiography running to sixty-eight typewritten pages. Last year, I wrote a biography of my father as a companion piece; typed the whole thing into proper form on my computer, and had a limited number of copies professionally printed and bound as a paper-back, titled *Willie Neal and Josephine, A Legacy of Love.* In that form, it became two hundred and three pages. From my viewpoint, it is exactly that, and while copies last, family members who are interested need only to contact me. Isaac Thompson Pratt and Nancy Jane Lowder had seven children, all born at or near Chatham Hill, Virginia:

1. Samuel James, born April 4, 1886, of whom more
2. Lorena Katherine, born January 1, 1888, of whom more
3. Mark, born November 21, 1889; died May 18, 1963, single. He went west early in life, working on ranches in Nebraska and Texas, where it is believed he may have worked for either or both of his half brothers, Oliver Pratt (1865) or Henry Thompson Pratt (1861), both of whom were very successful ranchers and cattle-men in Missouri and Texas. Mark is buried at the Ridgedale Methodist Church.
4. Anna Elizabeth, born March 21, 1891, of whom more
5. Walter Elbert, born July 3, 1893; married November 13, 1913 to Mary Lyde Meadows, a nurse, born 1890, daughter of John and Mahala Meadows. They had no children, but raised her nephew, Mack Morgan, from infancy. Walter was on crutches most of his adult life from a form of arthritis. He and Mary, and her brother, were brutally bludgeoned and shot to death by a hired man on their farm September 3, 1953, and are buried in Meadows Cemetery near Saltville, Virginia.
6. Josephine Davis, born September 3, 1895, of whom more
7. Laura Rebecca, born January 20, 1899, of whom more

The Isaac Thompson Pratt Home

Drawn by the author from descriptions given by
Josephine Davis Pratt Hurley; May 31, 1981

1ST FLOOR

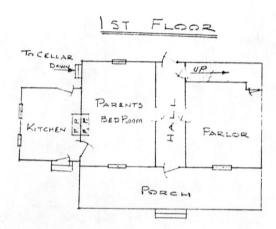

Parents Bed Room · Kitchen · Parlor · Hall · Porch · To Cellar Down · UP

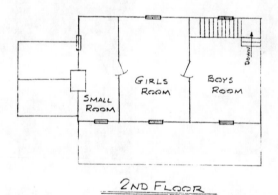

Small Room · Girls Room · Boys Room · Down

2ND FLOOR

Anna Elizabeth Pratt
1891

Lorena Katherine Pratt
1888

Josephine Davis Pratt
1895

Laura Rebecca Pratt
1899

The daughters of Isaac Thompson Pratt & Nancy Jane Lowder Pratt

Samuel James Pratt
1886

Walter Elbert Pratt
1893

Mark Pratt
1889

The sons of Isaac Thompson Pratt & Nancy Jane Lowder Pratt

Samuel James Pratt
1886-1965

This son of Isaac Thompson Pratt (1827) and his second wife, Nancy Jane Lowder (1858) was born April 4, 1886 at Chatham Hill, in Smyth County, Virginia; died April 18, 1965 at Knoxville, Tennessee, and is buried at Blacksburg, Virginia. Married June 12, 1918 at Jenkins, Letcher County, Kentucky, to Nannie Elizabeth Horne, born March 12, 1890 at Nottingham, Scott County, Virginia; died September 6, 1965 at Blacksburg. Her parents were Emmet N. and Louella Monarchus Horne. When I was about in the third grade, we visited Uncle Sam on his farm during one summer and had a wonderful time with our cousins. When we left, he gave me two baby, white rock chickens, which I carried home in a shoe box on the bus. Those two little chickens grew into a fat hen, and a large, proud rooster, and they were the start of a great flock, providing eggs and meat for our family for a number of years. His children also visited with our family on occasion. Four children, all born at Jenkins, Letcher County, Kentucky:

1. Mary Elizabeth, born March 1, 1919. Married March 24, 1940 Hugh Paschel Rice, Jr. born February 14, 1919 at Mendota, Washington County, Virginia, and died August 29, 1995, son of Hugh Paschel and Lillie White Rice. They had four children:

    a. James Paschel, born June 14, 1941 at Abingdon, Virginia; apparently married four times. First in May, 1958 to Joyce Taylor, and second December 28, 1965 to Barbara A. Mills; third and fourth unknown. He had two children from the first marriage and one from the second:

        (1) Gwendalyn Kay, born March 22, 1961
        (2) James Paschel, Jr.
        (3) Stacey Lynn, born March 9, 1976 at Colorado Springs, Colorado.

    b. Deborah Louise, born March 17, 1950 at Oak Ridge, Tennessee, and married twice. First, December 27, 1969 to Jerry Wayne Cooper, born March 1, 1945 in Heiskell, Knox County, Kentucky; and second in 1977 to Michael W. Rowland. One child, born to the first marriage:

(1) Keli Elizabeth, born March 8, 1972 at Oak Ridge

c. Gerald Lee, born January 1, 1943 at Pennington Gap, Virginia; died January 6, 1943 at Mendota, Virginia.

d. Susan Elizabeth, born May 20, 1961 at Oak Ridge, and married 1980 to Wayne Jennings.

2. Ella Louise, known as Eloise, born July 17, 1920; married November 25, 1939 to James Beverly Neal, Jr., born May 29, 1914 at Limestone, Washington County, Virginia. One son:

a. James Richard, born April 1, 1943 at Marion, Virginia. Married December 17, 1966 to Sarah Cole Parker, born September 26, 1944 in Newark, New Jersey, daughter of Charles Edward and Isabel Korherr Parker. They had three children:

(1) James Charles, born October 25, 1970 in Athens, Greece; died October 28, 1970; buried New York

(2) Susan Lowery, born January 30, 1972 at Harvey, Illinois.

(3) John Campbell, born July 16, 1976 at Oak Park, Illinois.

3. Sammy June, born June 26, 1923; married June 17, 1950 to John Gow Evans, Jr., known as Jack. He was born October 16, 1921 at Cambridge, Dorchester County, Maryland. One of the stories I have heard about my Uncle Sam Pratt is that, when they were expecting their third child, after two girls, he announced that the child would finally be Samuel James Pratt, Jr. When yet another girl was born, he settled for the contraction, Sammy June. Three years later, he finally got the son, but had used the name. After the second world war, Sammy June and I renewed our childhood contacts, together with cousin Roy Pratt Wolfe, in Washington, D. C., for a short period of time, where all of us were working. When Jack finally retired, they moved back to the eastern shore, at last report living in California, Maryland. They have one son:

a. John Gow, III, born May 12, 1959 at Toledo, Ohio; married and had one son:

(1) Colin William, born January, 1993

4. James Douglas, born January 5, 1926; died November 13, 1995 in Florida. Married August 27, 1949 to Mildred Frances

Crowder, born July 23, 1928 at Roanoke, Virginia. Two children, born at Roanoke:

a. Michael Allen, born March 17, 1958
b. Kimberley Anne, born July 6, 1959; married to Andrew Thomas Buckler, Jr. at Alexandria, Virginia, and has two children:
   (1) David Andrew, born February 28, 1987
   (2) Benjamin Daniel, born April 13, 1989

Anna Elizabeth Pratt
1891-1964

This daughter of Isaac Thompson Pratt (1827) and Nancy Jane Lowder Pratt (1858) was born March 21, 1891 at Chatham Hill, Virginia; died January 15, 1964 and is buried at Powell Valley Memorial Gardens Cemetery near Appalachia, Virginia. Married November 25, 1920 to Chester Hardin Wolfe, born September 15, 1898, son of George Hammond and Mary Gilby Wolfe. He is also buried at Powell Gardens. They had two sons:

1. Chester Hardin, Jr., born November 8, 1921 at Jenkins, in Letcher County, Kentucky; died February 1, 1994 at the University of Tennessee Hospital in Knoxville. For many years, he was the mayor of Middlesboro, Kentucky and, at his death, there were several news accounts of his life and accomplishments. As Bob Madon, mayor of Pineville, expressed it: "*In my estimation, he is the most efficient mayor I've ever known.*" For years, he battled arthritis which originated during his service in India during the second world war, resulting in replacement of both hips, and the amputation of one leg prior to his death. He was married May 8, 1944 to Jesse Allen, born February 5, 1921 in Middlesboro, Kentucky and they had one daughter:
   a. Rose Allen, born May 24, 1948 at Louisville, Kentucky. Her second marriage was on September 8, 1973 to Earl Dean Gordon, born August 26, 1943 at Middlesboro. One child born to each marriage, born at Middlesboro:
      (1) Robert Hardin, born May 3, 1969
      (2) Jessica Allen, born January 23, 1976

2.   Roy Pratt, born May 2, 1924 at Burdine, Kentucky, and died
November 23, 1987 at his country home near Charlottesville,
Virginia, known as *The Granary*. Married August 6, 1946 to
Elizabeth Jackie Gilbert, born December 9, 1924 at London,
Kentucky, daughter of Samuel H. and Lucy Cook Gilbert.
Both served in government posts at Seoul, during the Korean
War. Roy and Jackie were listed in *The Green Book*, a social
register of Washington, D. C., and were prominent in local
society, involved in many social activities, and entertained
their many friends often. They lived on upper Connecticut
Avenue, and spent their summer weekends at their home on a
small farm near Charlottesville. Roy was president of the
National Society of State Societies and a member of the
Touchdown Club. Both had been president of the Kentucky
State Society. Jackie was a senior editor of *Army Times
Publishing Company*, and has, for a number of years, been
Chairperson of the annual Cherry Blossom Festival. In
connection with that effort, she has been the guest of the
Japanese government in Tokyo on at least two occasions, as
well as other important trips. After Roy's death, Jackie has
remained in Washington, retired but still socially active, and
currently engaged in her own consulting business. They had
two daughters, born in Washington, D. C.:

a.   Jo Ann, born December 8, 1947; married in Washington
August 15, 1971 to Patrick Darricades, born in France, a
nephew of the Marquis Collier de la Marliere. They live
in Canada, and have two children:
   (1)   Eric Anthony Jaime, born September 7, 1976 in
   Hamilton, Ohio.
   (2)   Karen Nathalie Laurance, born June 1, 1979 at
   Burlington, Ontario, Canada.

b.   Nancy Dale, born April 20, 1949. She was a National
Cherry Blossom Princess, and married Randy Wilkey.
They make their home in California, and have a son:
   (1)   Sean Wolfe, born August 31, 1990 at Walnut
   Creek, California.

Lorena Katherine Pratt
1888-1958

This daughter of Isaac Thompson Pratt (1827) and Nancy Jane Lowder Pratt (1858) was born January 1, 1888 at Chatham Hill, Smyth County, Virginia, and died July 8, 1958 at Appalachia, Virginia. She was a public school teacher all her life, and was one of the author's favorite aunts. She visited with our family on many occasions during the early years, and stayed with us for weeks at a time during the summer hiatus from teaching. She was probably the closest to my mother of any of her other brothers and sisters. Only at her death did I learn part of that reason, when I, and most of the family, first met her daughter and grandchildren at the funeral. Aunt Lorena had a daughter, bearing the Pratt name:

1. Lorena Roberta, born September 16, 1920 and died November 19, 1986. Married to Aris Richard Plaatsman and lived in New York state. Divorced, they had a daughter and a son:
   a. Joy Elizabeth, born March 8, 1944; married John Lavin, who died 1987, and had a son:
      (1) Sean Richard, born June 16, 1966
   b. Aris Richard, Jr., born April 11, 1947; married Jackie Edson and had twin daughers:
      (1) Michelle, born July 10, 1971.
      (2) Christine, born July 10, 1971.

Lorena Roberta Pratt
1920-1986

Willie Neal Hurley
1895-1964

Josephine Davis Pratt
1895-1988

This daughter of Isaac Thompson Pratt (1827) and Nancy Jane Lowder Pratt (1858) was born September 3, 1895 at Chatham Hill, Smyth County, Virginia; died February 7, 1988 at Radford, Virginia in her ninety-third year. Married November 8, 1919 to Willie Neal Hurley, son of the Reverend David Pearson Hurley and Sarah Alberta Clementine Neikirk Hurley. He was born May 8, 1895 at Independence, Virginia, and died March 21, 1964 at their home in Radford. Both are buried at Sunrise Cemetery in Radford.

Josephine was a public school teacher most of her adult life, retiring in 1960 after serving fifteen years in the school system of Montgomery County, Maryland. Willie Neal had also been a teacher, a high school principal, and an athletic coach, but during those last fifteen years, had been employed as a statistician with the Department of Health, Education and Welfare in Washington. They retired to Radford, where Willie Neal had sisters living, and where their daughter, Josephine, lived with her husband and family.

After the death of Willie Neal, Josephine married second on June 7, 1970 to Hyter Anderson Loving of White Sulphur Springs, West Virginia, a widower with one grown son. His son served as best man at the wedding, and the author had the pleasure of giving away the bride, his own mother. Hyte was born May 22, 1893 and died January 13, 1984, after some fourteen wonderful years shared with mother. Josephine and Willie Neal had three children:
1.   Jacqueline Anne, born October 24, 1920, of whom more.
2.   Josephine Alberta, born March 22, 1923, of whom more.
3.   William Neal, Jr., born August 7, 1924, of whom more.

Jacqueline Anne Hurley
1920-

This daughter of Willie Neal Hurley (1895) and Josephine Davis Pratt Hurley (1895) was born October 24, 1920 at Jenkins, in Letcher County, Kentucky. Educated at Radford College (now Radford University) where she received both a BA and a BS in four years of college work, all with honors. Named in *Who's Who in American Colleges and Universities*. Holds a masters from the University of Delaware. Began a teaching career at the public school in Dublin, Virginia, later teaching French at the prestigious Tatnall School in Wilmington, Delaware. Associate in publication of *The Workers World at Hagley* in 1981; contributing author to *The Popular Perception of Industrial History* by Weible and Walsh in 1985; co-author of *Sophie du Pont, A Young Lady in America*, in 1987, and manager of the exhibit of Sophie's drawings in Washington, D. C. Married June 27, 1942 at Radford, Virginia, to Curtis M. Hinsley of Wyoming, Delaware. He was born October 9, 1917 and served in the navy from 1942 to 1946; returned to Hercules Powder Company; finished his career as Chief of Foreign Sales, located for three years at The Hague, Holland. Two children:
1.   Jacqueline Anne, born at Chattanooga, Tennessee, June 1, 1943. Married September 16, 1967 Randal C. Morrison, son

of Charles Harmon Morrison and Dorothy Sechrist Morrison. Jan, as she is always known, attended Randolph Macon for two years, and holds a BA, a masters and, in 1995, a doctorate from Ohio State. Randy has a BA from Ohio Wesleyan, and a masters from Ohio State. They have one daughter:

a. Laura Jo, born December 28, 1971 at Columbus, Ohio. She holds a BS from Oberlin College and is in her first year of pre-med at Cleveland, Ohio.

2. Curtis Matthew, Jr., born at Chattanooga, Tennessee on May 30, 1945. He is known as Kit, attended Tower School at Wilmington, Delaware, and the International School of The Hague, in Holland; received his BA from Princeton University; and a doctorate from the University of Wisconsin. He is an accomplished pianist, a professor of history at Northern Arizona University at Flagstaff, and the author of *Savages and Scientists, The Smithsonian Institution and the Development of American Anthropology, 1846-1910.* He was married August 18, 1968 to Rebecca Ann Snedden, from whom he was divorced. She was a daughter of Dr. and Mrs. Harold E. Snedden of Sandusky, Ohio, and a graduate of Vassar, summa cum laude, Phi Beta Kappa. He was married second July 21, 1995 at Ashland, Oregon, to Victoria Loree Enders, with all of his family in attendance. There were three children born to his first marriage:

a. Christopher Matthew, born October 4, 1969 at Madison, Wisconsin. He holds a BA from Princeton University

b. Sarina, born October 22, 1971 at Madison. She holds a BS in chemistry from Haverford College and in 1994, has started graduate studies at Syracuse University in veterinarian medicine.

c. Matthew Garritt, birthed at home by his parents October 4, 1975, at Hamilton, New York. In 1994, Matt is in his second year at Oberlin College, in the music department, studying classical guitar.

Left to right: Jacqueline Ann Hinsley Morrison; Curtis Matthew
Hinsley; Jacqueline Anne Hurley Hinsley; Curtis Matthew Hinsley, Jr.

Left to right: Rebecca, Kit, Matthew, Sarina & Christopher Hinsley

Left to right: Randy, Jan and Laura Jo Morrison

Josephine Alberta Hurley
1923-

This daughter of Willie Neal Hurley (1895) and Josephine Davis Pratt Hurley (1895), was born March 22, 1923 at Ivanhoe, Wythe County, Virginia, and always known in the family as "Sis." She and the author attended school together from second grade through high school graduation, and were extremely close. Sis won the local beauty contest, and I was the master of ceremonies. She was a Red Cross rated swimmer, and still plays tennis occasionally. She received her BA degree from Radford College, and appears also to have inherited some of her grandmother's artistic talents with oils and canvas. She was married February 3, 1945 at Waukegan, Illinois, to John Benjamin Spiers, Jr. of Radford,

Virginia. He was born December 12, 1926, son of Judge John B. Spiers and Maxine Graves Spiers. He served as a line officer in the navy during the second World War, in the Pacific Theatre, arriving in Japan at the close of hostilities. He received his BA degree from Hampden Sydney College and his law degree from the University of Virginia, with Order of the Coif. He is the surviving member of Spiers and Spiers, Attorneys at Law, and plans to retire during 1994. John is an avid motorcyclist, and he and Josephine have taken several extensive trips together, most notable of which was from Radford, Virginia, to Seattle, Washington and points in between, when both were well into their fifties. They were the parents of four children:

1. Sherry Anne, born June 19, 1950 at Radford, a graduate of Florida State University, and a practicing attorney in Tallahassee, Florida. Married November 5, 1988 to Philip Howard Spratt, who was born July 31, 1948 in Ottawa, Ontario, Canada, son of John Fenton Spratt and June Carol Thayer Spratt. They have one son:
    a. Alexander Philip, born December 24, 1991 in Tallahassee, Florida

2. Vikki Lynn, born March 22, 1953 at Green Cove Springs, Florida. Married March 21, 1988 at Waiplo Valley, Hawaii to Gianni Cesare Catellacci, born December 7, 1949 at Florence, Italy, a son of Fernando and Vanda Frandi Catellacci. She holds a masters degree in art therapy from Goddard College, Vermont, and was listed in *Who's Who in American Colleges and Universities* while attending Guilford College in Greensboro, North Carolina. They have a daughter:
    a. Alima Clara, born June 16, 1989 in Hawaii

3. John Benjamin, III, born September 23, 1954 at Radford. He holds a BA in journalism from the University of Georgia. Married first to Darliet Colley of Marion, Virginia on May 23, 1982 and had a son. Married secondly to Valerie Jean Paul on April 7, 1990, on Guam, where both were working when they met; a daughter. His children were:
    a. Justin Benjamin, born February 27, 1984 at Radford, and died in 1993

214

b. Lindsey Josephine, born January 28, 1991 on the island of Guam

4. Joanne, born November 22, 1955 at Radford. She is a teacher of learning disabled children, holding a BA from Radford College, a masters in special education from the University of Virginia, and a doctorate from Virginia Polytechnic Institute and State University. She was married on July 25, 1981 to Spero Moche, Jr., a merchant marine officer.

John Benjamin Spiers, Jr. & Josephine A. Hurley Spiers

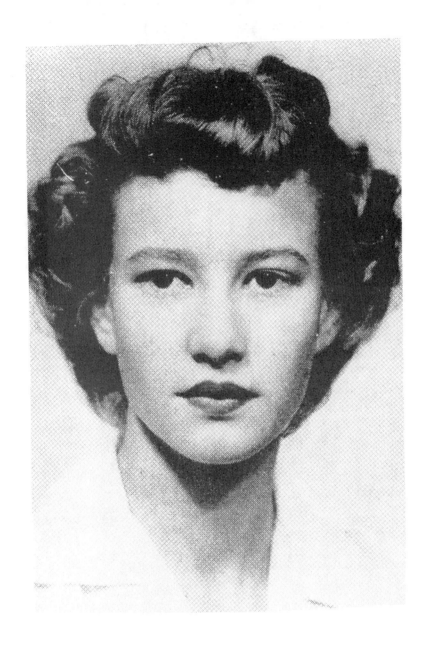

Josephine Alberta Hurley Spiers

John Benjamin Spiers, Jr.

John Benjamin Spiers, III

Sherry Ann Spiers Spratt & Alexander Philip Spratt

Philip Howard Spratt & Alexander Philip Spratt

Spero Moche, Jr. & Dr. Joanne Spiers Moche
And Best Friend

Vikki Lynn Spiers Catellacci & Alima Clara Catellacci

William Neal Hurley, Jr.
1924-

This son of Willie Neal Hurley (1895) and Josephine Davis Pratt Hurley (1895), was born August 7, 1924 at Princeton, Mercer County, West Virginia, and is the author of these papers. Serving in World War II in the navy as a bomb disposal specialist, he was a member of the assault and garrison forces that captured Eniwetok Atoll from the Japanese in the Marshall Islands campaign. He attended Northwestern University and the University of Virginia; was a licensed professional land surveyor in Maryland, Delaware and Virginia; managing partner of Hurley and Cissel Surveys in

Montgomery County, Maryland prior to joining Kettler Brothers, Inc., a major local building and development company. Retired as vice president the first of 1986, and lives in the new town of Montgomery Village, built by the company, now containing about 12,000 homes.

On the occasion of his retirement, he received a State Senate Resolution, and a Governor's Citation from the state of Maryland, recognizing his achievements and contributions to his community and state. On October 5, 1985, the local community board of directors saw fit to rename one of the larger parks in Montgomery Village the *William Hurley Park*, in recognition of his services to the community.

Left to right: John B. Spiers, III; Josephine A. Hurley Spiers;
William N. Hurley, Jr.; Curtis M. Hinsley;
Jacqueline Anne Hurley Hinsley; Jacqueline Ann Hinsley Morrison;
Laura Jo Morrison
c.1986

Bill and Kay Hurley

On May 11, 1987, Bill was awarded the Cross of Military Service by the United Daughters of the Confederacy at an impressive luncheon ceremony in Baltimore. On November 30, 1994, he received certification that his petition for the grant of Honorary Armorial Bearings and Crest was approved by Warrant to the Kings of Arms from The Most Noble Miles Francis Stapleton, Duke of Norfolk, Knight of the Garter, Knight Grand Cross of the Royal Victorian Order, Companion of the Most Honourable Order of the Bath, Commander of the Most Excellent Order of the British Empire, Earl Marshal and Hereditary Marshal of England, and by Letters Patent granted by Her Majesty, the Queen. Such Arms and Crest will be hereditary in the male line of descent and may be borne by such descendants.

The Arms are described as: Gules, three escallops in pale between two Flaunches invected Or each charged with a Flaunch

222

also Gules thereon a Cross Crosslet Or. And for the Honorary Crest upon a Helm with a Wreath Or and Gules A Cardinal (Richmondina cardinalis) proper holding in the dexter foot a Catherine Wheel Or. Mantled Gules doubled Or.

He was married June 6, 1953 at Washington, D. C. to Catherine Lamay Hines. She was born December 13, 1925 in Greensboro, North Carolina, a daughter of Paul Homer (1899) and Myrtle Elsie Peeples Hines (1901). They have two sons:

1. Bradley Allan, born February 5, 1947 in Washington. Married August 9, 1968 to Sharon Lee Mash, at Salt Lake City, Utah. She was born September 13, 1948 in Washington, D. C., although one of her ancestors was with the Brigham Young party in the settlement of Utah. Brad attended elementary school in Montgomery County, Maryland, and high school in Bangor, Maine, living with his grandmother Anderson. He attended Utah State and received his BA from Weber State University, followed by his masters. They live in Sandy, Utah, and have four children, the first two born at Murray, Utah, and the last two at Sandy:
   a. Monika Lynn, born November 16, 1976
   b. Karen Marie, born March 7, 1980
   c. Douglas Wayne, born December 31, 1982
   d. Le Ann Erin, born June 11, 1985
2. William Neal, III, born August 15, 1955. At the time of his birth, and announcement of his name by his proud parents, his grandfather stated that he was not, of course, the 3rd, since my father's name was actually Willie Neal, not William Neal. That meant, naturally, that I was not a junior, either! There was no birth certificate from 1895, but all the family had always called him by the full name, Willie Neal; his navy enlistment papers used that name; everything we could find verified that he was correct. So, I wrote to West Virginia for my own birth certificate and found that I was officially registered simply as: *Wm N. Hurley, Jr.* Mother told me that I was born at home, very early in the morning; in fact, on the kitchen table! She and dad told the doctor that I would be named for my father, and he took the responsibility of registering the birth. He apparently assumed that dad was William Neal,

rather than Willie Neal, and that's what happened to me. In any case, both my son and I bear the name with pride. Neal was educated at St. John's Episcopal Parish Church in Olney, Montgomery County, Maryland, and Bullis Prep at Potomac. That completes the circuit from the original immigrant to Maryland, who appears in the records of St. John's Episcopal Parish Church in Prince George's County. He served for two years in the merchant marine service, traveling to many interesting ports of call. In January, 1985, he received his BA in accounting from the University of Maryland, and a masters degree in 1994. He is a Certified Management Accountant, and a fellow in the Life Management Institute. He is currently employed as contracts manager for MCI in Washington, D. C. He was married June 7, 1986 in Montgomery Village, Maryland, to Kathleen Ann O'Sullivan. She was born March 30, 1962 at the old Providence Hospital in Washington, daughter of Patrick Joseph O'Sullivan, the fifth, who was born December 23, 1934 in Washington; and Frances Elaine Coufal O'Sullivan, born January 2, 1940 in Baltimore. Kathleen is a 1984 graduate of Catholic University, with a degree in chemistry and a sub-concentration in finance. In 1992, she received her masters as well. She was a materials chemist and section chief with the Bureau of Engraving and Printing, specializing in postage stamp papers, inks and adhesives. Their children are in the tenth generation of the Hurley families who are in lineal descent from Daniel Hurley (1658), the Irish immigrant to Maryland, and native-born Americans. They live in a home they had built to their design specifications, near both of their families, and have three children, all born at Shady Grove Hospital, Gaithersburg, Maryland:

a. Bridget Nora, born March 6, 1990. Her name is taken from those of her two maternal great-great grandmothers. Her mother's paternal great grand-parents were Patrick Joseph and Bridget O'Connor O'Sullivan of Ireland. Her mother's maternal great grandparents were William Garfield Smith and Nora Belle Elzey Smith, of Maryland.

b. William Daniel, born February 24, 1992. His first name continues the fourth generation of the name through his father, his grandfather and his great grandfather (in spite of the Willie Neal origin!). The second name is that of Daniel Hurley of 1658, the original immigrant, and the progenitor of all of the Hurleys I have researched.

c. Katherine Ann, born June 1, 1995. Her first name honors both her mother, Kathleen, and her paternal grandmother, Catherine Lamay Hines Hurley, combining the spelling of the two names. Her middle name respects the memory of her maternal great grandmother, Ann Mary Smith Coufal.

Neal, Kathleen and Kathryn
1995

William Daniel Hurley and Bridget Nora Hurley

Laura Rebecca Pratt
1899-1926

This daughter of Isaac Thompson Pratt (1827) and Nancy Jane Lowder Pratt (1858) was the eighteenth child born to his two marriages, and in his seventy-second year. She was born January 20, 1899 at Chatham Hill, Smyth County, Virginia; died July 25, 1926 at Akron, Ohio; buried at Bent Ridge Cemetery, Meta, Pike County, Kentucky. Married August 16, 1921 Clarence Donaldson, and had two daughters:

1. Annette Dale, born August 16, 1922 at Pikeville, Kentucky and married March 20, 1943 to Quentin Roosevelt Justice. They had three children, the first born at Lexington, Kentucky and the last two at Pikeville:
   a. Daniel Quentin, born August 5, 1944; married January 18, 1964 to Gatha Dale Robinson, and had a son:
      (1) Daniel Shannon, born January 11, 1966, Pikeville. He and Tara Young have one son:
         (a) Hunter Brooklynn, born April 7, 1994
   b. John Laurance, born March 2, 1954; November 27, 1976 to Liddie Renee Wells and had a son:
      (1) Joshua Lee, born June 8, 1978
   c. Thomas Dale, born August 4, 1955; married December 31, 1977 to Brenda Gale Cisco and had a daughter:
      (1) Crystal Gale, born August 7, 1978 at Pikesville
2. Rebecca Jean, born January 11, 1924 at Burdine, Letcher County, Kentucky; married August 17, 1945 to Jesse James Baxter, Jr., born June 11, 1914 at Spears, Kentucky; died February 25, 1996 at Lexington, Kentucky; son of Jesse James and Stella Alford Baxter. They have a son:
   a. James Edward, born October 14, 1947 at Lexington, and married October 2, 1976 to Judy Hicks Meyer, and had two children:
      (1) Laura Joan, born October 21, 1977 at Lexington
      (2) Janie Elizabeth, born March 27, 1984 and adopted October 27, 1987

CHAPTER 16

Marshall Pratt
1735-1784

In my small library, I have a copy of an unpublished booklet setting forth the genealogy of Averill and Maggie Pratt, including the Pratt, Holliday and Forgey families, written in 1950 by Earl Pratt. It was given to me by James Pratt, then living at Oak Ridge, Tennessee. Neither of us can establish a connection to the families here under study, but perhaps it exists, and the inclusion of the data here may assist another researcher in uncovering the missing link.

In the booklet, it is reported that Marshall Pratt, at the age of 19, took part in the Battle of Great Meadows, or Fort Necessity, fought by Colonial troops under George Washington on July 3, 1754. As a result of the battle, Marshall Pratt was one of sixty soldiers who collectively received a grant of 28,627 acres of land, commonly known as *The Savage Grant*, reportedly so named for the sergeant leading the troops. The grant is described in complete detail, including the names of the recipients, in *Virginia Military Land Grants*, by Symmes. As an interesting aside, it is reported that the Chief Surveyor of the grant was Sir William Crawford, who was burned at the stake by the Indians at Chillicothe.

It is also of some interest to recall that the company was under the command of Colonel Joshua Fry, who was thrown from his horse and died from those wounds earlier in the campaign. Fry was a well-known military leader, originally from the eastern section of Virginia, but later moved to Albemarle, near the home of Thomas Jefferson. It was Joshua Fry and Peter Jefferson who together prepared a comprehensive map of Virginia, Maryland, and other east coast areas in 1751. George Washington was his second in command, and assumed command of the troops, with title of Colonel. The battle at Fort Necessity was perhaps one of the first engagements in which Washington held command, and he was forced to surrender to the French.

The same book indicates that another grant of fifty acres was made to this Marshall Pratt for military service, which he sold to Washington on April 14, 1774. This was also the date on which the owners of the *Savage Grant* gathered at Mount Vernon to agree on a division of the entire tract into sixty separate parcels. The grant included what are now the municipalities of Huntington, Ceredo, Guyandotte, Kenova and Barboursville, in West Virginia; as well as Catlettsburg, Kentucky.

Marshall was born c.1735 in Accomack County, Virginia, and is shown on a roll call of Woodard's Company of the Colonial Militia, dated September 25, 1757. He is said to have been 22 years of age; five feet, three inches tall; a planter by trade; enlisted from Northampton County; fair complexion; black hair; and under the heading of remarks, *a small man.*

The wife of Marshall has not been reported to me, but he apparently had several children, all born in Virginia. There were at least three sons, one of whom reportedly settled in Kentucky. This sounds very much like the *"three brothers story"* that is prevalent in genealogical studies but, in any case, the two brothers reported to me were:

1. Jesse, who finally settled in West Virginia. A little bit of family history reports that, on one occasion, Jesse was asked by his mother to fetch an armfull of firewood; he went out to get it and did not return home for eight years, but came in carrying an armfull of wood. He was married in Cabell County, West Virginia, November 30, 1809 to Sallie Forgey.

2. Joshua, born in 1784; married October 13, 1831 in Lawrence County, Ohio to Sarah Forgey. Although the names Sarah and Sallie are confusing, it appears that the two girls here are not one and the same person, and that the two brothers did, in fact, both marry a Forgey. The papers from which this information was taken indicate that Joshua was the first of the family to move from Virginia to Ohio, and that he was a *post natal* child; that is, born after the death of his father. As such, according to local superstition of the times, he was possessed with the ability to blow his breath into the mouths of small children and babies, and cure what was then known as "thrush," a rash or breaking out, within the mouth cavity, for

which there was no other known cure. Joshua had seven children, all apparently born in Lawrence County, Ohio:

a. James, born November 21, 1832; went to Kansas
b. Roxey, born February 13, 1835; married Joel Eearles.
c. John, born March 15, 1837; served as a Confederate soldier, wounded at or shortly after the Battle of Shiloh. Surrendered with his brother Nimrod at Perryville, while considering desertion, and sent to St. Lous, Missouri, where they took the Oath of Allegiance and were released. After returning to Ohio, both he and Nimrod joined a Kentucky company in the Union Army, and finished the war in federal service. Married to Charlotte Earles and had three children:
    (1) Averill; married to Maggie Etta Holliday, of whom more
    (2) Andrew; married Anna Holliday, sister of Maggie
    (3) Sarah, married Henry Keeney.
d. Andrew, born January 25, 1839; perhaps married May 3, 1868 in Lawrence County, Ohio to Eliza Pemberton.
e. Nimrod, born May 2, 1841. See story above relative to his brother John, and their adventures during the Civil War. Married in Kentucky; lived at Catlettsburg, and had two sons: Frank and Willie.
f. William, born June 9, 1845; married April 11, 1869 to Elizabeth Mount, and had at least one son and perhaps three daughters.
g. Nancy, born February 7, 1847. She was perhaps married September 30, 1868 in Lawrence County, Ohio, to James O. Martin.

Averill Pratt
m/1891

This son of John Pratt (1837) and Charlotte Earles Pratt, was born in Ohio, and married c.1891 to Maggie Etta Holliday. She was originally named Marietta, and her name was changed after her marriage. They lived at South Point, Ohio and were the parents of seven children:

1. Pearl A., a daughter, born June 9, 1892; married to Zelda Watters, and had four children:
   a. Hilda; married Dr. William Temple; lived in Covington, Kentucky, and had no children.
   b. Keith, married Mary Green and had four children: Pat, Mike, Rodney and Jean Lee.
   c. Frank Pratt.
   d. Wanda Pratt, married Joe Hoy. They lived at Kalamazoo, Michigan, and had four children: Shelley, Thomas, Susan and Joseph.
2. Nellie, born April 26, 1894; died April 25, 1964. Married to John A. Ashworth; lived at Ironton, Ohio, no children.
3. John Earl; married December 24, 1928 to Edna Dean. He was an attorney in Ironton, Ohio, and the author of the papers from which this information has been derived. Two children:
   a. Margaret Anne; married Ralph R. Kelley, a pharmacist. Lived at Boynton Beach, Florida; four children: Kaye, Kara, Mark and Laura.
   b. Dean; married Barbara Metzger. Lived at Sewanee, Tennessee where he studied for the ministry. Three children: Jennifer, Melinda and Eric.
4. Charles M., born August 3, 1899; died December 21, 1972. Married Stella Draper; no children.
5. James Carl; married Edna Lynd, and had a son:
   a. John Carl, a veterinarian, married; two sons: David and Eddie.
6. Inez, a retired school teacher; lived at Ironton, Ohio; single.
7. Arno, formerly a school teacher, and then a Methodist minister who lived at Winter Haven, Florida and married twice. First to Nellie Smith, and second to Ernestine Jones. Six children.

CHAPTER 17

Jonathan Pratt
1714-1781

This early member of the Pratt family is included here in order to preserve a fairly substantial record, although no evidence has been discovered as yet linking him to the Pratts who are the principal individuals now under study. In 1990, W. M. Pratt and his wife, from Kennewick, Washington, were visiting in my home county of Montgomery, in Maryland. At the Mormon library in Salt Lake City, they had seen a copy of my first genealogical effort, *The Ancestry of William Neal Hurley, III,* printed in 1985, in which a section was devoted to the Pratt families. They contacted me on arrival in the area, and we had a day or so of pleasant visiting with them, and two of their daughters. They gave me a copy of a small pamphlet, entitled *Pratt Profiles, The Saga of a Pratt Family, The (Probable) Ancestry of and Some Descendants of Jonathan Pratt of Newberry County, South Carolina,* written by Grace Pratt Thomas, but not published. Incidentally, the children of W. M. Pratt are part owners of the major development firm known as *Folger-Pratt,* one of the more important, well-known commercial firms in the Washington metropolitan area.

Jonathan Pratt appears in deed records of Orange County, Virginia as early as June 25, 1740, at which time he purchased a tract of land containing 200 acres from Richard Mauldin, located on branches of the Robinson River. On July 22, 1741, he purchased from Martin Duett a tract of 150 acres on the great fork of the Rappahannock River near the thoroughfare mountain road. Present day roads in this area (now Madison County, Virginia) are United States route 29, and state road 231. Along the latter, there is a very small, simple, cross-road area known as Pratts, undoubtedly named for the family. Another deed, acknowledged May 22, 1748, contains a lease from Henry Shorter for 100 acres in the fork of the Rappahannock River upon Beaver Dam.

According to IGI records of the Mormon Church, Jonathan was born about 1714. He was apparently married twice; first about 1739 to an unknown girl, born about 1718; his second wife being Mary, widow of Christian Redman, and the mother of a son and daughter from that marriage: John and Katherine Redman.

A deed dated May 15, 1775, in Culpeper County, Virginia, was executed by John Redman, Jonathan Pratt and Mary Pratt, his wife, conveyind lands which formerly belonged to Christian Redman. It should be noted that Culpeper County was formed in 1748 from part of Orange County, and that Jonathan Pratt lived in the area that became part of the new county.

In 1768, Jonathan made a deed of gift to his son, James, for 180 acres of land, for natural love and affection. He also gave a tract of 150 acres to his son, Jonathan Pratt, Jr., for natural love and affection, which was part of the original land he had acquired. Each of these gifts was to become effective upon the death of their father. In 1762, Jonathan assigned the right of use and possession of a tract of land along the Mountain Road to Robert Mansell for a peior of twenty years dating from 1762. This would lead to an assumption that Jonathan may have had a daughter who married to Robert Mansell. Records of Virginia and South Carolina indicate that members of the Pratt, Mansell and Redman families lived near each other, and were presumably related.

The will of Jonathan is dated October 24, 1777 and probated May 4, 1781, indicating that he probably died early that year. He left his principal estate to his son Thomas, and gave to his wife's daughter Katherine Redman, a bed and one cow. The inventory of estate was taken August 20, 1781, and indicates that he was rather well-to-do for the time.

Following the death of his father, James Pratt conveyed the property that had been given to him to his brother Thomas, by deed dated August 23, 1781. At that time, James was said to be of Bedford County, Virginia. Jonathan Pratt, Jr., also conveyed his lands as gifted by his father, to his brother Thomas in 1769, at which time Jonathan, Jr. was said to be living in Montgomery County, Virginia.

233

Jonathan Pratt appears to have been the father of at least three sons, and perhaps a daughter, all presumed to have been born from his first marriage, probably in Orange County, Virginia:

1. Thomas, born c.1740, of whom more
2. James, born c.1742, of whom more
3. Jonathan, Jr., born about 1745, of whom more
4. A daughter, perhaps, married to Robert Mansell.

Thomas Pratt
1740-1814

This son of Jonathan Pratt (1714), probably his eldest, was born c.1740, probably in Orange County, Virginia. Married Mary Ann, and died c.1814 in Culpeper County, Virginia. He was probably married in the early 1760s, and appears in several transactions of land in Culpeper and Madison Counties. He lived in Culpeper at the time of his death, but the original tract of land which he inherited from his father was in Madison, created from Culpeper in 1792.

Distribution of his estate, dated 1815, is found in Will Book 1, page 43, in which his heirs are mentioned by name. His wife is not mentioned in the distribution, and is presumed to have either predeceased her husband, or to have received her one-third dower prior to distribution of the remainder. This may be the same Thomas Pratt shown as head of household in the 1810 census of the county. The family included one male over 45 years (Thomas); one male 26 to 45; one male under 10; one female 26 to 45 (perhaps Mary Ann); and eleven slaves. Their children, all born in Culpeper County, Virginia, included:

1. Elizabeth, born c.1762; died c.1807 in Rockcastle County, Kentucky. Married c.1782 in Culpeper County, Virginia, to James Graves.
2. Josiah, born c.1764; died before December 28, 1827 in Culpeper County, Virginia. Married there December 16, 1789 to Mary Beckham.
3. Susannah.
4. Thomas, Jr., married first January 7, 1796 to Elizabeth Smith and second December 2, 1812 to Martha (Patsy) Terrell, both

in Culpeper County, Virginia. He moved to Warren County, Missouri, and probably died there. It is interesting to note that Henry Thompson Pratt (1861), a half-brother of the author's mother, spent the last part of his life in Warrensburg, Missouri where he is buried.

5. Jonathan, married in Culpeper County on February 5, 1803 to Hannah Roberts; and died c.1815 in Madison County.

6. Jane; married in Culpeper County March 4, 1800 to Briscoe Smith; and died before 1815. At least one daughter:
   a. Mary Ann.

7. Jesse; married in Culpeper County, February 24, 1813 Milley Johnson, and died late in 1818.

8. James.

James Pratt
1742-1804

This son of Jonathan Pratt (1714) was born c.1742 in Orange County, Virginia. We have previously reported the deed of gift in 1764 to James from his father, and the fact that James conveyed the property to his brother after the death of their father. Prior to 1774, James had removed to Bedford County, Virginia, where, in 1778, he purchased a tract of land containing 350 acres from Henry Huff, located on the head of Glady Creek, and a little more than a year later, sold the property to William Overstreet, at which time his wife, Mary, signed the deed with her mark. At a court held March 27, 1780, he was permitted to keep an ordinary at the fork of the road near Otter River. On March 2, 1782, James purchased from John Talbot of Campbell County, Virginia, a tract of land containing 770 acres on the head of Amos's Branch.

On December 9, 1799, one James Pratt (perhaps this one), was brought to court on charges that he had feloniously struck and wounded Isham Going on the night of November 18, with a hickory stick on the left side of his head, so that he died. The case was heard, at which time James plead not guilty, but was ordered taken to the jail, and from there to the district court in New London. We do not now know the outcome of this action, nor whether we are here dealing with the right James Pratt.

By the Court of February, 1804, James had died, and one third of his estate was allotted to his widow, Mary. Various deeds, court and chancery records reveal the names of seven of the children. In at least one case, mention is made of the one-eighth share of the estate, suggesting that there were eight children, although we can now report only seven:

1. Mary, born c.1766; married in Bedford County, Virginia April 6, 1786 to Durester (or Drury) Foster. She died after 1822, and had apparently left Virginia.

2. James, Jr.; married Lucy Flint, daughter of Richard Flint; and died after 1810. In 1806, he was living in Rockbridge County, Virginia.

3. Lucy, born c.1775, probably in Bedford County, Virginia, and married after 1806 to James Woodford. At least one child:
   a. Nancy.

4. Judah, or Julia, born c.1780, and married August 3, 1801 in Franklin County, Virginia, to Jesse Wilks. Moved out of Virginia, and died after 1822.

5. William; married in Franklin County January 13, 1817 Julia Brockman.

6. Joshua, born c.1787, probably in Bedford County. The small pamphlet mentioned at the beginning of this chapter suggests that this may be the same Joshua Pratt who was married to Sarah Forgey in Ohio, but that does not seem to be the case. The documentation sent to me relative to Joshua Pratt (1784), son of Marshall Pratt (1735) as reported in Chapter 16 is too well presented to be dismissed. It was that Joshua, and not this one, who was the husband of Sarah Forgey, which see.

7. Jesse, leaving children mentioned in the will of his father:
   a. Joshua
   b. Jane
   c. Polly
   d. Hugh, born c.1809 in Virginia, of whom more

Hugh Pratt
1809-

This son of Jesse Pratt (and grandson of James Pratt of 1742) was born c.1809 in Virginia; married July 15, 1834 in Lawrence County, Ohio to Judith M. Pratt, born in Virginia. Both died in Center Township, Hancock County, Indiana. Nine children, first two born in Lawrence County, and the rest in Hancock County, Indiana:

1. Calpurna, born 1836; married March 9, 1862 Julian Moore.
2. William F., born 1838; died December 24, 1905 at Greenfield, Hancock County, Indiana. Married March 14, 1862 to Martha E. Marsh.
3. Jesse D., born 1843; died April 26, 1884 at Hancock. Married October 4, 1865 Jemima E. Simmons.
4. Rosa Ann, born 1845.
5. Joshua J., born 1847
6. Julia M., born 1854
7. Adelia R., born 1858; married March 18, 1876 to George M. Jackson.
8. Emma E., born 1862, and married August 6, 1885 to Hiram N. Barrett.
9. Marshall Valandingham, born January 15, 1864; died January 28, 1942 in Hancock County, Indiana. Married December 10, 1885 to Armilda Ellen Johnson, born May 21, 1866. At least two children:
   a. Leslie Hugh, born March 18, 1888; married March, 1907 to Wynema E. Wilson.
   b. Harry Johnson, born May 16, 1894; died March 9, 1895

CHAPTER 18

Jonathan Pratt, Jr.
1745-1802

This son of Jonathan Pratt (1714), was born c.1745, probably in Orange County, Virginia. As has been reported earlier, he received a deed of gift from his father in 1769 in Culpeper County, which he later sold to his brother, Thomas (1740) after the death of their father. In 1781, when he sold the property, he was said to be of Montgomery County, Virginia. No record has been found of Jonathan Pratt, Jr. in that county, so we assume he lived there only for a short time, and perhaps owned no property.

We will attempt to prove here that this Jonathan Pratt, Jr. is the same individual found later in Newberry County, South Carolina. He is known to have married Elizabeth Hughes, daughter of Blackmore Hughes, probably early in 1770. Blackmore Hughes was found in records of Hanover County, Virginia, where he is shown as a planter and a builder. Most of the records of that county were destroyed, but he is mentioned there from c.1748 to c.1763. By 1778, he had moved to Henry County, Virginia, and was that year appointed tax assessor of the county, where he died c.1786.

Four of his children: Blackmore, Jr.; George; John; and Mary (wife of Jesse Abston), lived and owned land in Bedford County, Virginia, and remained there until their deaths, with the exception of Blackmore Hughes, Jr., who moved to Kentucky. When the elder Blackmore died in August of 1786, he left to his daughter Elizabeth Pratt the sum of 30 pounds, and directed that the 100 acres of land lying at the White Falls on the Smith River be sold and the money be given to her. It should be remembered that Patrick County was created from Henry County in 1791, five years after the death of Blackmore Hughes, Sr. From personal knowledge, the author is well aware of a location in Patrick County known as Smith River Falls, a popular picnic and recreation area, which may be the area in which the 100 acres was located. Smith River flows near the line between Patrick and Franklin Counties, so this must be the general area in which Jonathan lived.

There is a deed dated September 21, 1779 from Jonathan Pratt of Henry County, to Humphrey Burditt of Pittsylvania County, for a tract of land containing 79 acres. Also, on January 31, 1787, Jonathan Pratt, now of Franklin County, Virginia, conveyed 200 acres to William Swanson of the same county. (Franklin was created from parts of Henry and Bedford Counties in 1786). Both tracts are described as being on the Blackwater River near the mouth of Bull Run. Both deeds were witnessed by one John Pratt, not otherwise identified. In order to be a legal witness, he must have been born by 1758 or so, which may suggest that he was yet another son of Jonathan Pratt, the elder, or at least a close relative.

Jonathan, Jr. was a member of the Henry County State Militia and marched in Thomas Smith's Company from Henry County to assist General Nathaniel Green at the battle of Guilford Courthouse on March 15, 1781.

With the death of his wife's father in 1786, and the sale of his property in 1787, it appears probable that Jonathan, Jr. left Virginia and moved to South Carolina. He appears there in the Old Ninety-six District, which was later Newberry County, in the 1790 census. On September 11, 1795, he purchased 100 acres of land from Richard Mansell. This transaction is our best evidence that we are here dealing with the same Jonathan Pratt, Jr., of Culpeper, Madison and Henry Counties, Virginia. Richard Mansell was a son of Robert Mansell, who had been given the use of a certain tract of land by Jonathan Pratt, Sr. in 1762. We had earlier suggested that Robert Mansell was married to a daughter of the earlier Jonathan; if that is correct, then Richard Mansell would be a first cousin of our Jonathan Pratt, Jr. It is a well-known fact that immigrations in this period were seldom by a single family, but generally by groups of families, moving together, who were also more often related than not. We believe that this set of circumstances fairly well establishes that the Jonathan Pratt of Newberry, South Carolina, is one and the same with the Jonathan Pratt, born c.1745 in Culpeper County, Virginia.

Jonathan became very active in the purchase of real estate in South Carolina, and apparently for a time lived in Fairfield County, returning to Newberry. On January 9, 1796, he purchased two tracts of 35 acres and 50 acres on Richard's spring branch. On May 5, 1796, he bought from George Johnson all of his land in Newberry County on "*the other side of a certain creek below the line of said Pratt.*" On January 13, 1797, he bought from William Malone 100 acres on Enoree River, and a branch called Gossell's Creek. On May 30, 1796, he bought a 43 acre tract from James Vardiman on Heller's Creek.

Jonathan died, probably early in 1802, without leaving a will. Administration was granted on March 8, 1802, and inventory was taken on March 17. The inventory included farm and household items, including four beds, two plows, tools, two horses, sixteen geese, nine head of cattle and sixty-one hogs. Jonathan was a distiller of whiskey, and the inventory included stills and casks, tubs and quantities of small grain. His widow, Elizabeth, and other family members are mentioned in the sale of the estate. Also mentioned as purchasers of items were Richard and John Mansell, sons of Robert Mansell.

Records indicate that Jonathan was a man who possessed numerous talents. He was a large landowner, well educated, a distiller of whiskey, operator of a singing school, a riding school, and a finishing school. Books were included in his inventory, and he had made a pledge to his church, which was paid out of his estate. From available records, the children of Jonathan Pratt, Jr., and his wife, Elizabeth, appear to have included the following:

1. John, perhaps, but questionable
2. George, born c.1774, of whom more
3. William, born c.1776, of whom more
4. Mary, born c.1777, of whom more
5. A daughter, perhaps Sarah, born c.1780. One Sarah Pratt was married to Gideon Nelson before 1800, and by that date was the mother of one son and one daughter. Her husband's name appears in the settlement of estate of her father, but her's does not. By 1819, Gideon sold land, and his wife, Sarah, signed to relinquish her dower rights. The census records of 1800 through 1870 raise questions as to whether or not Sarah, who appears in the 1850 census by name, with her actual age stated, is in fact the daughter of Jonathan Pratt, Jr., or a

second wife of Gideon Nelson, when ages are taken into account for the entire family. Gideon and his family were still in Newberry County, South Carolina during the 1830 census, but moved to Talbot County, Georgia, some time after that, where he died in 1856, leaving a widow and several children, one of whom was:

a.   Gideon, Jr.
6.   Frances, born March 1, 1784, of whom more
7.   Milley, probably born in Virginia, but perhaps in Newberry County, South Carolina. Nothing is known of her except that in each of the estate returns of her father, she received an equal share with the other children. It was once thought that she and Mary were the same individual, but that does not seem to be the case, in that, at the same time that Milley received a share of the estate, John Hutchinson (who had married Mary) also received an equal share. From old family letters of the mid 1800s, it appears possible that Milley may have married Benjamin Gage, since the letters refer to "old uncle Ben Gage."
8.   John Jonathan, born c.1791, of whom more

George Pratt
1774-1813

This son of Jonathan Pratt, Jr. (1745) and Elizabeth Hughes Pratt, was probably born c.1774 in Orange County, Virginia. He moved with his parents and grew to manhood in Newberry County, South Carolina. On September 4, 1796, he received two grants of land in the county, then Old Ninety-six District. He was married June 1, 1799 in Newberry County to Elizabeth. Her last name is reported as "School" on family group sheets of the Mormon church, born c.1775, but the source of that information is not known. He is shown in the census of 1800 with a wife and a daughter under the age of five.

About 1811, George left South Carolina, and moved to Knox County, Tennessee, where he settled along Bull Run Creek. He was enlisted on July 30, 1813 in Knoxville to serve in the War of 1812 as a private in Captain Graham's 1st Regt of Riflemen. Barely two months later, he contracted disease and died at Fort Ball, Canada on September 15, 1813. His widow, Elizabeth, tried over a period of years to prove her claim for a widow's pension, which was finally granted in 1855 at the rate of $4.00 per month. She was then living in Union County, which had been created from part of Knox County, Tennessee about 1850. The children were:

1. David, born c.1800 in Orange County, Virginia, according to the family group sheets, but more likely Newberry County, South Carolina, since his father probably moved there with David's grandparents prior to his marriage in 1799. David would have moved as a youngster with his family in 1811 to Knox County, Tennessee. The census of 1850 for that county includes David's family, there stating that he was born in Virginia, so that remains questionable. David married Sarah Mitchell on March 2, 1837, born c.1820 in Tennessee. His family of seven children were all born in Knox County:
   a. Eathalena, born 1838. Probable the same Eatha M. M. Pratt shown on Mormon records as married October 2, 1856 to William Perry in Knox County.
   b. Charles A., born 1840; perhaps the same individual who was reported married March 24, 1867 in Knox County to Elizabeth J. Tummins (or Lummins).
   c. Mathise, born 1842
   d. Louisa, born 1844
   e. Elizabeth, born 1847; perhaps the same who was married October 12, 1880 to Henry Browning in Knox County.
   f. Thomas, born 1847
   g. Joseph, born 1850
2. John, born 1801 in Newberry County, South Carolina, as were the rest of the children, and married to Mary.
3. Willis, born 1804
4. Mary, born 1806
5. James, born 1807; married in 1834 to Lucinda Bullock.
6. Thomas, born 1807. This may well be Thomas Robert Pratt, who moved to Putnam County, Indiana; then to Wisconsin; and finally to Missouri. Family tradition holds that Thomas died c.1884 while visiting a brother in Kentucky, although it appears that his brother Willis remained in Tennessee. A son:
   a. Willis Layton.

William Pratt
1776-1832

This son of Jonathan Pratt, Jr. (1745) and Elizabeth Hughes Pratt, was born c.1776 in Virginia, and moved with his parents to Newberry County, South Carolina when he was in his early teens; and is listed there as one of the pupils in his father's singing school. He was party to a deed in 1802, with his mother, selling 43 acres of land on Heller's Creek. Shortly after that, he left South Carolina and removed to Greene County, Tennessee. There were already a number of Pratts in that and neighboring counties, and he may have found relatives there.

He did find a wife, and was married there under a marriage bond dated March 27, 1806 to Isabel or Isabella Hall. Records reportedly held by their son, Jonathan Blackmore Pratt, stated that she was born in Ireland. He moved his family to Knox County, Tennessee, and settled in the Bull Run Valley, where, in 1812, his wife died, leaving him with four small children, the first listed. As has been noted just above, his brother, George Pratt (1774) had apparently arrived in Bull Run Valley about a year before the death of William's wife.

One Richard Taylor and his wife, Hannah Vernon Taylor, had moved from Stokes County, North Carolina, and settled in the Bull Run Creek valley area. One of his daughters, Susannah Taylor, had been married to William Halbert, and moved to Tennessee as well. William Pratt, now needing a mother for his small children, married Rebecca Worth Taylor, another of the daughters of Richard and Hannah Vernon Taylor. Years later, Jonathan Blackmore, son of William Pratt from his first marriage, would marry Susannah Halbert, a daughter of the sister of his stepmother.

William and his second wife had eight children, some born at Bull Run Creek, and some in White County, and probably the last two in Hardin County, all in Tennessee. William sold land in White County in 1825, and may have shortly thereafter moved to the Holland Creek area in Hardin County. He appears in the 1830 census of Hardin and reportedly died there about 1832.

Some family records indicate that Rebecca Worth Taylor Pratt died in Alabama in 1843, and since the marriage of one of her sons,

Christopher Columbus Pratt, was found there in 1844, and the 1850 census shows that George Taylor Pratt's daughter, Elizabeth F., was born in 1844 in Alabama, the family is probably correct. The Halberts were also found in Lauderdale County, and adjoining Limestone County, Alabama. The children of William Pratt were:

1. Jonathan Blackmore, born January 18, 1807, of whom more.
2. William Buchanan, born February 19, 1809 near Greenville, Greene County, Tennessee; married Mary Ann Smith.
3. Cynthia Ann, born 1819, probably at Bull Run Creek in Knox County, Tennessee; died c.1828
4. Rebecca Isabella, born October 10, 1811, probably at Bull Run Creek; married William Lloyd.
5. Thomas, born c.1812, probably at Bull Run Creek
6. George Taylor, born c.1813, probably at Bull Run Creek, in Knox County, Tennessee. Married to Mary Ann and in 1850, was living in Monroe County, Mississippi.
7. Ezekiel Lyon, born January 26, 1816 at Caney Fork River in White County, Tennessee. Moved to Mississippi and lived in Pontotoc County, where he married his first wife, Frances Lodaska Whitten, in November of 1846, according to family records. However, according to family group sheets found in the Mormon library, it is likely that he married his first wife in White County, Tennessee, where his first son was reportedly born, and moved to Mississippi after that event. After the death of Frances Lodaska, he was married second to Minerva Faulkner. He removed to Utah in the 1850s and settled in Tooele; moved to Dixie for a while; and died in Salt Lake City, August 10, 1907. The one son reported was:
   a. Francis M., born c.1848 in White County, Tennessee.
8. Elizabeth, born February 29, 1821 at Caney Fork River, in White County, Tennessee. Married Berry H. Lloyd and apparently moved to Lauderdale County, Alabama, as B. H. Lloyd (apparently her husband) performed the marriage ceremony there of her brother, Christopher Columbus Pratt, and Margaret Ann Fowler.
9. Frances Eufracia, born c.1823, probably at Caney Fork, White County, Tenneses. Married March 5, 1846 in Monroe County, Mississippi to William H. Martin, son of Seth and

Frances Halbert Martin. In 1860, they lived in Tishomingo County, Mississippi.

10. Pratt, Martin Hughes, born c.1825
11. Christopher Columbus, born March 29, 1819 at Caney Fork River, White County, Tennessee. Married June 3, 1844 Margaret Ann Fowler in Lauderdale County, Alabama.
12. Daughter, apparently stillbirth born 1827, probably in Hardin County, Tennessee.

Jonathan Blackmore Pratt
1807-1890

This son of William Pratt (1776) and Isabel Hall Pratt was born January 18, 1807 at Greenville, in Greene County, Tennessee. Named for his grandfather, Jonathan Pratt (1745), and his great grandfather, Blackmore Hughes, he was married January 6, 1832 in Tennessee to Susannah Halbert, daughter of William and Susannah Taylor Halbert. She was born May 15, 1812 in Tennessee and died October 28, 1891 at Holden, Mallard County, Utah. Jonathan Blackmore Pratt died April 11, 1890 at Deseret, Mallard County, Utah. His family is included for several generation in the Ancestral Files of the Mormon church, to which the interested reader is referred. The family moved between 1838 and 1840 to Missouri, and after 1848 to Utah, with little question at some point having joined the Church of Jesus Christ of Latter Day Saints. They had children, briefly described here:

1. Rebecca Ann, born October, 1834, in Hardin County, Tennessee; married Edward Ricks
2. Martha Jane, born June 25, 1836, in Hardin County, Tennessee; died October 18, 1889 at Grantsville, Utah. Married November 9, 1857 to James Mitchell Worthington, born January 3, 1831 at Old Brighton, Beaver County, Pennsylvania, and had children, born at Grantsville, in Tooele County, Utah:
   a. Angeline Martha, born September 21, 1858
   b. James Henry, born July 2, 1860; married to Martha Downs, born June 3, 1862 at Withington, Lancaster, England. Six children.

c.   Susanna Rachel, born September 3, 1862; married to August Wilhelm Rytting, born May 13, 1860 at Waksala, Uppsala, Sweden

d.   Sample Steven, born March 10, 1865

e.   Edward Joseph, born March 29, 1867

f.   Franklin Richard, born July 18, 1869

g.   Alice Ann, born September 1, 1871; married Edward Eli Poulton, born October 9, 1865 at Coalville, Summit County, Utah. Four children.

h.   Princetta, born November 2, 1874

i.   Warren William, born September 7, 1876

3.   Mary Caroline, born February 26, 1838, in Hardin County, Tennessee; married Clayborn Montgomery Elder, born there February 26, 1838. Children, first two born at Grantsville, Tooele County, Utah:

a.   Clayborn Pratt, born August 1, 1859; married first Isabel Stark, and second Annie Maria Rasmine Petersen, born September 21, 1871 at Mt. Pleasant, Sanpete County, Utah. He had five children.

b.   Mary Louisa, born June 5, 1861; married Price Williams Nelson, born August 29, 1855 at San Bernadino, and had eleven children, and numerous grandchildren.

c.   William David, born February 4, 1864 at Duncans Retreat, Washington County, Utah; married Emma Ann Black, born April 11, 1874 at Kanosh, Millard County, Utah.

d.   Jonathan Pratt, born January 14, 1867 at Virgin City, in Washington County, Utah; married Bertha Ann Dewsnup, born July 20, 1874 at Fillmore, Utah. Eighteen children.

e.   Ellen Isabel, born July 10, 1870 at Mountain Dell, Utah; married Samuel Nutter Stanworth, born March 21, 1865 at Duncan, Utah. Six children.

4.   Uphrasia Isabella, born July 13, 1840 at Aberdeen, Monroe County, Missouri. Married William Addington Martindale, born June 11, 1814 at Washington, Wayne County, Indiana, and had children:

a. Alonzo, born April 30, 1859 at Grantsville, Utah; married Mary Elizabeth McIntosh, born there December 4, 1864. Thirteen children.

b. John Albert, born July 5, 1862 at Tooele, Utah; married Elizabeth Jean Wright, born April 13, 1862 at Salt Lake City, Utah. Eight children.

c. Susanna Isabell, born March 26, 1864 at Grantsville, Utah; married James Keller Dayley, born June 10, 1862 at Richmond, Utah. Eleven children.

d. William Lyman, born January 18, 1867 at Virgin City, Utah; married Helen Agnes Lewis, born January 22, 1876 at Slaterville, Weber County, Utah. Eight children.

e. Minnie, born c.1869 at Virgin City, Utah

f. Athan Thomas, born January 18, 1871 at Virgin City and married to Angeline Amelia McMurray, born February 23, 1876 at Grantsville, Utah.

5. William Halbert, born May 8, 1844 in Tishimingo County, Missouri; married Ann Elizabeth Burgess, born June 11, 1843 at Marshfield, England. They had children, born at Duncan's Retreat, Washington County, Utah:

a. Elizabeth Susanna, born April 3, 1865; married Hyrum Franklin Wright, born there October 27, 1865. Seven children.

b. William Franklin, born April 27, 1867; married Elizabeth Elinor Tolbert, born August 27, 1875 at Kamas, Summit County, Utah. Ten children.

c. Jonathan Burgess, born June 28, 1869; married Emma Alldredge, born August 31, 1876 at Lehi, Utah and had seven children. Married second Almira Celestial Knight, born July 28, 1881 at Kingston, Utah and had four more children.

d. Thomas Henry, born December 3, 1873; married Jane Marinda Harmon, born January 10, 1877 at Holden, Utah. Six children.

e. James Halbert, born October 29, 1876.

6. Elizabeth Frances, born October 1, 1846 in Tishimingo County, Missouri; married John Clayborn Montgomery Elder,

born January 2, 1827 at Rutherford, Tennessee. Children, the first five born in Washington County, Utah:

a. Martha Susannah, born May 4, 1864
b. James Edward, born November 4, 1865; married Julia Rhoana Workman, born January 27, 1880 at Hillsdale, Utah. Nine children.
c. Hyrum Pratt, born December 1, 1867
d. Annie Elizabeth, born November 5, 1869; married Calvin Kelsey, born October 16, 1856 in Salt Lake County, Utah. Seventeen children.
e. Walter Wallace, born June 19, 1871; married Mary Angeline Page (or Adams), born October 27, 1878 at Paria, Washington County, Utah. Twelve children.
f. Agnes Etey, born June 5, 1874 in Beaver County, Utah; married Thomas George Theobald, born March 26, 1874. Eight children.
g. Franklin Pratt, born January 19, 1877 in Kane County, Utah; married Permelia Jane Page, born March 28, 1885 at Snyderville, Summit County, Utah. Eight children. Perhaps married second to Jane Evert.
h. Ira Milton, born January 2, 1880 at Glendale, in Kane County, Utah; married Fannie Holiday.
i. Parley Pratt, born September 25, 1882 at Snowflake, in Navajo County, Arizona; married Anna Elizabeth Johnson, born February 8, 1885 in Millard County, Utah and had five children. Married second Magdalene Rawlinson, born November 10, 1887 at Oak City, Utah and had six more children.
j. Charles Pratt, born January 5, 1885 at Duncan's Retreat, Utah.
k. Edgar Pratt, born April 2, 1887 at St. George, Utah
7. John Wesley, born c.1848 at Itawamba, Missouri

Mary Pratt
1777-

This daughter of Jonathan Pratt, Jr. (1745), was born about 1777 in Virginia, before her parents moved to South Carolina. She married John Hutchinson in Newberry County, South Carolina, and they are found in the 1800 census of the county, although John had purchased land in Fairfield County in January of 1798 on Terrible Creek, a branch of Broad River, adjoining the lands of Robert Mansell. Mary died prior to April 2, 1849, when her husband wrote his will, probated July 11, 1849. An equity case shows his date of death as May 29, 1849, and demonstrates that he was a man of means, possessing a number of slaves and material goods. He left a very large estate, including about 1,500 acres of land, valued at twenty-five thousand dollars, and numerous slaves. He had already given several slaves to each of his daughters, and the land and remaining slaves went to his grandchildren, sons of his only son, John Hutchinson, Jr., who had predeceased his father. He named his brother-in-law, John J. (Jonathan) Pratt, of Union County, Tennessee, with two other men, as executors and guardians of the minor children. They declined the appointment at his death, and the probate judge, James P. Stewart, proceeded to administer the estate, distributing all the legacies, except that left to the grandchildren. Finally, a suit was filed in equity, November 13, 1854, to sell the lands and settle the estate. The children were:

1. Mary, born c.1796; married Cornelius Nevill and had children:
   a. Joseph W., born 1831
   b. John M., born 1833
   c. C., a daughter, born 1835
   d. Laura, born 1836
2. Nancy R., married to Gordon
3. Frances, married to Haynie
4. Elizabeth, married to William Nevill
5. John, Jr., married to Mary; father of at least:
   a. John P.
   b. Robert O.
   c. Thomas C.
   d. William B.
   e. Jonathan P.
   f. James S.
   g. Mary E.

Frances Pratt
1784-

This daughter of Jonathan Pratt, Jr. (1745) and his wife, Elizabeth Hughes Pratt, was born March 1, 1784 in Virginia, and moved to South Carolina, with her parents. William Haynie Summers, of Turin, Coweta County, Georgia, is a descendant of this family, and reportedly holds a family Bible of the Cates family, which contains valuable information relative to this family. Frances was married in Newberry County, South Carolina, August 7, 1807 to Asa Cates, born December 31, 1781 in Orange County, North Carolina, son of Robert and Sarah Cates. In 1844, Asa and Frances moved to Turin in Coweta County, Georgia, where their daughter, Nancy, had moved some years before. There, on December 28, 1844, for four dollars, Asa purchased a tract of 100 acres from his son-in-law, Elijah Summers. The couple appears in the 1850 census for Coweta County, but not thereafter, and their death dates are not known. Children, all born in Newberry County, South Carolina:

1. Nancy, born January 20, 1809; married November 8, 1832 to Elijah Summers. Moved to Turin, Coweta County, Georgia, where she died July 13, 1886.
2. Jonathan, born November 11, 1810; died the same day.
3. John H., born October 18, 1811; died 1854 in Coweta County. Married 1841 to Acelina Walton.
4. Robert A., born August 11, 1813; married Adana Zimmerman in 1845.
5. Walter A., born September 15, 1815; died December 11, 1820
6. Sarah Frances, born September 12, 1817; married February 3, 1841 in Coweta County, Georgia, to Ezekiel Haynes.
7. Mary E., born July 29, 1820; married in Coweta County July 29, 1848 to James E. Walton.
8. Martha, born July 13, 1823, and married in Coweta County July 25, 1875 to Reason Mobley.

John Jonathan Pratt
1791-1860

This son of Jonathan Pratt, Jr. (1745) and Elizabeth Hughes, was born January 11, 1791 in Newberry County, South Carolina. When grown, he moved to neighboring Union County, where he settled in the town of Unionville, and married Dorcas Eliza Moore, born c.1797, a daughter of Alexander Moore and Dorcas Ervin Moore. John Jonathan Pratt was a Probate Judge for twenty-one years, as well as a prominent merchant and shoe manufacturer. In the 1850s, he moved to Alabama, settling in Cherokee County at McGhee's Bend, near Leesburg. He died in 1860; Dorcas died in 1871, and both are buried in the cemetery in the bend.

He and Dorcas were parents of several children, many of whom were reportedly quite intelligent and talented. A biographical sketch of one of their sons, Dr. Alexander Moore Pratt, appearing in the *North Alabaman*, states that he had three sisters who possessed rare literary attainments; one a playwright of considerable ability, and who had translated many foreign periodical magazines, novels and other literature into the English language; another who had written several novels and histories of the United States. The third sister was an extensive traveller, having crossed the Atlantic Ocean no less than a half dozen times, and visited all the provinces and principal cities of Europe, and personally met several of the potentates. The names of the sisters, unfortunately, were not provided.

The census of 1850 for Union County, South Carolina, shows John Pratt as head of household at age 59, planter and an Ordinary (Justice); his wife Dorcas at age 53; Adalina at age 20; Jonathan at age 19 and a student of law; Eliza at age 17; Adolpha at age 11; and Lucy Herndon at age 4. The family, perhaps all of them born at Unionville, included:

1. Alexander Moore, apparently the eldest of the children, and not living at home at the time of the 1850 census. At the age of eighteen, he began the study of medicine, graduating from Charleston College; the Jefferson of Philadelphia; and the Stuyvesant of New York. He practiced for two years in his home state, and then moved to Carnesville, Georgia, where he

251

married Martha Freeman, daughter of Dr. Henry Freeman. In 1857, he moved to Cherokee County, Alabama, and to Centre in 1860, where he was assigned to the position of Post Surgeon until the end of the War Between the States. He developed *Pratt's Peerless Purgative*, which was sold in the drug store of his son, Paul, for many years. He had at least two children:

    a.   Paul F., who died at about twenty-three years of age

    b.   Mary, known as Mamie, but took the name Marie later; married R. B. Smyer. Lived in Birmingham, Alabama

2.   Adalina, born c.1830; married to Ockendon of Montgomry, formerly of Greenville.

3.   John Jonathan, Jr., born April 14, 1831 in Unionville, Union County, South Carolina. Graduated with a BA in 1849 from Cokesbury College, and began a career in newspaper work, during which time he studied law and worked in various small towns in South Carolina and Alabama. Moved to Centre in Cherokee County, Alabama, where he was married in 1852 to Julia R. Porter, daughter of Benjamin F. Porter. In 1854, he and his wife went abroad and lived in England for a number of years. Frustrated at writing by hand, he invented a writing machine which he called the *Pterotype*, the first practical typewriter and the forerunner of the Remington. In 1864, he received a provisional patent from the British Patent Office, and on December 1, 1866, received British Patent No. 3,163 for his machine. He exhibited the device before the Society of Arts, the Society of Engineers in London, and the Royal Society of Great Britain. The significant difference in Pratt's machine was that the type characters were arranged on a single revolving wheel as opposed to a type bar. He returned to his home in Centre, Alabama, and that year received a United States patent for his typewriter. In 1882, he received another patent, and sold the device to the Hammond Company, at which time he moved to Brooklyn, New York, where the machines were made, and continued to make improvements until his death. His biography appears beginning at page 173, in *Dictionary of American Biography*, Volume VIII, edited by Dumas Malone. He became something of a legend in Centre,

where the Professional Business and Women's Club have made a memorial park at the location of his family cemetery a few miles outside town, and planned to establish a typewriter museum there in his honor. He had children:

a. Isabelle Julia
b. Stella

4. Eliza, born c.1833; apparently married to E. F. Herndon. There is some confusion here; the 1850 census of her father's household included a four-year old named Lucy Herndon, who must have been a granddaughter, born c.1846. Eliza was also in the household, at the age of 17, obviously not the mother of that child. There may have been an older daughter married to a Herndon, the mother of the child in the census report.

5. Adolpha, born c.1839; married to S. C. Fouche, and lived in Chattanooga, Tennessee. Believed to be the world traveller mentioned in the sketch of her brother, Dr. Alexander Pratt.

6. Lila, married a Speer, and lived in St. Augustine, Florida.

CHAPTER 19

Miscellaneous Pratt Family Members

During the course of research, a number of references to Pratt family members has been discovered, although the individuals named have not yet been identified within the large family group now under study. That information will be reported here to preserve the data for further research. Perhaps some reader can make the necessary connection.

Oliver Pratt
1853-

This individual and at least part of his family was found in the 1910 census of Supervisor's District #8, Cooper County, Missouri. It was found somewhat by accident, while checking census returns relative to my mother's half-brother, Henry Thompson Pratt (1861), who was known to have died in Missouri. It is also known that Henry Thompson and his brother, Oliver Pratt (1865), went west as young men from their home in Virginia.

Henry Thompson's first child was born in Nebraska in 1890; his second 1893 in Iowa; and he arrived in Warrensburg, Missouri in 1896, where his third child was born. The whereabouts of Oliver are not as clear, but he is known to have been in or near Encinal, Texas on March 6, 1910, when he was named a trustee of his local church. The unknown Oliver in Missouri was also some twelve years older than mother's half-brother. There can therefore be no question that the Oliver Pratt in the census of 1910 for Cooper County, Missouri, is a different individual. What attracted my attention was that, according to the census reports, this second Oliver was born in Virginia, as were both of his parents. His wife, Mary E., was born c.1857 in Iowa. Her father was born in Pennsylvania, and her mother in Missouri. They had one son listed in the census:
1. William B., born c.1893 in Missouri

John M. Pratt
1831-1905

According to a copy of a family Bible found in the Library of the Mormon Church at Salt Lake City, this John M. Pratt lived in Tennessee. It is reported that a short sketch of his life appears on page 910 of a *History of Tennessee, With Sketches of Gibson, Orion, Weakley, Dyer and Lake Counties,* published in Nashville in 1887, which I have not researched. A construction of his family from the Bible indicates that he was born November 30, 1831 and died May 3, 1905. Married in Gibson County, Tennessee, October 26, 1854, to Sarah V. Smith, born February 10, 1840 at the home of Mrs. M. A. Smith, who was probably her mother. The Bible lists a number of children, all apparently those of this couple, three of whom died within a matter of days of each other:

1. James Manley, born September 2, 1856, and died October 14, 1893
2. William Zachariah, born July 21, 1858; died January 29, 1868
3. Jasper LaFayet, born May 24, 1864; died January 26, 1868
4. Robert G., born June 2, 1866; died February 1, 1868
5. Cora E., born June 29, 1869; probably the same who married January 14, 1892 in Gibson County, Tennessee to T. L. Oliver
6. Joseph E., born February 12, 1870
7. Arthur, born October 12, 1874
8. Pearl V., born September 27, 1877; died July 4, 1908
9. Edward T., born August 21, 1879
10. Essie, born July 5, 1881

William Pratt
1734-1797

This individual is described in *The Pratt Family of North Carolina and Alabama, with Sketches of Allied Families, Including Beavers, Vernon and Hampton,* compiled by Margaret U. Lofquist in 1966, and found in the library of the Daughters of the American Revolution in Washington, D. C.

This William is found in records of Abbeville County, South Carolina, where he married Emma Hays, and perhaps was married second January 28, 1783 to Mary Drennen. Family tradition holds that three Pratt brothers "came over" or "came south" and that one of them was killed by Indians. This is a new version of one of the oldest stories I have found, in several family histories. It is often reported that three brothers arrived, usually from England or Ireland, and that one returned home, or went west or south, and was never heard from again. I have discussed this legend with a number of other researchers, and they, too, have come across the story in their family lines. We can only assume that someone reaches back as far as they can recover, and something leads them to develop this family "legend" of three brothers.

William was apparently in South Carolina as early as 1756. He served as a private in the Revolution, and operated a grist mill on Little River. He died in 1797; his estate was administered March 28, 1797; and an inventory was made May 3, 1797. Children were:

1. Sarah, born South Carolina in 1756; died 1858 at the age of 102. Married Cador Gantt, born April 15, 1771, and died December 2, 1845. No children; both buried at Little River Baptist Church Cemetery in Abbeville County.
2. Mary; married Josiah Burton; born c.1763. Both of them died in Abbeville County, South Carolina. Her will was written August 6, 1829 and proven November 27, 1829. His estate was administered September 5, 1829. Children were:
    a. Robert, born 1783; married Sarah Hall
    b. Sarah, born 1786; married Winston Hall
    c. William, born 1790; married Elizabeth
    d. Caleb, born 1792; died 1860. Married Dicey Smith
    e. John, born 1796; married Elizabeth Pruitt
    f. Elizabeth, born 1797; married Samuel Black, and lived in Walker County, Alabama
    g. Peter S., born 1801; married Harriet Martha McGee
    h. Mary, born 1810; died 1866. Married Joshua Ashley
    i. Josiah, married Sally Osborn; may have died in Mexican War
3. Joseph, born January 1, 1768; died April 7, 1826. Married April 15, 1793 to Elizabeth Jones, and had children:
    a. Emmy, or Amy, born 1794; died 1869. Married 1812 to Samuel Young.

b. Sarah, born 1796; died 1866. Married 1815 to William Young.

c. William, born 1798; died 1863. Married 1823 to Martha Murdock. At least one son:

  (1) Charles Felix, born 1824, of whom more

d. Thomas, born 1800; died 1826

e. Joseph, born 1803; died 1826

f. Elizabeth, born 1806; married 1826 John McConnell.

g. Mary, born 1809; died 1816

h. John, born 1812; died 1849; and married 1867 to Nancy Harkness

i. Nancy, born 1820; died 1826

j. Caroline, an adopted niece, born 1809, and died 1867; married Thomas Crawford.

4. William, Jr.; married and said to have had nine children. Moved to Kentucky.

5. Susannah, married Tyre Gantt, brother of Cador Gantt. Lived in Franklin County, Indiana during 1815. It has also been reported that Susannah was perhaps a daughter of her brother, William Pratt, Jr., though doubtful.

6. James, born March 31, 1788; died September 14, 1828, and married to Sarah, born November 26, 1790; died April 25, 1840. They had children:

a. John, born 1808; died 1888. Married Mary Key.

b. William, born 1811, and died 1842. Married to Louisa Robertson

c. Robert, born 1817; married Louisa

d. Daughter; married Timothy Thomas

e. Daughter; married William L. Cunningham

f. Daughter; married James B. Key

g. Elizabeth; married Lewis C. Clinkscales

h. Sarah A.; married John T. Miller

7. David, probably the youngest child; apparently married a daughter of Austin Smith, and had at least one child:

a. Almina

Charles Felix Pratt
1824-1901

This son of William Pratt (1798) and Martha Murdock, was born October 19, 1824 in Abbeyville County, South Carolina. He was married there July 2, 1845 to Gabrilla Ann Callahan, born there July 3, 1823, daughter of John and Nancy Pinson Callahan. It appears that Charles Felix moved shortly after marriage to Rome, in Chattanooga County, Georgia, where his first seven children were born. He must have then moved to Dirtown, in the same county, where his last two children were born. Some time after 1864, he moved to Iowa, where he died October 23, 1901 at Crescent, Pott County. His wife died there January 23, 1902. The children were:

1. John W., apparently a twin to Nancy Elizabeth, born June 2, 1846; died July 25, 1924. Married to Mary Etta Motz.
2. Nancy Elizabeth, born June 2, 1846; died February 12, 1917, and married to Edmond Levi McKinney.
3. James Arthur, born September 14, 1848; died February 9, 1934. Married to Mary Agnes Twomey.
4. Sylvester Valentine, born April 10, 1852; died September 23, 1907. Married December 10, 1878 Margaret Tomenia Currie.
5. Martha Ann, born August 12, 1854; died July 6, 1871
6. Emma Matilda Eleanor, born August 24, 1856, and died September 2, 1943. Married Charles Daniel Watts.
7. Phoebe Jane, born August 11, 1859; died December 23, 1841. Married January 13, 1889 to John Newton Boyd.
8. Charles Felix, Jr., born November 10, 1861; died July 28, 1928 at Sioux Falls, South Dakota. Married to Maria Darling Butterworth, born June 26, 1869 in Dow City, Iowa; and died December 14, 1927 at Sioux Falls. We can assume that the wedding took place in Pott County, Iowa, where the family had moved from Chattanooga County, Georgia, some time after 1864. Ten children, the first four born at Council Bluffs, Iowa; the next four in Missouri Valley, Iowa; and the last two in South Dakota:
    a. Rolla, born February 18, 1893; died July 25, 1964
    b. Forrest, born January 18, 1895

c.   Floyd, born February 3, 1897; died September, 1897
d.   Bessie Geneva, born September 7, 1898
e.   Hugh, born October 20, 1900
f.   Joy Delight, born March 16, 1903; died August, 1928
g.   Fred, born November 29, 1904
h.   Beulah, born April 24, 1907
i.   Ward, born September 21, 1909 at Seneca, South Dakota
j.   Robert Winifred, born June 26, 1912 at Winifred, South Dakota

9. Leona Mary Frances, born February 28, 1864; died October 14, 1930. Apparently married twice: first December 25, 1884 to Milton, and second to Clement Hough.

Wilburn Pratt
c.1880-

This information was sent to me in October, 1979, by Les Donaldson of Phoenix, Arizona. We have yet to make a connection to the other Pratt families under consideration. Wilburn was a son of Steve Pratt, living in eastern Kentucky around Hindman, Leburn and Prestonburg. Les surmises from other ages that Wilburn was born c.1880 and that his father, Steve, was born c.1850. Wilburn was married to Lucy, and they had several children, including:

1. Albert
2. Alvin
3. Clark Elhannon, born c.1897
4. Ida
5. Rainey
6. Sarah
7. Dovie, born c.1909; married to Chester Campbell Donaldson, and the mother of our correspondent, Les Donaldson.

Isaac Pratt
1802-

The information following was assembled through letters with Eddy Pratt during 1983. He was then living in Clinton, Tennessee. This Isaac Pratt was born c.1802, either in Virginia, or Rockingham County, North Carolina. He appears in the census of 1830 for Hawkins County, Tennessee. By 1840, he is found in the neighboring county of Grainger, where he lived until his death sometime in the 1870s.

The 1830 census of Hawkins County carries one Thomas Pratt, a Revolutionary War soldier, born c.1769 and married to Sarah Garrison, daughter of Isaac Garrison, IV. It has been suggested that Thomas may be the father of Isaac, but a number of researchers believe that not to be the case. The 1820 pension application of Thomas does not mention a son of Isaac's age; also Thomas' wife lists her sole heir in 1852 as being Polly Pratt, in Hawkins County, Tennessee.

Isaac was married to Sarah Jones, born in Virginia c.1801. She was perhaps the daughter of Joshua Jones, who appears in the neighboring household in the 1839 Hawkins County census. There were eleven children:

1. James Alexander, born 1824; married first Elizabeth Evans; second Mary A. Thompson, daughter of Spencer Thompson, (1794) and Susannah Montgomery Thompson (1801)
2. Mary, born 1826; married Balis Evans.
3. George Washington, born 1827; married first Mary Smith, and second Priscilla Clowers.
4. William, born 1830; married first Emaline Davis and second Mary. Moved with his family to Texas in the 1880s
5. Elisha, born 1832; married Ann Eliza Pemberton
6. Isaac, Jr., born 1835; married August 6, 1858 in Jefferson County, Tennessee, to Rachel Pierce
7. Jack Lafayette, born 1838; married Lucy Ann Hodges. This is the great, great grandfather of Eddy Pratt, my correspondent.
8. Joseph Henry Harris, born 1839; married Martha Potter
9. Joshua, born 1843; married Sarah Bridgewaters. Reported killed in the Civil War, perhaps enlisted in Confederate army at Bristol, Virginia. One son:
   a. Thomas J.
10. Edna, born 1843
11. Frances Adeline, born 1846; married first Nicholas Owens; second James Brannon; third, Allen Jasper Kelley.

Charles Pratt
1888-1944

Charles was born May 31, 1888 at Leas Spring, in Grainger County, Tennessee. Reported on Mormon church records, his father was James P. Pratt and his mother was Mollie Holder Pratt. He was married November 3, 1907 at Knoxville, Tennessee to Ella Cooper, daughter of George Cooper. Six children, born Knoxville:

1. Raymond Leroy, born April 10, 1910; died September 14, 1925
2. Juanita, born February 7, 1915; married December, 1933 to Sam G. Hill
3. William Cody, born January, 1917, an infant death
4. Nellie, born October 22, 1918; married August 22, 1948 to William Clyde Baker
5. Eugene, born August 13, 1920; married June, 1944 to Isabella Jean Eads
6. Charles Henry, born June 1, 1922; married December, 1946 to Sue Dunlap

Zephaniah Pratt
m/1790

This individual is found in several entries of the records of the Mormon Church, in the general lists for the state of Kentucky. He is reported there as having married Keziah Lancaster on December 30, 1790 in Bourbon County, Kentucky. It would appear that he moved about 1793 to Logan County, and once again about 1796 to Christian County, both in Kentucky, where he died about December 18, 1808. leaving a will. Several children are reported, probably not in the order of birth:

1. Nancy, born c.1791 in Bourbon County, Kentucky
2. Elizabeth, born c.1792
3. Susan, or perhaps Susanna, as mentioned in her father's will; born c.1794 in Logan County, Kentucky
4. William, born c.1795 in Logan County
5. Phebe, born c.1797 in Christian County, Kentucky. Probably married there February 7, 1817 to William Clark.

6. Henrietta
7. Mary
8. Patsey
9. Sarah
10. John
11. Zephaniah, Jr.

Military Service Records

Some of the following references appear within the text, but not nearly all of them. Each individual has the surname Pratt:

Daniel M. Private, Co. B, 31st Regt, NC, CSA. Enlisted in Anson County at age 22, October 3, 1861. Wounded in the right hip at Fort Harrison, Va on or about September 30, 1864. Accounted for through December, 1864.

David: Private, 1st Co. A, 36th Regt, NC (2nd Regt NC Artillery), CSA. Enlisted in Hanover County March 8, 1862. Transferred to 2nd Co. I, 10th Regt (1st Regt NC Artillery) in November, 1863. Accounted for through October, 1864.

Francis Marion: Private, Co. K, 52nd Regt, NC, CSA. Enlisted in Forsyth County at age 28, May 10, 1862. Captured at Falling Waters, Md, July 14, 1863; sent to Baltimore. Confined at Point Lookout, Md August 17, 1863. Paroled there March 3, 1864 and received for exchange at City Point, Va March 6, 1864. Reported on duty with the Division wagon-train July to December, 1864.

G. I.: Private, Co. L, 17th Regt, NC (1st Organization), CSA. Place and date of enlistment not known. Captured at Roanoke Island February 8, 1862 and paroled at Elizabeth City February 21, 1862.

Garland, Jr.: Private, Co. D, 45th Regt, NC, CSA. Enlisted from Rockingham County at age 24, March 11,

1862. Died in hospital at Richmond about February 5, 1863 of pneumonia.

George Morgan: Corporal, 2nd Co. G, 40th Regt NC (3rd Regt NC Artillery), CSA. Resided as a farmer in Orange County, where he enlisted at age 21, March 11, 1862. Transferred to Co. E, 13th Battalion, NC Light Artillery, November 4, 1863. Promoted to Sergeant, May 20, 1864. Paroled at Greensboro April 27, 1865

George T.: Private, Co. C, 4th Regt, Va Infantry, CSA. Son of Madison Pratt (1816), born 1843 in Pulaski County, Va; enlisted March 14, 1862 at Newburn, Va. Wounded in left leg December 13, 1862 at battle of Fredericksburg, Va. Severely wounded at Gettysburg July 3, 1863 while serving in the Stonewall Brigade under Brig Gen James A. Walker. Full report appears in the text.

George W.: Private, Co. D, 45th Regt, NC, CSA. Enlisted from Rickingham County at age 22, March 11, 1862. There were five Pratt boys in this company. George W. was wounded in the arm at Spottsylvania Courthouse, Va about May 19, 1864. Absent, wounded, through February, 1865

H. B.: Chaplain, Field and Staff, 63rd Regt, NC (5th Regt, NC Cavalry), CSA. Presbyterian minister in Orange County; appointed Chaplain to rank from February 1, 1863. Resigned November 14, 1863 by reason of the "*desultory and unsettled life.*"

Howell T.: Private, Co. D, 45th Regt, NC, CSA. A farmer in Rockingham County; enlisted in Wayne County May 8, 1862. Wounded in the hand at or near Spotsylvania Courthouse, Va, May, 1864. In hospital at Richmond August 13, 1864 with a contusion of the left hip; returned to duty August 17, 1864; present until February 26, 1865 when he was reported absent without leave. Paroled at Greensboro, NC, May 24, 1865.

J. H.:	Private, Co. H, 38th Regt, NC, CSA. Enlisted at Camp Holmes, near Raleigh, April 5, 1864.
James A.:	3rd Sergeant, Co. F, 54th Regt, Va Infantry, Reynold's Brigade, Stephenson's Division, Hood's Corp, Army of Tennessee, CSA. Son of Madison Pratt (1816). Record of service complete in text.
James R.:	Corporal, Co. A, 45th Regt, NC, CSA. Born in Rockingham County, NC where he enlisted at age 28, March 11, 1862. Mustered in as private; promoted to corporal September, 1862. Died in camp of disease near Drewry's Bluff, Va. December 12, 1862.
John:	Private, Co. D, 6th Regt, NC, CSA. Enlisted in Mecklenburg County, at age 26, May 28, 1861. Wounded in the leg at Malvern Hill, Va July 1, 1862. Captured at Gettysburg July 3, 1863 and confined at Fort Delaware. Paroled and transferred for exchange March 19, 1865 to Aikens Landing, James River, Va. Paroled at Morgantown May 16, 1865.
John A.:	Private, Co. D, 45th Regt, NC, CSA. Enlisted from Rockingham County, NC at age 27, March 11, 1862. Died of disease April 12, 1862; place not reported.
John L.:	1st Lieutenant, Co. K, 21st Regt, NC, CSA. A farmer in Forsyth County, NC; enlisted at age 26 on June 11, 1861. Mustered in as sergeant and elected to 1st Lieutenant to rank from April 27, 1862. Captured at Stephenson's Depot, Va, July 20, 1864. Confined at Camp Chase, Ohio until paroled and transferred to Boulware's and Cox's Wharfs, James River, Va and received for exchange March 11, 1865. He was perhaps promoted to Captain at some date.
John Marion:	Captain, Co. L, 50th Regt, Va Infantry, CSA. Son of Nicholas H. Pratt (1811). Record set forth in the text.

John P.: Private, Co. A, 45th Regt, NC, CSA. Born in Rockingham County, NC where he enlisted at age 32, March 26, 1862. Wounded slightly at Gettysburg July 3, 1863; captured there about July 5, 1863; confined at Fort Delaware until transferred to Point Lookout about October 15, 1863. Released there January 25, 1864 after taking Oath of Allegiance, and joining United States service.

Josephus: Sergeant, Co. I, 13th Regt, NC, CSA. Enlisted from Rockingham County at age 18, May 3, 1861. Mustered in as private; promoted to sergeant February 25, 1863. Wounded in left thigh and captured at Gettysburg July 1/5, 1863. Hospitalized at Chester, Pa and transferred to City Point, Va for exchange September 23, 1863. Captured April 2, 1865 on South Side Railroad near Petersburg, Va; confined at Hart's Island in New York Harbor; released June 18, 1865 after taking Oath of Allegiance.

Little J.: Private, Co. F, 37th Regt, NC, CSA. Enlisted in Wilkes County at age 21, September 24, 1861. Died September 20/30, 1862; cause and place unknown.

Pleasant W.: Private Co. E, 22nd Regt, NC, CSA. Enlisted in Guilford County at age 21, May 23, 1861. Mustered in as corporal but reduced in rank. Discharged about January 24, 1862 by reason of disability. Reenlisted same company February 22, 1862; wounded at Frayser's Farm, Va, June 30, 1862. Reported absent without leave in September, 1862. Returned to duty; wounded in the head at Chancellorsville,Va, May 1/4, 1863. On detail as teamster June, 1863 through October, 1864. Captured at Petersburg, Va, April 3, 1865; confined at Hart's Island, New York Harbor until released June 17, 1865 after taking the Oath of Allegiance.

R. H.:　　　　　　Private, Co. G, 18th Regt, NC, CSA. Enlisted
　　　　　　　　September 5, 1864 at Camp Holmes, NC. Killed
　　　　　　　　at Jones' Farm, Va September 30, 1864.

Richard:　　　　Private, Co. F, 45th Regt, NC, CSA. Born in
　　　　　　　　Henry County, Va; enlisted Rockingham County,
　　　　　　　　NC at age 21, March 11, 1862. Died in hospital
　　　　　　　　at Richmond on or about December 2, 1862 of
　　　　　　　　"*phthisis*," which Webster defines as pulmonary
　　　　　　　　tuberculosis.

S. M.:　　　　　Private, Co. B, 31st Regt, NC, CSA. Enlisted in
　　　　　　　　Anson County, March 13, 1864. Captured at
　　　　　　　　Cold Harbor, Va, June 1, 1864; confined at Point
　　　　　　　　Lookout, Md. Transferred to Elmira, New York,
　　　　　　　　July 12, 1864; paroled there October 11, 1864
　　　　　　　　and transferred to Venus Point, Savannah River,
　　　　　　　　Ga, where he was received November 15, 1864
　　　　　　　　for exchange.

Thomas:　　　　Sergeant, Co. K, 45th Regt, NC, CSA. Enlisted
　　　　　　　　in Forsyth County at age 21, March 22, 1862.
　　　　　　　　Mustered in as private; promoted to sergeant be-
　　　　　　　　tween July, 1862 and February, 1863. Killed at
　　　　　　　　Gettysburg about July 3, 1863

Thomas H.:　　Private, Co. K, 45th Regt, NC, CSA. Resided in
　　　　　　　　Rockingham County; enlisted from Wake County
　　　　　　　　at age 30, September 1, 1862. Wounded in the
　　　　　　　　chin and captured at Gettysburg, July 1, 1863.
　　　　　　　　Hospitalized there and transferred to hospital at
　　　　　　　　David's Island, New York Harbor, July 23, 1863.
　　　　　　　　Died in hospital of wounds, July 26, 1863.

William:　　　　Private, Co. C, 8th Regt, NC, CSA. Born at
　　　　　　　　Charleston, South Carolina; occupation Seaman.
　　　　　　　　Enlisted in New Hanover County at age 38, Au-
　　　　　　　　gust 4, 1861. Captured at Roanoke Island on
　　　　　　　　February 8, 1862; paroled at Elizabeth City Feb-
　　　　　　　　ruary 21, 1862. Exchanged August, 1862. Trans-
　　　　　　　　ferred to Confederate States Navy May 24, 1864.

William H.:　　Private, Co. A, 1st Regt, NC, CSA. Enlisted in
　　　　　　　　Chowan County, NC at age 19, May 18, 1861.

Wounded and captured at Sharpsburg, Md, September 17, 1862; confined at Fort McHenry, Md until paroled and sent to Fort Monroe, Va. for exchange, October 18, 1862. Admitted to hospital in Richmond, October 23, 1862, with a wound on the left shoulder and transferred to Goldsboro, April 3, 1863. Admitted to hospital at Danville, Va, October 12, 1864; carried on the muster rolls through December, 1864. Paroled at Greensboro, May 10, 1865.

William H.: Private, Co. D, 45th Regt, NC, CSA. Enlisted in Rockingham County at age 22, March 11, 1862. Captured at Winchester, Va, September 19, 1864 and confined at Point Lookout, Md. Released about October 17, 1864 after taking the Oath of Allegiance and joining United States Army, and assigned to Co. C, 4th Regt, US Volunteer Inf.

William J.: Private, Co. I, 13th Regt, NC, CSA. Enlisted in Rockingham County at age 40, May 3, 1861. Discharged August 1, 1862 by reason of being over-age.

William R.: Corporal, Co. K, 52nd Regt, NC, CSA. Enlisted in Forsyth County at age 21, March 22, 1862. Mustered in as private; promoted to corporal between July, 1862 and February, 1863. Captured at Gettysburg, July 3, 1863. Confined at Fort Delaware until transferred to Point Lookout, Md, October 20, 1863. Died there of unreported causes, March 6, 1864.

BIBLIOGRAPHY

American Historical Society. *History of Virginia, 1924*

Banks, *Descendants of John Pratt*, 1900

Block, Maxine, Editor. *Current Biography, Who's News and Why*, New York: H. W. Wilson Company, 1940

Bockstruck, Lloyd DeWitt. *Virginia's Colonial Soldiers*

Boddie, John Bennett. *Southside Virginia Families.*

Burke. *Burke's Peerage and Baronetage.*

_____. *The General Armory*

Chalkey, Lyman. *Records of Augusta County, Virginia, 1745-1800*

Coldham, Peter Wilson. *The Bristol Register of Servants Sent to Foreign Plantations 1654-1686*, 1988

_____. *Complete Book of Emigrants, 1607-1660*

Colket, Meredith B, Jr. *Founders of Early American Families*

Creekmore. *Early East Tennessee Taxpayers*

Crozier. *The General Armory*

Filby. *Passenger and Immigration Lists Index.*

Fry, Joshua & Jefferson, Peter. *Map of Virginia, North Carolina, Pennsylvania, Maryland, New Jersey 1751.* Montgomery County, Md Library, Atlas Archives.

Gose, George B. *Pioneers of the Virginia Bluegrass*

Hamlin, Charles Hughes. *Virginia Ancestors and Adventurers.* 1975

Hardy, Stella Pickett. *Colonial Families of the Southern State of America.* 1981

Hayden, Horace Edwin. *Virginia Genealogies, a Genealogy of the Glassell Family.* 1973.

Hurley, William N., Jr. *Hurley and Related Families.* Gaithersburg, Md.: Sir Speedy, 1992

_____, *The Ancestry of William Neal Hurley, III*, Chelsea, Michigan: BookCrafters, 1985

_____. *Pratt, Lowder And Related Families.* Gaithersburg, Md.: Sir Speedy, 1992

Lofquist, Margaret U. *Pratt Families of North Carolina and Alabama*, with sketches of allied families. 1966. DAR library, Washington, D. C.

Lovelace, Jane Pratt. *The Pratt Directory, 1995 Revised Edition.* Chandler, Arizona. Ancestor House, 1995

MacLysaght, Edward. *Irish Families, Their Names, Arms and Origins*

Meade, Bishop William. *Old Churches, Ministers and Families of Virginia.*

Morgan, Claritta H. *Births and Deaths, 1853-1871, Pulaski County, Virginia.* Pulaski public library.

_____. *Marriage Licenses Issued 1850-1900, Pulaski County, Virginia.* Pulaski public library.

Mormon Church, Genealogical Library. Archival family group sheets and other records.

_____. *International Genealogical Index.* North Carolina, Tennessee, Maryland, Pennsylvania, Ohio, Kentucky, Alabama, Virginia and other states.

Pratt, Earl. *Genealogy of Averill Pratt and Maggie Pratt, Including the Pratt, Holliday and Forgey Families.* Manuscript: 1950.

Pratt, Kenneth Charles. *Abraham, The Father of us All, A Pratt Family History.* Oxford, Connecticut: Privately printed. 1968.

Preston. *History of Southwest Virginia*

Rubin, Louis D., Jr. *Virginia, A History.* New York, W. W. Norton & Company, 1977

Schreiner-Yantis, Nettie. *Archives of the Pioneers of Tazewell County, Virginia.*

_____. *Wythe County, Virginia, 1800 Tax Lists and Abstracts of Deeds, 1796-1800*

Smith, Annie L. *Virginia Quit Rents, 1704*

Symmes. *Virginia Military Land Grants*

Tepper, Michael. *Emigrants to the Middle Colonies*
_____. *Passengers to America*

Thomas, Grace Pratt. *Pratt Profiles, The Saga of a Pratt Family, Descendants of Jonathan Pratt of Newberry County, South Carolina.* Manuscript; 1984.

Torrence, Clayton. *Virginia Wills and Administrations, 1632-1800*. Baltimore, Maryland: Genealogical Publishing Co., 1978

Trimble, David B. *Southwest Virginia Families*

Tyler's Quarterly, Historical and Genealogical Magazine. *Genealogies of Virginia Families.*

Unknown Author. *High on a Windy Hill*. Cemetery records of southwest Virginia. Mormon Temple Library, Salt Lake.

_____. *Annals of Tazewell County, Virginia.* Tazewell County Library, Tazewell, Virginia

_____. *Grayson County, Virginia, A History*

_____. *Appalachian Ancestors*, May 30, 1986

_____. *Simon Newcomb Pratt*, 1917.

_____. *Matthew Pratt and his Descendants*, 1890

_____. *Phineas Pratt and Descendants*, 1897

_____. *Thomas Pratt, One Line of Descendants*, 1963

_____. *Descendants of Lieutenant William Pratt*, 1864

Virginia State Library and Archives, Richmond. Wills, estates, inventories, births, deaths, marriages, deeds and other reference works relative to counties of Virginia.

Wayland, John W. *Virginia Valley Records*

Williams, Joseph Edward & Eleanor Talbert. *Too Early To Be A Talbert*. Manuscript, 1986

Wilson, Goodridge. *Smyth County History and Traditions*, Radford, Virginia: Commonwealth Press, Inc., Reprint 1976

INDEX

All names appearing in the text are indexed, with each of the pages on which the individual appears. To distinguish between those persons with the same name, dates will generally follow the index entry. A plain date indicates the date of birth or nearly so; entries reading d/1789 indicate the date of death; m/1879 indicates the date of marriage. Some of the more common names, such as John, Sarah and others, will appear with no dates and numerous page references. Almost without exception, they will refer to more than one individual.

Asbridge, Hedgeman, 22
Asbury, George W. 1836, 159
Asbury, Minnie M. 1880, 159
Asbury, Rebecca E. 1837, 159
Ashley, Danny Ray, 108
Ashley, Joshua, 256
Ashley, Ray Gentry, 108
Ashworth, John A., 231
Atchison, Ivey Jean, 94
Atkins, David Brian 1977, 158
Atkins, James Thomas 1979, 158
Atkins, Robert, Jr., 158
Atwell, Evangeline Kay, 101
Atwell, Nancy, 167, 193
Atwood, Edward, 90
Ausel, See Hansel
Autery, No given name, 74
Avino, Autumn 1984, 62
Avino, Gina Marie, 62
Ayers, Laura, 67
Bach, Bonnie Kathleen, 18
Bach, Courtney, 72
Bach, Harlan, 72
Bach, Ike, 71
Bach, Logan, 72
Bailey, Alexander, 22
Bailey, Dixie, 67
Bailey, No given name, 69
Bailey, Rita, 161
Baker, Donna Rae, 177
Baker, Eric Samuel 1986, 139
Baker, Harold W., 88
Baker, Harold W., Jr., 88
Baker, Harriet, 88
Baker, Jeffery, 88
Baker, Jesse Nash 1985, 139
Baker, Robert, 139
Baker, William Clyde, 261
Baldwin, Herman, 112
Baldwin, Lillie Elizabeth, 45
Baldwin, Nancy Lee 1942, 112
Bales, Lillian, 46
Balls, Ralph Verl, 178
Bamford, Dorothy Jane, 95
Banks, Anna, 72
Banks, Asbury, 71, 72

Banks, Calvin, 72
Banks, Cleary Mullins, 72
Banks, Clifford, 71
Banks, Cora, 72
Banks, Floyd, 72
Banks, Gladys, 71
Banks, Henry, 71
Banks, John, 72
Banks, Leck, 71
Banks, Lenis, 71
Banks, Leona, 71
Banks, Linda, 71
Banks, Lumy, 71
Banks, Montgomery, 71
Banks, Ollie Profitt, 72
Banks, Orbin, 71
Banks, Orville, 71
Banks, Pecola Trent, 72
Banks, Roy, 72
Banks, Verlin, 71
Banks, Walker, 71
Bannister, John James 1919, 54
Bannister, John James, Jr. 1945, 54
Bannister, Margaret Ellen 1947, 54
Bannister, Sadie B., 54
Bannister, William C., 54
Barner, Shirley, 60
Barney, Velma, 191
Barrett, Hiram N., 237
Bartels, Larry Bruce 1939, 60
Bartels, Laura Ann 1965, 60
Bartels, Melissa Jo 1967, 60
Bartels, Michelle Marie 1969, 60
Bartels, Roy, 60
Bates, P. R., 82
Batty, Juanita, 46
Baumgardner, Clay, 40
Baxter, James Edward 1947, 227
Baxter, Janie Elizabeth 1984, 227
Baxter, Jesse James, Jr., 227
Baxter, Laura Joan 1977, 227
Beck, Stephen, Dr., 42
Becker, Carol Pratt 1958, 54
Becker, Walter F., 54
Becker, Walter Francis 1956, 54
Beckman, Mary, 234

Brandt, Walter 1882, 15
Brandt, William 1886, 15
Brannon, James, 260
Brattin, Jenny, 93
Breeding, No given name, 137
Breedlove, Rebecca, 158
Brewer, Beverly June 1928, 57
Brewer, Charles Dean 1935, 57
Brewer, Charles Jefferson 1900, 57
Brewer, Emma K. 1886, 17
Brewer, Howard Robert 1924, 57
Brewer, James Milton, 57
Brewer, Jason Dean 1968, 57
Brewer, Jerry, 71
Brewer, Tricia Elaine 1971, 57
Bridgeman, Martha Ellen 1863, 39
Bridgewaters, Sarah, 260
Brinser, Brian K. 1958, 92
Brinser, Emily Jeanette 1988, 92
Brinser, Sarah Elizabeth 1985, 92
Brinser, Will Foster 1981, 92
Brockman, Julia, 236
Brooks, Alexander Jackson 1813,
    167, 170, 171, 174
Brooks, Mary Ann Barbara 1862,
    167, 170
Brooks, Nancy Eliza Snow 1857,
    167, 171
Brooks, Nancy Jane 1857, 167, 171
Brooks, Susan Sarah 1859, 167, 174
Brooks, Thomas, 167
Brown, Afton, 191
Brown, Arduth, 191
Brown, Birdie M., 196
Brown, Bonnie Mae, 191
Brown, Clora Louise Daniels, 192
Brown, Delores Virginia 1925, 18
Brown, Edith, 83
Brown, Edna 1917, 191
Brown, Elizabeth McCormick, 83
Brown, Fannie Eliza 1906, 24
Brown, Frank W., 83
Brown, Gale Taylor 1921, 191
Brown, Glen 1921, 191
Brown, Joseph Norman 1889, 191
Brown, Lori 1956, 62

Brown, Mamie, 127, 136
Brown, Michele Marie, 112
Brown, Robert W., 83
Brown, Robert W., Jr., 83
Brown, Sarah C. 1898, 150
Browning, Henry m/1880, 242
Buchanan, Albert E. 1872, Dr., 45
Buchanan, Blanche Beatrice 1905,
    151
Buchanan, Cora, 157
Buchanan, Edna, 45
Buchanan, Emma Carrie 1842, 44
Buchanan, Felix Grundy, 104
Buchanan, Florence D., 116
Buchanan, Herman, 101
Buchanan, Hickman Spiller, 45
Buchanan, John, 100
Buchanan, Jonathan, 159
Buchanan, Larry Malcolm, 159
Buchanan, Laura Marie, 45
Buchanan, Lee Etta, 121
Buchanan, Lolen, 44
Buchanan, Louise, 105
Buchanan, Louise 1898, 120
Buchanan, Margaret Louise 1887,
    104
Buchanan, Nancy B., 44
Buchanan, Nina Kate 1907, 150
Buchanan, Pearl 1890, 123
Buchanan, Ruby Pauline, 153
Buchanan, Samuel Lee, 159
Buchanan, T. G., 116
Buchanan, Thomas Theopolus, 123
Buchanan, W. H., 123
Buchanan, W. P., 150
Buchanan, Warren, 45
Buchanan, William Worth 1880, 151
Buck, Henry Edison 1924, 41, 42
Buck, Minnie Vernon, 95
Buckler, Andrew Thomas, Jr., 206
Buckler, Benjamin Daniel 1989, 206
Buckler, David Andrew 1987, 206
Budvorson, Glen Lee, 185
Budvorson, Gunnar 1902, 185
Budvorson, Richard Ned, 185
Budvorson, Vivian Beatrice, 185

Calfee, Susan C. 1849, 85
Calhoun, Verna Mae, 107
Call, Lucy Elvira, 191
Call, Mildred, 108
Call, Ronald Dean, 152
Callahan, Arthur H. 1892, 18
Callahan, Bessie H. 1896, 18
Callahan, Cora E. 1888, 18
Callahan, Effie 1895, 18
Callahan, Gabrilla Ann 1823, 258
Callahan, Jesse C. 1904, 18
Callahan, John, 258
Callahan, Maud Lee 1891, 18
Callahan, Sarah 1899, 18
Callahan, Thomas Livey 1856, 18
Callahan, William Harrison 1889, 18
Campbell, Alaine Juiton 1959, 109
Campbell, Andrew, 100
Campbell, Andrew Jackson 1885, 12
Campbell, Anne Elizabeth 1959, 110
Campbell, Arthur, Col. 1743, 98,
    100
Campbell, Billie Jean, 108
Campbell, Brenda, 103
Campbell, Catherine Travis 1956,
    110
Campbell, Charles Edward 1960,
    110
Campbell, Charles Meade 1928, 109
Campbell, Charles, Captain, 100
Campbell, Courtney Anne 1983, 106
Campbell, Crystal Leann 1981, 109
Campbell, David G. 1883, 12
Campbell, David P. 1837, 17
Campbell, David Price 1947, 106
Campbell, David Price, Jr. 1976, 106
Campbell, Dorothy 1921, 112
Campbell, Dougal, 99, 100
Campbell, Duncan, 100
Campbell, Duncan 1645, 100
Campbell, Edgar 1914, 112
Campbell, Elizabeth Christine 1979,
    106
Campbell, Elizabeth D. 1837, 99
Campbell, Ellen Louise 1947, 105
Campbell, Ellen Marie 1989, 108

Campbell, Eloise 1910, 111
Campbell, Emily B. 1839, 99
Campbell, Emma Florence 1907,
    111
Campbell, Eva 1905, 102
Campbell, Florence Kathryn 1911,
    104
Campbell, Frederick 1900, 18
Campbell, Gabe Sanders 1976, 105
Campbell, Gary Raymond 1989, 111
Campbell, George 1922, 103
Campbell, George Allen 1915, 105,
    110
Campbell, George Ringo 1846, 46,
    101, 102, 104, 111
Campbell, George Sanders 1949,
    105
Campbell, Gertrude Mae 1882, 101
Campbell, Gilbert Leon 1957, 109
Campbell, Grundy Sanders 1921,
    107
Campbell, Harrison 1904, 18
Campbell, Harry Eugene 1880, 101,
    111
Campbell, Harry Eugene, Jr. 1921,
    113
Campbell, Hattie 1895, 17
Campbell, Henry P. 1858, 101
Campbell, Howard 1902, 18
Campbell, Hugh, 100
Campbell, Inez 1925, 103
Campbell, Isaac 1838, 12
Campbell, Jack Pratt 1987, 111
Campbell, Jackson Pratt 1931, 105,
    110
Campbell, James Allan 1936, 112
Campbell, James Allen 1945, 105
Campbell, James Arthur 1877, 99,
    101, 104
Campbell, James Arthur, 2nd 1954,
    109
Campbell, James Arthur, III 1989,
    110
Campbell, James Clyde 1912, 104
Campbell, James Clyde, Jr. 1944,
    104

Campbell, James Howard 1955, 107
Campbell, James M. 1851, 101
Campbell, James S. 1891, 12
Campbell, Jane 1931, 103
Campbell, Jean Elizabeth 1916, 106
Campbell, Jerome B. 1854, 101
Campbell, John 1674, 100
Campbell, John 1849, 101
Campbell, John Buchanan 1918, 106
Campbell, John Buchanan, Jr. 1943, 106
Campbell, John E. 1888, 12
Campbell, John, Capt. 1738, 100
Campbell, John, Capt. 1741, 100
Campbell, John, II, Capt 1738, 99
Campbell, John, III, Capt. 1768, 99
Campbell, Jonathan Everett 1991, 110
Campbell, Jonathan Roy 1989, 107
Campbell, Joseph Meade 1986, 110
Campbell, Josey Robert 1986, 110
Campbell, Julian Arthur 1926, 108
Campbell, Justin Edward 1988, 110
Campbell, Kellie Alane 1968, 112
Campbell, Kerry Lynn 1974, 105
Campbell, Kimberly Ann 1964, 112
Campbell, Kristen Nicole 1983, 110
Campbell, Kristen Victoria 1984, 107
Campbell, Laura Jane 1897, 12
Campbell, Laura Sue 1967, 111
Campbell, Lisa Marie 1970, 104
Campbell, Lois Delila, 182
Campbell, Louise 1927, 103
Campbell, Louise S. 1841, 99
Campbell, Maggie 1890, 17
Campbell, Margaret 1839, 100
Campbell, Margaret 1924, 113
Campbell, Margaret Ann 1924, 108
Campbell, Margaret Sanders 1953, 107
Campbell, Martha Jo 1953, 105
Campbell, Mary Adaline 1844, 99
Campbell, Mary Helen 1907, 103
Campbell, Mary Louise 1912, 111, 143

Campbell, Minnie 1897, 17
Campbell, Myrtle 1893, 17
Campbell, Nancy Caroline 1958, 110
Campbell, Nancy J. 1882, 12
Campbell, Nancy Jean, 103
Campbell, Nellie 1919, 112
Campbell, Nora C. 1859, 101
Campbell, Patrick, 100
Campbell, Raymond 1907, 18
Campbell, Raymond Arthur 1960, 111
Campbell, Richard Noel 1957, 108
Campbell, Robert Jackson 1957, 110
Campbell, Rosemary Gass 1942, 105
Campbell, Rush S. 1835, 99
Campbell, Samuel, 11
Campbell, Sandra, 103
Campbell, Sandra Keele 1953, 108
Campbell, Sandra Lee 1956, 107
Campbell, Sarah Ellen 1962, 110
Campbell, Spottswood Mitchell 1804, 46, 98, 99, 101
Campbell, Susan Beth 1949, 108
Campbell, Thomas Meade 1953, 109
Campbell, Thomas Meade, Jr. 1976, 109
Campbell, Virginia Lynn 1959, 107
Campbell, White David, 100
Campbell, William Claude 1961, 108
Campbell, William Enzer 1875, 101, 102
Campbell, William H. 1910, 103
Campbell, William Hal 1986, 107
Campbell, William Harold 1923, 108
Campbell, William, Col. 1745, 98, 100
Campbell, Zelia, 92
Canoles, Donald Wayne, 112
Cardwell, Louis, 14
Carson, Kit, 126
Carson, Martha Loraine 1866, 126, 127, 131, 136, 162
Carson, William, 126
Carter, Bettie Sue 1933, 158

278

Carter, Beverly, 158
Carter, Christopher, 159
Carter, Daisy Ruth 1935, 158
Carter, Donald Hugh 1937, 158
Carter, Edward, 103
Carter, James Wesley, 157
Carter, Janet Faye 1943, 159
Carter, Jesse 1774, 9
Carter, Kevin Keith, 159
Carter, Lewis, 9
Carter, Lois Christine 1932, 157
Carter, Nancy 1800, 6, 8, 9, 10, 16, 20
Carter, Patsy 1941, 141
Carter, Raymond Lee 1942, 158
Carter, Raymond Scott, 158
Carter, Robert Buchanan 1911, 157
Carter, Robert Buchanan, Jr. 1945, 159
Carter, Samuel Joe 1948, 159
Carter, Steve, 158
Carter, Timothy Joe, 159
Carter, Tina, 158
Carter, Toni, 159
Carter, Valentine S., 14, 16
Carter, Vicky, 159
Carter, Wayne, 159
Carter, William, 158
Carver, Charles Douglas, 177
Carver, Florence Idell, 177
Carver, George 1893, 177
Carver, Harold Murray, 177
Carver, Irma May 1918, 177
Carver, Marvin George, 177
Carver, Parley Pratt, 194
Carver, Willard Ivan, 177
Cassell, Lillian A., 87
Castell, Jane, 87
Catellacci, Alima Clara 1989, 214
Catellacci, Fernando, 214
Catellacci, Gianni Cesare 1949, 214
Catellacci, Vanda Frandi, 214
Cates, Asa 1781, 250
Cates, John H. 1811, 250
Cates, Jonathan 1810, 250
Cates, Martha 1823, 250

Cates, Mary E. 1820, 250
Cates, Nancy 1809, 250
Cates, Robert, 250
Cates, Robert A. 1813, 250
Cates, Sarah, 250
Cates, Sarah Frances 1817, 250
Cates, Walter A. 1815, 250
Caudill, Doris Ann, 112
Chamber, William Pollock, 194
Chamberlain, Ralph Jean, 172
Chancy, Henry, 74
Chandler, Wilson Call, 191
Cheney, Aaron Linden 1893, 170
Cheney, Clyde Leon 1895, 170
Cheney, Crystal Pearl 1914, 170
Cheney, Elam, 170
Cheney, Ezekiel Thomas 1872, 170
Cheney, Harriet Glenda 1901, 170
Cheney, Harris Bennett, 170
Cheney, Mervin Ezekiel 1897, 170
Cheney, Monta Kreal, 170
Cheney, Thaddeus Faugne 1905, 170
Cheney, William Thadd 1892, 170
Cherry, Ellen, 191
Chisler, Beth Anne 1971, 154
Christensen, Andrew, 170
Christensen, Archibald 1886, 195
Christensen, Bernard Englebert 1893, 195
Christensen, Frayne Wilford, 173
Christensen, John Christian 1883, 173
Christensen, Olive Bernice, 173
Christoferson, Kathy, 64
Christoferson, Louis, 64
Christoferson, Lynn, 64
Christoferson, Robert, 64
Christoferson, Shirley, 64
Chumbley, Alma Joan 1910, 197
Chumbley, Elizabeth 1869, 78, 82
Chumbley, Joseph D. 1850, 78, 82
Chumbley, Margaret J., 83
Cisco, Brenda Gale, 227
Clancy, Catherine, 167
Clapp, Martha Elizabeth, 109
Clark, Albert 1894, 22

Clark, Alice 1896, 22
Clark, Carrie 1893, 22
Clark, Charles 1892, 22
Clark, Charles Champ, 151
Clark, Charles Champ, III 1980, 151
Clark, Charles Champ, Jr., 151
Clark, Charlie, 101
Clark, Elsie 1890, 22
Clark, Frederick, 174
Clark, Jackie, 160
Clark, James Benjamin 1986, 151
Clark, Jesse 1884, 22
Clark, John H. 1859, 22
Clark, Mae, 191
Clark, Minnie 1908, 22
Clark, William, 261
Clark, William Thompson 1982, 151
Claspill, James Martin, 15
Classil, Joseph, 14
Clayson, Alice 1907, 183
Clear, Annie Evelyn 1919, 147
Clear, Beverly Rose, 121
Clear, H. F., Jr., 121
Clear, Harve Franklin, 147
Clement, Eva Viola 1899, 191
Clement, Gale Wilford, 191
Clement, Hollis Demont, 191
Clement, Leslie 1914, 191
Clement, Mary Irene, 185
Clement, Mary Ora, 183
Clement, Nyla Grace, 191
Clement, Ray Lynn 1920, 191
Clement, Rhea 1920, 191
Clement, Thomas Leslie 1892, 191
Clement, Thomas Ross, 191
Clements, John H., 41
Clements, Philip Andrew, 40
Clements, Talitha Cumi 1820, 40
Clinkscales, Lewis C., 257
Clowers, Priscilla, 260
Clyde, Lola Lucy 1904, 185
Coates, Marvin Leroy, 183
Coates, Murry D., 182
Coe, Gayle Louise, 74
Cofer, Mark Scott 1963, 91
Cohen, Mary Cecilia, 104

Cole, David Austin, 97
Cole, Eleanor, 107
Cole, Warren Arthur 1965, 97
Coleman, Sarah Ann 1898, 23
Coleman, T. A., 136
Colewall, Alice Marie, 197
Colley, Darliet, 214
Collins, George, 68
Collins, Mary, 148
Compton, Raymond, 194
Connell, Gae Bernice, 191
Contreras, John, 140
Cook, Anne Beatrice 1914, 142
Cook, Carol Anne, 142
Cook, Catherine Lynn 1970, 141
Cook, Charles William 1935, 141
Cook, Geoffrey Fred 1961, 141
Cook, George Fred 1911, 141
Cook, George Fred, Jr. 1940, 141
Cook, Henry H., 141
Cook, Henry Samuel 1905, 141
Cook, Henry Samuel 1942, 142
Cook, Hobart Holmes 1909, 141
Cook, Hobart Holmes, Jr. 1941, 141
Cook, Irene Neal, 142
Cook, James Lee 1945, 141
Cook, James Lee, Jr. 1973, 141
Cook, Kimberley Lynette 1962, 141
Cook, Lucy, 207
Cook, Mary Gray 1938, 141
Cook, Mattie Mae 1906, 141, 142
Cook, Patsy Ann 1933, 141
Cook, Peggy Jean 1944, 141
Cook, Scott 1970, 142
Cook, William D., 141, 142
Coombs, Joseph, 43
Cooper, Ella, 261
Cooper, George, 261
Cooper, James Oliver, Dr., 104
Cooper, Jerry Wayne 1945, 204
Cooper, Kathy 1945, 104
Cooper, Keli Elizabeth 1972, 205
Cooper, S., General, 89
Coopwood, Elta, 104
Copenhaver, William H., 54
Corrico, Sally m/1822, 37

Cottle, Lyle Jay, 192
Coufal, Ann Mary Smith, 225
Coufal, Frances Elaine 1940, 224
Coulson, Douglas, 52
Coulthard, Edna Lee 1879, 151
Courtney, John Wesley, 42
Cowan, Mahlon Susong, 91
Cowan, Sallie Nancy, 91
Cox, Benjamin, 116
Crabtree, Betty Anne 1942, 142
Crabtree, Birdie Jane 1941, 142
Crabtree, Edna, 140
Crabtree, James Thomas 1907, 142
Crabtree, Lucille, 140
Crabtree, No given name, 116
Crabtree, Tabor, 140
Craighead, Allen Tooney 1928, 142
Craneck, James, 57
Craneck, Maureen, 57
Crawford, Thomas, 257
Crawford, William, Sir, 228
Cross, Benjamin 1940, 92
Cross, Beulah, 19
Cross, Harry, 92
Cross, Nell Pratt 1968, 92
Cross, Spencer Benjamin 1972, 92
Crouere, Suzanne Marie, 143
Crouse, April 1974, 151
Crowder, Mildred Frances 1928, 206
Crowdis, Iva Pearl, 170
Cunningham, William L., 257
Currie, Margaret Tomenia, 258
Curtis, Max, 188
Curtis, Susan Clarissa 1888, 190
Cusworth, Eliza, 171
Cutwright, No given name, 22
Cypher, Min, 140
Dace, Eliza Jane, 22
Dace, Elizabeth, 15
Dace, James M., 15
Dace, Michael Edward, 15
Dace, O. E., 15
Dailey, Laura Beth, 91
Dalton, David Herbert, 181
Dameron, Jettie 1921, 141
Dancy, Blaine James, 105

Dancy, James Clyde 1947, 105
Danewood, Cindy, 57
Danewood, Dale, 57
Danewood, Donald, 57
Danewood, Roy, 57
Darnell, Hazel Stall, 19
Darr, Alexander 1838, 166
Darr, Alonzo 1874, 167
Darr, Annette 1872, 167
Darr, Betty, 166
Darr, Eliza Penelope 1865, 166
Darr, George 1867, 166
Darr, James 1876, 167
Darr, Mary Susan 1868, 166
Darr, May 1870, 167
Darricades, Eric Anthony Jaime
     1976, 207
Darricades, Karen Nathalie Laurance
     1979, 207
Darricades, Patrick, 207
Davis, Emaline, 260
Davis, Ida Marion 1890, 187
Davis, W. M., 115
Dayley, James Keller 1862, 247
de la Cour, Edmund, 52
de la Marliere, Marquis Collier, 207
Dean, Alan, 102
Dean, Edna, 231
DeBord, Aaron David 1975, 63
DeBord, Alda, 121
DeBord, Amber Nicole 1980, 63
DeBord, Andrew B. 1849, 63, 120
DeBord, Ashley 1977, 63
DeBord, Beattie Lee, 121
DeBord, Charles, 63
DeBord, Curtis, 120
DeBord, David 1946, 63
DeBord, David Porter, 121
DeBord, Deborah Jean, 123
DeBord, Della, 63
DeBord, Donald, 121
DeBord, Edith Glenna 1924, 121
DeBord, Edna, 120
DeBord, Emily Jane, 121
DeBord, Ethel Marie 1911, 121
DeBord, George Wiley 1890, 123

281

DeBord, Glen, 120
DeBord, Harold Eugene 1926, 123
DeBord, Henrietta 1887, 123
DeBord, Henry H. 1893, 123
DeBord, Jeffrey Blake, 121
DeBord, John, 120
DeBord, John Thompson 1878, 121
DeBord, John William, 121
DeBord, Joseph Michael, 123
DeBord, Kenneth, 63
DeBord, Louise Miller 1915, 123
DeBord, Mable, 120
DeBord, Mariam 1928, 123
DeBord, Martha Henderson, 121
DeBord, Martha Jane 1830, 165
DeBord, Mary Ovella 1920, 121
DeBord, Mattie S. 1895, 123
DeBord, Mildred, 63
DeBord, Nancy Jane 1834, 165, 166
DeBord, Nancy Virginia, 121
DeBord, Nannie R. 1881, 123
DeBord, Nannie Virginia 1909, 121
DeBord, Opal, 121
DeBord, Opal 1917, 123
DeBord, Phyllis, 63
DeBord, Raymond Lee 1916, 121
DeBord, Raymond Lee, Jr., 121
DeBord, Reese B. 1897, 63, 123
DeBord, Robert Edward 1922, 121
DeBord, Robert Edward, Jr., 121
DeBord, Sarah, 120
DeBord, Sharon, 63
DeBord, Susan Margaret 1907, 121
DeBord, Thomas P. 1884, 123
DeBord, Walter Beattie 1913, 121
DeBord, William B. 1918, 121
DeBord, William John 1876, 120, 123
DeBord, Woodrow Wilson 1914, 123
Delaney, Addie Margaret, 91
Delp, Daniel Wayne, 158
Delp, Danny, 158
Delp, Jo Ann, 109
Delp, Joe, 109
Dennison, No given name, 28
Denniston, Margaret, 25

Derey, Celeste Tatum 1971, 92
Derey, Clifford Walter 1942, 92
Derey, Jill Pratt 1959, 92
Derey, Sally Jane 1944, 92
Derey, Samuel, 92
Derey, Vernon Foster 1904, 92
Derey, Walter Leaton 1974, 92
Deskins, Ruth, 112
Dewsnup, Bertha Ann 1874, 246
Diarmid, Scott, 53
Dickenson, Fannie Karen 1956, 95
Dickenson, James Samuel 1921, 95
Dickenson, James Samuel, Jr. 1965, 95
Dickenson, James William, 95
Dickess, Leo, 121
Dimeler, Glenda, 112
Dixon, Alice Eveline 1872, 179
Dixon, Aloa, 182
Dixon, Anatha 1917, 182
Dixon, Arta May, 181
Dixon, Asael Harold 1888, 182
Dixon, Asael Jenkins, 182
Dixon, Beulah, 181
Dixon, Charles Harvey 1894, 180
Dixon, Elsie Katherine, 181
Dixon, Elsie Mae 1891, 182
Dixon, Elwood Grow, 180
Dixon, Emma Fern 1898, 180
Dixon, Forest B., 181
Dixon, Gloria Ethlyn, 182
Dixon, Grace, 181
Dixon, Harold Grow, 181
Dixon, Harvey 1844, 179
Dixon, Harvey Wells 1907, 181
Dixon, Harvey, Jr. 1874, 180
Dixon, James Frederick 1904, 180
Dixon, John Frederick 1879, 181
Dixon, John Pritchett, 181
Dixon, Kenwood LeDair, 182
Dixon, Kittie Calpurnia 1877, 181
Dixon, Kittie Virginia 1908, 181
Dixon, Lowell Don, 182
Dixon, Mary Elizabeth 1871, 179
Dixon, Myrtle Vivian, 181
Dixon, Nordessa, 182

Fulks, Catherine m/1814, 39
Fulks, Christopher Columbus 1876, 38
Fulks, Columbus Nicholas 1891, 37
Fulks, Dewey Lavander 1898, 37
Fulks, Elizabeth 1807, 37
Fulks, Elizabeth 1813, 34
Fulks, Elizabeth 1841, 34, 36
Fulks, Elizabeth m/1822, 34
Fulks, Ellen 1875, 38
Fulks, Elsy W. 1864, 39
Fulks, Emily 1834, 34, 36
Fulks, Ernest 1900, 37
Fulks, Gilly S. 1854, 39
Fulks, Hannah 1799, 36
Fulks, Henrietta 1862, 39
Fulks, Hester A. 1863, 39
Fulks, Jake 1871, 38
Fulks, James 1830, 34
Fulks, James Andrew 1923, 37
Fulks, James R. 1855, 36
Fulks, Jane 1896, 37
Fulks, Jarod J. 1860, 39
Fulks, John 1881, 39
Fulks, John Henry, 39
Fulks, John M. 1804, 37
Fulks, John S. 1852, 39
Fulks, Joseph 1806, 34, 36
Fulks, Joseph 1845, 34, 36
Fulks, Kelly 1868, 37
Fulks, Kelly Lloyd 1903, 37
Fulks, Laura 1864, 37
Fulks, Leah, 36
Fulks, Leah 1831, 36
Fulks, Leah 1832, 34
Fulks, Letitia 1809, 37
Fulks, Lettie J. 1866, 39
Fulks, Lucetta C. 1856, 39
Fulks, Margaret, 39
Fulks, Margaret 1877, 38
Fulks, Mary, 198
Fulks, Mary J. 1847, 39
Fulks, Mary m/1810, 25, 26, 27, 28, 29, 32, 33, 34, 44, 65, 69, 77, 98, 99, 115
Fulks, Nancy 1801, 37

Fulks, Nancy 1805, 36
Fulks, Nancy W. 1869, 38
Fulks, Nellie 1856, 36
Fulks, Nicholas 1750/60, 33
Fulks, Nicholas 1831, 37, 39
Fulks, Nicholas m/1790, 25, 32, 34, 44, 98
Fulks, Nicholas m/1810, 36
Fulks, Orran 1786, 38
Fulks, Patsy, 36
Fulks, Paul 1926, 37
Fulks, Polly 1800, 36
Fulks, Polly 1831, 34, 36
Fulks, Ray Lavander 1925, 37
Fulks, Rebecca 1781, 36
Fulks, Rebecca m/1811, 38
Fulks, Reuben 1847, 34
Fulks, S. A. 1848, 39
Fulks, Sally 1837, 34
Fulks, Sally Ann 1822, 37
Fulks, Samuel 1837, 34
Fulks, Samuel Adams 1836, 36
Fulks, Samuel d/1837, 36
Fulks, Samuel L. 1819, 38
Fulks, Sara 1875, 38
Fulks, Sarah 1843, 34, 36
Fulks, Temperance 1790, 38
Fulks, Thomas 1828, 39
Fulks, Thomas S. 1812, 38
Fulks, Virginia 1841, 34
Fulks, W. S. 1844, 39
Fulks, Weyland 1873, 38
Fulks, William, 36
Fulks, William 1761, 38
Fulks, William 1786, 38
Fulks, William 1804, 34
Fulks, William Green 1859, 39
Fulks, William m/1800, 36
Fulks, Wilson 1797, 38
Fullen, Vida 1962, 108
Fullen, William, 108
Fuller, Alexander 1877, 174
Fuller, Fanny Adell 1876, 174
Fuller, George Arthur, 195
Fuller, Mary Elizabeth 1878, 174
Fuller, Susan Sarah 1878, 174

Fuller, Thomas Eldridge, 174
Fuller, Thomas Eldridge 1875, 174
Fuller, Thomas Eldridge, Jr. 1847, 174
Fults, George, 35
Gage, Benjamin, 241
Gangi, Amy Marie 1984, 112
Gangi, Brian Michael 1980, 112
Gangi, Gary Frank 1949, 112
Gangi, Lynn Campbell 1948, 112
Gangi, Peter, 112
Gangi, Terry Jean 1956, 112
Gannaway, M. A., 86
Gannaway, T. M., 86
Gannaway, Virginia 1871, 86
Gantt, Cador 1771, 256, 257
Gantt, Tyre, 257
Gardner, Andrew T., 121
Gardner, Captain, 88
Gardner, D. M., 87
Gardner, Denny Pratt, 87
Gardner, Emma Sue, 121
Gardner, James Hugh, 121
Gardner, James T., 121
Gardner, Mack, 87
Gardner, Marvin M. 1905, 87
Gardner, Richard, 161
Gardner, Tammy Lynn 1974, 161
Garnand, James, 82
Garnand, Jennie L. 1857, 82
Garnand, Nancy, 82
Garner, Alice M. 1876, 16
Garrison, Isaac, IV, 260
Garrison, Sarah, 260
Gass, John M., 105
Gass, Mary Graham 1919, 105
Gass, Nannie Lee 1894, 53
Gass, Rose, 53
Gass, S. E., 53
Gates, Cynthia Diane 1956, 152
Gaudiosi, Christine Cynthia, 106
Gibson, Franklin D., 96
Gibson, Lauren Kay-Lee 1994, 96
Gibson, Matthew Samuel 1968, 96
Gilbert, Elizabeth Jackie 1924, 207
Gilbert, Mary Ann 1942, 154

Gilbert, Samuel H., 207
Gilby, Mary, 206
Gillespie, John, 179
Gillespie, Mary Jane 1840, 179, 182, 184
Gillespie, Virginia Edna 1915, 141
Gilley, Beatrice 1905, 161
Gilmer, Lydia Shoemaker, 96
Glover, Winifred Tremble, 110
Glovier, Nina Jane, 147
Glovier, Robert Blaine, 147
Goff, John, 169
Goforth, Margaret Green, 21
Going, Isham, 235
Golihorn, Mabel, 44
Gonzales, Brandt 1971, 153
Gonzales, Carroll Lynn 1950, 152
Gonzales, Justin Lynn 1987, 153
Gonzales, Stefanie 1972, 153
Goodman, No given name, 121
Gordon, Earl Dean 1943, 206
Gordon, Jessica Allen 1976, 206
Gordon, No given name, 249
Gordon, Robert Hardin 1969, 206
Graddy, Dorothy, 19
Graddy, Rufus Allen 1887, 19
Graham, H. H., 22
Graham, Marie 1920, 189
Graham, No given name 1859, 69
Graham, Ruth, 159
Gran, Michael D., 59
Graves, James, 234
Graves, Maxine, 214
Gray, Ruby Lois 1907, 184
Green, Elgin, 101
Green, Mary, 231
Green, Jackie 1958, 146
Green, Nathaniel, General, 239
Green, Valerie Joy, 51
Gregory, Basil Carson 1927, 160
Gregory, Buford Lynwood 1919, 159
Gregory, Donna Lynn 1954, 160
Gregory, Kenneth Kera 1930, 160
Gregory, Lloyd Haskell 1923, 159
Gregory, Payton Howard 1895, 159
Gregory, William Howard 1950, 160

Hansel, Gilbert L. 1885, 10
Hansel, Henry H. 1849, 10
Hansel, John W. 1843, 10
Hansel, Lawrence A. 1857, 10
Hansel, Mary E. 1850, 10
Hansel, Nancy J., 10
Hansel, Sarah Jane 1845, 10
Hansel, Sterling Pierce 1860, 10
Hansel, William E. 1890, 10
Hansell, Henry H. 1805, 10
Hansen, Ann 1935, 184
Hansen, Bertha Elizabeth, 62
Hansen, Bertha Maggie, 184
Hansen, James Lee, 184
Hansen, Martha Elaine, 184
Hansen, Mary Ellen, 184
Hansen, Nels 1881, 184
Hansen, Vennes May, 184
Hansen, Wilford Nels, 184
Hansen, William Lamonte 1909, 184
Hansom, Mamie Elizabeth, 88
Hardy, Dauna 1916, 189
Harkness, Nancy, 257
Harmon, Ava 1897, 11
Harmon, Bethanie, 13
Harmon, Della M. 1877, 11
Harmon, Edward Rhudy, 147
Harmon, Effie Catherine 1885, 11
Harmon, Elmer 1889, 11
Harmon, James Page, 11
Harmon, Jane Marinda 1877, 247
Harmon, Janet, 158
Harmon, John 1884, 11
Harmon, John Milton 1852, 11
Harmon, Lizzie 1887, 11
Harmon, Oral 1908, 11
Harmon, Raymond 1905, 11
Harmon, Stephen 1885, 11
Harmon, Susannah 1775, 9
Harmon, Thadius 1892, 11
Harris, Harriet 1841, 170
Harris, Patsy, 109
Hart, Michael, 158
Hart, Rita, 158
Hart, Ronald, 158
Hart, Wesley, 158

Hartley, Verna, 176
Hatfield, Cookie, 105
Hatton, Lerlee, 71
Havens, Rachel, 59
Hawkes, John Burns, 189
Hawkins, Alberta, 108
Hawkins, Benjamin F., 190
Haworth, Cecil, 92
Haworth, Virginia 1916, 91
Hawthorne, Charles Walter, 110
Hawthorne, Sarah Catherine 1990, 110
Hawthorne, Stephen Campbell 1993, 110
Hawthorne, Terry R. 1953, 110
Haynes, Ezekiel, 250
Haynie, No given name, 249
Hays, Emma, 255
Hayter, Amanda Jane, 93
Hayter, Harry, 68
Hayter, Myrtle, 68
Hayter, Whitley, 68
Heath, James Daniel, 109
Heath, Janet 1960, 109
Heavers, Debra Lynn 1965, 146
Hegsted, Rebecca 1878, 192
Helbert, Kevin Ron 1966, 91
Helbert, Kolton Parker 1994, 91
Helton, Gilmer, 103
Hendrick, Marshall, 56
Henegar, Ovella, 153
Heninger, Elizabeth Ann 1833, 193
Heninger, Frances Katherine 1873, 194
Heninger, Lavinia, 196
Heninger, Margaret Letner 1839, 193
Heninger, Phillip, 193, 196
Heninger, Reese Thompson, 194
Herndon, E. F., 253
Herndon, Ellen Marie, 108
Herndon, Lucy 1846, 251, 253
Herron, Fern Marie 1921, 16
Hewlett, Margaret Ann Stewart, 185
Hiatt, Clarence Rodolphus 1881, 169

Hiatt, David Hastings 1855, 168, 178
Hiatt, Geneva Deseret 1897, 169
Hiatt, Joel Walter, 184
Hiatt, John William 1878, 168
Hiatt, Lizzie Velettie 1893, 169, 178
Hiatt, Sara Frances 1888, 169
Hicks, Mary Frances m/1874, 38
Hiersoux, Carol, 158
Hill, Ada 1862, 23
Hill, Sam G., 261
Hines, Catherine Lamay 1925, 223, 225
Hines, Paul Homer 1899, 223
Hinsley, Christopher Matthew 1969, 211
Hinsley, Curtis Matthew 1917, 210
Hinsley, Curtis Matthew, Jr. 1945, 211
Hinsley, Jacqueline Anne 1943, 210
Hinsley, Matthew Garritt 1975, 211
Hinsley, Sarina 1971, 211
Hodge, Martha Carrolin, 168
Hodges, Lucy Ann, 260
Hodgson, Andrew James 1994, 91
Hodgson, Anthony Dewayne 1966, 91
Hodgson, Bruce Washington, Jr. 1942, 91
Hodgson, Janice Dawn 1968, 91
Hodgson, Lisa Darlene 1964, 91
Hodgson, Michael Bruce 1995, 91
Hoffman, Elke, 113
Hogan, No given name, 22
Hoge, Kent Howe 1940, 142
Hoge, Monty Crabtree 1967, 142
Hoge, Scott 1971, 142
Hogston, John, 68
Holberton, Hazel Richmond, 196
Holbrook, Kenneth Barlow, 181
Holbrook, Marise, 182
Holdaway, Hattie, 110
Holdaway, Mary Blair 1897, 195
Holder, Molly, 261
Holdren, Elizabeth Mae 1894, 176
Holiday, Fannie, 248

Holliday, Anna, 230
Holliday, Maggie Etta, 228, 230
Holliday, Marietta, 230
Holmes, Cleo, 176
Holmes, Lamar Lindsay, 181
Holoman, Mebane, 46
Homes, Alex, 68
Honaker, Ruby 1877, 86
Honaker, S. P., 86
Honaker, Susan J., 86
Hopson, Noah, 110
Hopson, Rhonda Lynn 1964, 110
Horan, Debra, 150
Horne, Emmet N., 204
Horne, Nannie Elizabeth 1890, 204
Horton, Marian, 74
Horton, Virginia Tennessee 1891, 152
Hough, Clement, 259
Houston, Lawrence, 194
Howell, Elizabeth, 46
Howell, Gordon 1860, 78
Hoy, Joe, 231
Hoy, Joseph, 231
Hoy, Shelley, 231
Hoy, Susan, 231
Hoy, Thomas, 231
Hubble, Annie, 147
Hubble, Chad Eric 1971, 102
Hubble, David Owen 1984, 153
Hubble, Jerry Dean 1954, 153
Hubble, Robert Nathan 1981, 153
Hubble, Ronald, 102
Hudson, Carol Sue 1952, 102
Hudson, Christopher Allen 1971, 102
Hudson, Cynthia Jo 1957, 103
Hudson, Jack Allen, 102
Hudson, Jack Allen, Jr. 1950, 102
Hudson, Mary Elizabeth, 174
Hudson, Rosanna, 174
Hudson, Teresa Ann 1956, 102
Huff, Henry, 235
Hughes, Blackmore, 238, 245
Hughes, Blackmore, Jr., 238

Hughes, Elizabeth, 238, 240, 241, 243, 250, 251
Hughes, George, 238
Hughes, John, 238
Hughes, Mary, 238
Hull, Ira, 9, 11
Hulsey, William H., 14
Humes, William, 26
Humphrey, Mildred, 97
Hunt, Russel Frank, 184
Huntsman, Ida Rebecca 1873, 196
Huntsman, Isaiah, 196
Hurley, Bradley Allan 1947, 223
Hurley, Bridget Nora 1990, 224
Hurley, Daniel 1658, 224, 225
Hurley, David Pearson 1861, 209
Hurley, Douglas Wayne 1982, 223
Hurley, Jacqueline Anne 1920, 210
Hurley, James F. 1827, 85
Hurley, Josephine Alberta 1923, 210, 213, 214
Hurley, Karen Marie 1980, 223
Hurley, Katherine Ann 1995, 225
Hurley, Le Ann Erin 1985, 223
Hurley, Monika Lynn 1976, 223
Hurley, William Daniel 1992, 224
Hurley, William Neal, III 1955, 223
Hurley, William Neal, Jr. 1924, 210, 220, 223
Hurley, Willie Neal 1895, 209, 210, 213, 220, 223, 225
Hurst, Cora, 87
Hutchinson, Elizabeth, 249
Hutchinson, Frances, 249
Hutchinson, James S., 249
Hutchinson, John, 241, 249
Hutchinson, John P., 249
Hutchinson, John, Jr., 249
Hutchinson, Jonathan P., 249
Hutchinson, Mary, 249
Hutchinson, Mary 1796, 249
Hutchinson, Mary E., 249
Hutchinson, Nancy R., 249
Hutchinson, Robert O., 249
Hutchinson, Thomas C., 249
Hutchinson, William B., 249

Huttiball, Kristie Elizabeth, 180
Hyland, Mary, 40
Isenhour, Billie Jean, 95
Isgrig, Walter Franklin 1872, 11
Ivers, Mary Anne 1936, 143
Jackson, Allyn Boyd, 181
Jackson, Charity m/1843, 39
Jackson, Ellen, 22
Jackson, George M., 237
James, Katherine, 197
Jarvis, Olivea Jane 1892, 19
Jefferson, Peter, 228
Jefferson, Thomas, 228
Jenkins, Alice, 45
Jenkins, Ethel Christina 1893, 182
Jenkins, Hannah, 177
Jennings, Wayne, 205
Jensen, James Lewis 1886, 183
Jensen, Leonard Charles 1897, 171
Jensen, Norma Lois, 183
Jett, Charles Everett 1959, 146
Johansen, Blanche Nancy, 173
Johansen, Earl Jay 1916, 173
Johansen, Florence Sena 1920, 173
Johansen, Hugh Noyle 1911, 173
Johansen, Moroni 1876, 173
Johansen, Neal 1922, 173
Johansen, Nola Ruth 1928, 173
Johansen, Pearl May, 173
Johansen, Ray Arvil 1909, 173
Johansen, Robert Kay 1930, 173
Johansen, Vea 1918, 173
Johns, Cloretta, 58
Johnson, Anna Elizabeth 1885, 248
Johnson, Armilda Ellen 1866, 237
Johnson, Betty, 108
Johnson, Donna Darlene, 176
Johnson, George, 240
Johnson, Inger Elizabeth, 172
Johnson, Julia Ann, 29
Johnson, Lenna Clariece, 184
Johnson, Milley, 235
Johnson, Ralph, 60
Johnson, Rue Flavilla 1894, 18
Johnson, Vada Louise, 184

Johnston, Nancy Hilton Albert 1790, 118, 164, 165, 179, 186
Johnston, William, 165
Jones, Amanda Sanderson, 183
Jones, Edith Mae, 169
Jones, Eleanor Ann 1862, 195
Jones, Elizabeth, 256
Jones, Erasmus, 32
Jones, Ernestine, 231
Jones, Jason Campbell 1972, 108
Jones, John S. 1949, 108
Jones, Joshua, 260
Jones, Kathleen, 75
Jones, Mary, 111
Jones, Sarah 1801, 260
Jones, Walter S., 108
Jonston, Rachel 1840, 85
Joplin, Coleman, 166
Jordan, Anna Margaret 1949, 140
Jordan, Carolyn Alvina 1939, 139
Jordan, Deborah 1963, 139
Jordan, Elizabeth, 140
Jordan, Helen, 140
Jordan, James Robert 1945, 140
Jordan, Jeynne, 140
Jordan, John David, 140
Jordan, John Frederick 1938, 139
Jordan, Oliver Joseph, 139
Jordan, Oliver Joseph, Jr., 139
Jordan, Pamela, 140
Jordan, Richard Jerome 1942, 140
Jordan, Rosemary 1947, 140
Jordan, Russell, 140
Jordan, Ruth, 139
Jordan, Samuel Joseph, III 1941, 139
Jordan, Samuel Joseph, Jr. 1908, 139
Jordan, Sandra, 139
Jordan, Shannon, 140
Jordan, Thomas, 139
Jordan, William J., Capt., 83
Justice, Crystal Gale 1978, 227
Justice, Daniel Quentin 1944, 227
Justice, Daniel Shannon 1966, 227
Justice, Grace, 121
Justice, Hunter Brooklynn 1994, 227
Justice, John Laurance 1954, 227

Justice, Joshua Lee 1978, 227
Justice, Quentin Roosevelt, 227
Justice, Thomas Dale 1955, 227
Kay, Mary Jane, 96
Keeney, Henry, 230
Keesee, Daniel Richard 1956, 158
Keesee, Harley Thomas 1931, 157
Keesee, Howard Thomas 1952, 157
Keesee, Judy Beth 1955, 158
Keesee, Michelle Dawn 1989, 158
Keesee, Patsy Elizabeth, 110
Keesler, Ella Fountain, 51
Keheley, Scott, 102
Kelley, Allen Jasper, 260
Kelley, Kara, 231
Kelley, Kaye, 231
Kelley, Laura, 231
Kelley, Mark, 231
Kelley, Ralph R., 231
Kells, Frank, 46
Kells, James Thomas, 46
Kelly, Ebba, 67
Kelsey, Calvin 1856, 248
Kenneburg, Jennie Dolores, 195
Kennerson, Harry, 63
Kent, Madison Cecil 1890, 179
Kern, Margaret Christina, 46
Key, Clara, 15
Key, James B., 257
Key, Mary, 257
Keyes, Mahlon E., 22
Keys, Birdie, 22
Keys, Eva, 22
Keys, Rosie May 1887, 22
Keys, Theresa, 22
Keys, Thomas, 22
Keys, William 1855, 22
Killian, Lavon Hardcastle, 191
Kimberlin, Catherine 1828, 10, 12, 21
Kimberlin, Mary 1835, 12
Kimberlin, Rinard 1806, 16
Kimberline, Mary 1835, 16
Kimer, Edward Stephen, 173
King, Edith May, 191
King, Jennie Isabelle 1900, 166

King, Marvin, 88
Kinne, Helen Aimee, 61
Kinzer, Viola Jane, 95
Kirby, Margaret Ann, 159
Kister, Frederick, 35
Kister, Hannah, 35
Kitchen, Leora Maude, 174
Knight, Almira Celestial 1881, 247
Knowles, Ethel Virginia, 196
Kolstedt, Dave, 90
Kolstedt, Robert, 90
Kolstedt, William, 90
Korherr, Isabel, 205
Kotschorek, John, 94
Kotschorek, Tracey Lynne 1965, 94
Kowa, Deborah 1958, 143
Kranek, James, 57
Kranek, Maureen, 57
Krueger, Bernhard, 46
Krueger, Charles John 1904, 46
Krueger, Robert Dale 1958, 46
Kuper, Gilbert R., 51
Kuper, Gilbert R., Jr. 1972, 51
Kuper, Ward Hawkins 1974, 52
LaFleur, Faith Denae 1987, 109
Laird, Vera 1906, 188
Lamb, Roy, 174
Lamie, Alicia Lorraine 1979, 152
Lamie, Betty Kay 1949, 152
Lamie, Carl Carson 1953, 152
Lamie, Gary Lee 1958, 153
Lamie, James Travis 1975, 152
Lamie, James Wesley 1977, 152
Lamie, John A., 116
Lamie, John Mantz 1957, 153
Lamie, Lee Garfield 1931, 152, 153
Lamie, Mark Pratt 1958, 153
Lamie, Murphy Franklin 1994, 153
Lamie, Pattie Jean 1960, 153
Lamie, Raymond Etny 1884, 152
Lamie, Raymond Franklin 1952, 152
Lamie, Trenton Lee 1976, 152
Lamie, Troy Etny 1977, 152
Lamie, Vicki Jean 1955, 152
Lamie, Walter Early, 153
Lamie, William Franklin 1926, 152

Lamson, Jack Alan 1949, 59
Lamson, Jill Ann 1949, 59
Lamson, Mary Virginia 1943, 59
Lamson, William Aloysius, 59
Lamson, William Maxwell 1906, 59
Lamson, William Maxwell, Jr. 1943, 59
Lancaster, Keziah m/1790, 261
Land, Jane Elizabeth, 61
Land, John, 61
Larkins, Buddy Glen, 188
Larsen, Alta Alura, 184
Larsen, Boyd Neureen, 184
Larsen, Burton, 172
Larsen, Christian, 172
Larsen, Estella, 184
Larsen, Hannah Zelma 1896, 195
Larsen, Helen Zelma 1896, 195
Larsen, Henry Erastus 1879, 184
Larsen, Ila Winona, 184
Larsen, John Darrell, 184
Larsen, John Frederick 1875, 172
Larsen, Leo Christian, 172
Larsen, Maria Theresa, 184
Larsen, Vernon Frederick, 172
Larson, Kenneth James 1967, 161
Larson, Kenneth R., 161
Larson, Robert Paul 1970, 162
Lavin, John, 208
Lavin, Sean Richard 1966, 208
Lawson, Clay, 74
Leazer, Laura Francine, 157
Leazer, Sampson P., 157
Ledbetter, Candy, 51
Ledbetter, Daniel Alexander, 51
Ledbetter, Jeffrey Brown, 51
Ledbetter, Joseph Brown, 51
Ledbetter, Joseph Brown, Jr. 1945, 51
Ledbetter, Molly Lanier, 51
Ledbetter, Pattie Pratt 1942, 51
Lee, Alice Evelyn 1890, 179
Lee, Amber Pauline 1992, 96
Lee, Benjamin Rogers, Jr. 1956, 153
Lee, Catherine Vernon 1925, 95
Lee, Cecil Dixon 1913, 180

293

Lee, Christopher Donald 1971, 97
Lee, Christopher Nasaib 1966, 94
Lee, Clyde Dixon 1911, 180
Lee, Connally Litchfield 1862, 93, 95
Lee, Dorothy Helen 1927, 95
Lee, Edna May 1904, 180
Lee, Erin Lynda 1992, 94
Lee, Essie Idella 1892, 180
Lee, Estella 1887, 168
Lee, Fredric Arthur 1907, 168
Lee, Gregory Neal 1956, 96
Lee, Harold Dixon 1908, 180
Lee, Harry James 1908, 168
Lee, Henry Morgan 1855, 93
Lee, Henry Morgan, Jr. 1912, 94
Lee, Howard Closson 1878, 168
Lee, Howard Hampton 1909, 93
Lee, Howard Hampton, III 1956, 94
Lee, Howard Hampton, Jr. 1933, 94
Lee, Hyrum Bracken 1865, 179
Lee, Hyrum Dixon 1894, 180
Lee, Isaac Harvey 1896, 180
Lee, Jack Thomas 1932, 96
Lee, James Donald 1945, 97
Lee, James Mobley, 93
Lee, James Thomas 1903, 93, 95
Lee, James Thomas 1987, 96
Lee, Janie Sue 1939, 96
Lee, Lawrence Howard, 168
Lee, Loy Homer 1877, 168
Lee, Mary Juanita 1898, 180
Lee, Metta Fern, 180
Lee, Michael Thomas 1958, 96
Lee, Patsy Carol 1942, 97
Lee, R. N., 168
Lee, Ralph Hamilton 1905, 93
Lee, Rector Lawrence 1881, 168
Lee, Rector Leonard 1904, 168
Lee, Robert Edward 1898, 93
Lee, Roy Dixon 1901, 180
Lee, Russell, 180
Lee, Sharon Arlene 1967, 97
Lee, Shirley Ann 1935, 94
Lee, Thomas Loy 1846, 167
Lee, Thomas William, 168

Lee, Tyler Remington 1994, 94
Lee, Viola Desseretta 1882, 168
Leesemann, Louis C. 1833, 41
Lehmkuhl, Albert, 63
Lehmkuhl, Allan, 63
Lehmkuhl, Betty, 63
Lehmkuhl, Madeline R. 1921, 63
Leonard, Clarence E., 109
Leonard, Jane 1960, 109
Leonard, Margaret Elizabeth, 55
Leonard, Ray, 148
Leonard, Shirley Marie 1953, 148
Lester, Aaron Michael 1990, 109
Lester, Brittany Campbell 1976, 109
Lester, David Michael, 108
Lester, Melvin Cecil, 108
Lester, Terrence Patrick 1969, 108
Lewis, Bruce, 74
Lewis, Helen Agnes 1876, 247
Lindsay, William, 194
Little, Louellen, 71
Little, Mildred A., 110
Lloyd, Berry H., 244
Lloyd, William, 244
Lohmann, No given name, 13
Long, George Washington 1863, 166
Long, James Edward, 166
Long, Lynda, 104
Long, Susanna Frances, 168
Lott, Linda Faye, 158
Louthan, Jane, 194
Loving, Hyter Anderson 1893, 210
Low, Nora, 182
Lowder, Annie Liza 1861, 118, 198
Lowder, George Washington 1830, 118, 198
Lowder, Nancy Jane 1858, 116, 117, 120, 198, 199, 204, 206, 208, 209, 227
Lowman, Blanche L. 1897, 82, 83
Lowman, Catherine, 82
Lowman, David, 82
Lowman, Lena, 82
Lowman, Lillian, 82
Lowman, Ruby, 82
Lowman, William David 1865, 82

Lummins, Elizabeth J., 242
Lundgren, Anna Maybell, 172
Lynch, Florence, 103
Lynd, Edna, 231
Lyons, Earl Dean, 176
Lyons, M. Susanne, 111
Mabe, Reuben, 27
Machaido, Eunice, 58
Machen, Ada Lucille, 188
MacNeil, Herbert, 155
Madon, Bob, 206
Magee, Aletta, 180
Magruder, Olivia Epps 1852, 45
Magruder, P. H., 45
Magruder, Sallie, 45
Mallow, Mary Olive 1917, 19
Malone, Dumas, 252
Malone, William, 240
Maloyed, Ashley Jo 1981, 106
Maloyed, J. B., 105
Maloyed, James Curtis, 105
Manning, Floy, 176
Mansell, John, 240
Mansell, Megan Pratt 1979, 152
Mansell, Richard, 239, 240
Mansell, Richard Herbert 1944, 151
Mansell, Robert, 233, 234, 239, 240, 249
Mansell, William Matthew 1981, 152
Marara, Amelia, 161
Marlow, John, 38
Marlowe, Mary Etta, 42
Marsh, Martha E., 237
Marshall, Ann, 65
Marshall, Elizabeth, 75
Marshall, William, 39, 65
Martin, Fred 1912, 102
Martin, Helen, 102
Martin, James O., 230
Martin, Nancy 1931, 102
Martin, Peggy 1934, 103
Martin, Seth, 244
Martin, William H., 244
Martindale, Alonzo 1859, 247

Martindale, Athan Thomas 1871, 247
Martindale, John Albert 1862, 247
Martindale, Minnie 1869, 247
Martindale, Susanna Isabell 1864, 247
Martindale, William Addington 1814, 246
Martindale, William Lyman 1867, 247
Mash, Sharon Lee 1948, 223
Mathena, No given name, 146
Matherley, James Edward, 150
Mauldin, Richard, 232
Maxey, Frank Holcomb 1910, 111
Maxey, Harry Eugene 1935, 111
Maxey, Jenifer Kathleen 1966, 111
Maxey, Michele Susanne 1961, 111
Maxey, Robert Eugene 1955, 111
Maxey, William Eric 1960, 111
Maxey, William Frank 1934, 111
Maxey, William Harry 1959, 111
Mays, Margaret Louise, 46
Mays, No given name, 103
McAlister, William Thomas Davidson, 191
McArthur, Roy 1877, 196
McArthur, Sarah Elizabeth, 174
McBride, General, 13
McBride, Illa Artell 1902, 192
McCall, K. Andrew, 61
McCarty, Charles, 44
McCarty, Enoch J. 1818, 44
McCarty, J. M. "Bud", 44
McCarty, Jack, 44
McCarty, James, 44
McCarty, Lucille, 44
McCarty, Mary, 44
McCarty, Sidney, 44
McCarty, Virginia, 44
McCarty, William, 44
McClain, Sarah, 43
McClure, Ray, 162
McConnell, John, 257
McCoy, Mary, 100
McCrary, Angelynn, 28, 29, 41

Monson, Iretta Arvina 1912, 184
Monson, Olive 1895, 185
Montgomery, Richmond 1858, 85
Montgomery, Susannah 1801, 260
Moore, Alexander, 251
Moore, Anderson, 37
Moore, Dorcas Eliza 1797, 251
Moore, Julian, 237
Morehead, Harry L., 53
Morehead, Laura Belle 1921, 53
Moretz, Daniel, 95
Moretz, Rebecca Elizabeth 1980, 95
Moretz, Stephen Roger 1953, 95
Morgan, Alice, 109
Morgan, Mack, 199
Morrell, Patricia Ann 1960, 153
Morrison, Charles Harmon, 211
Morrison, Laura Jo 1971, 211
Morrison, Randal C., 210
Morton, Leonard M. 1859, 166
Morton, Minnie, 157
Morton, No given name, 167
Moses, Lois, 159
Mosier, Anna 1866, 39
Moss, No given name, 16
Motley, James Hershel, 95
Motley, Valerie Michelle, 95
Motz, Mary Etta, 258
Mount, Elizabeth, 230
Mower, Inez Lapriel 1909, 184
Mower, Lula Almira, 172
Mulhausen, James, 66
Mundy, Annie Jane 1889, 178
Mundy, James, 178
Munroe, Joseph Edsel 1945, 104
Munroe, Lonnie B., 104
Munroe, Lonnie Edsel 1914, 104
Munroe, Margaret Jean 1940, 104
Murdock, Charles H., 175
Murdock, Martha, 257, 258
Murphy, Lulu, 187
Murray, Allison Taylor 1984, 157
Murray, Christopher Keith, 157
Murray, Melissa Elaine 1982, 157
Murray, Vera 1917, 123
Musgrove, Lorene, 54

Musgrove, Sandra Diane 1951, 54
Musgrove, Williams Jenning, 54
Musick, Deborah 1964, 141
Myers, Fannie Mae, 61
Neal, Amanda 1986, 144
Neal, Brandon 1983, 144
Neal, Christopher 1981, 144
Neal, David Michael 1948, 144
Neal, Edna, 58
Neal, Frances, 58
Neal, James Beverly, Jr. 1914, 205
Neal, James Charles 1970, 205
Neal, James Frederick 1937, 143
Neal, James Richard 1943, 205
Neal, Jann Marie 1956, 144
Neal, Jessica Tate 1987, 143
Neal, John Campbell 1976, 205
Neal, John Christian 1995, 143
Neal, Michael Windsor 1955, 143
Neal, Nancy Carol 1958, 143
Neal, Patricia Beth 1957, 143
Neal, Regina Anne 1955, 143
Neal, Stephen Allen 1953, 143
Neal, Stephen Allen, Jr. 1988, 143
Neal, Susan Lowery 1972, 205
Neal, Tammy Caroline 1967, 144
Neal, Terri Lynn 1969, 144
Neal, William Cook 1931, 112, 143
Neal, William Frederick 1905, 142
Neal, William Oscar, 142
Neal, William Watson 1991, 143
Necessary, Judith Ann, 121
Necessary, Robert T., 121
Necessary, Wallace, 121
Neel, Elizabeth Gail 1950, 102
Neel, John Campbell 1971, 102
Neel, Vernon H. 1910, 101
Neel, William Campbell 1944, 101
Neely, David, 109
Neeves, Myra Lynn 1957, 107
Neeves, Roy Lee, 107
Neff, Malissa, 22
Neibaur, Newel Jacobs, 191
Neikirk, Sarah Alberta Clementine
    1866, 209
Nelson, Douglas, 191

Pratt, Adeline, 72
Pratt, Adolpha 1839, 251, 253
Pratt, Agnes 1904, 86
Pratt, Agnes Gertrude 1914, 147, 157
Pratt, Albert, 259
Pratt, Albert Paris 1897, 18
Pratt, Alexander 1861, 13
Pratt, Alexander 1890, 12
Pratt, Alexander Moore, Dr., 251, 253
Pratt, Alexander R. 1832, 7, 9, 12, 16, 17
Pratt, Alice Lillian 1894, 46
Pratt, Alicia Maria 1896, 17
Pratt, Alma Lavonne 1935, 126, 131, 134
Pratt, Alvin, 259
Pratt, America A. 1845, 45, 54, 55, 59, 63
Pratt, Amy 1794, 256
Pratt, Andrea Carole 1951, 151
Pratt, Andrew, 1, 230
Pratt, Andrew 1839, 230
Pratt, Ann, 148
Pratt, Anna Elizabeth 1891, 199, 206
Pratt, Annie Laura 1901, 145
Pratt, Annie Lee 1931, 155
Pratt, Annie V. 1897, 86
Pratt, Archie J. 1894, 17
Pratt, Arno, 231
Pratt, Arthur 1871, 82
Pratt, Arthur 1874, 255
Pratt, Aspasia Louise 1899, 17
Pratt, Averill m/1891, 228, 230
Pratt, Babel, 5
Pratt, Bable, 4
Pratt, Benjamin, 5
Pratt, Bernard 1784/94, 7
Pratt, Bessie Geneva 1898, 259
Pratt, Bettie 1875, 82
Pratt, Betty Ruth 1940, 161
Pratt, Betty Sue 1933, 155
Pratt, Beulah 1907, 259
Pratt, Brenda Joy 1960, 153
Pratt, Brooks 1903, 86

Pratt, Callie, 87
Pratt, Calpurna 1836, 237
Pratt, Carac Francis 1888, 19
Pratt, Carl Day 1891, 28, 41, 71
Pratt, Caroline 1809, 257
Pratt, Carrick N. 1880, 11
Pratt, Charles 1830, 3
Pratt, Charles 1888, 261
Pratt, Charles A. 1840, 242
Pratt, Charles Arthur 1940, 157
Pratt, Charles Dow 1864, 43
Pratt, Charles E. 1872, 11
Pratt, Charles Edward 1873, 68, 116, 120, 145, 150, 151, 155, 157
Pratt, Charles Edward 1975, 51
Pratt, Charles Edward, Jr. 1911, 147
Pratt, Charles Elwood, 74
Pratt, Charles Felix 1824, 257, 258
Pratt, Charles Felix, Jr. 1861, 258
Pratt, Charles G., 87
Pratt, Charles Henry 1881, 49
Pratt, Charles Henry 1922, 261
Pratt, Charles Jason 1983, 148
Pratt, Charles M. 1899, 231
Pratt, Charles McCready 1909, 51
Pratt, Charles McCready, Jr. 1939, 51
Pratt, Charles Rawson 1920, 131
Pratt, Charles Sayers 1877, 85, 86
Pratt, Charles Sayers 1907, 90
Pratt, Charles Sayers, 111 1967, 90
Pratt, Charles Sayers, IV, 90
Pratt, Charles Sayers, Jr. 1938, 90
Pratt, Charles Walter 1951, 148
Pratt, Charlotte Jean 1935, 157
Pratt, Christopher Columbus 1819, 244, 245
Pratt, Cindy, 69
Pratt, Clarence 1882, 69, 72, 74
Pratt, Clarence Pritchett 1907, 147
Pratt, Clarence, Jr. 1918, 74
Pratt, Clark Elhannon 1897, 259
Pratt, Clementine Cumi 1841, 41
Pratt, Cleveland 1892, 19
Pratt, Clifford 1905, 74
Pratt, Clifton Jackson 1907, 71

Pratt, Coe DeWayne 1972, 75
Pratt, Columbus Benjamin
   Alexander 1893, 18
Pratt, Comfort, 4
Pratt, Cora Adeline 1897, 71
Pratt, Cora E. 1869, 255
Pratt, Cynthia Ann 1800/10, 7, 9, 12,
   16, 20, 21
Pratt, Cynthia Ann 1819, 244
Pratt, Daisy B. 1875, 86
Pratt, Dallas Norman 1899, 46
Pratt, Dana Rae 1977, 154
Pratt, Daniel M. 1839, 262
Pratt, David, 5, 231, 257, 262
Pratt, David 1800, 242
Pratt, David 1934, 87
Pratt, Dean, 231
Pratt, Deborah Jean 1963, 154
Pratt, Donald Gary, 163
Pratt, Donald Ray 1921, 162
Pratt, Donald Stuart, 87
Pratt, Dott Clarence 1932, 155
Pratt, Dovie 1909, 259
Pratt, Eathalena 1838, 242
Pratt, Eddie, 231
Pratt, Eddy, 259, 260
Pratt, Edith E. 1880, 82
Pratt, Edith Mable 1918, 148
Pratt, Edna 1843, 260
Pratt, Edna 1904, 162
Pratt, Edna E. 1876, 49
Pratt, Edna Virginia 1930, 152
Pratt, Edward 1671, 2
Pratt, Edward T. 1876, 85, 86
Pratt, Edward T. 1879, 255
Pratt, Edyth Adelaide 1913, 92
Pratt, Eleanor Pritchett 1944, 150
Pratt, Eliot Forson 1971, 51
Pratt, Elisha 1832, 260
Pratt, Eliza 1833, 251, 253
Pratt, Elizabeth, 71, 137, 257
Pratt, Elizabeth 1762, 234
Pratt, Elizabeth 1792, 261
Pratt, Elizabeth 1806, 257
Pratt, Elizabeth 1821, 244
Pratt, Elizabeth 1847, 242

Pratt, Elizabeth 1875, 13
Pratt, Elizabeth C. 1813, 26, 28, 29,
   41, 65, 66
Pratt, Elizabeth F. 1844, 244
Pratt, Elizabeth Frances 1846, 247
Pratt, Elizabeth Susanna 1865, 247
Pratt, Elizabeth Tate 1916, 53
Pratt, Elizabeth Ward Cranston
   1982, 51
Pratt, Ella Louise 1920, 205
Pratt, Ellen 1917, 51
Pratt, Elwin Richard 1921, 19
Pratt, Emma E. 1862, 237
Pratt, Emma Hathaway 1865, 43
Pratt, Emma Matilda Eleanor 1856,
   258
Pratt, Emmy 1794, 256
Pratt, Enoch, 3
Pratt, Eric, 231
Pratt, Essie 1881, 255
Pratt, Eugene 1920, 261
Pratt, Eva, 137
Pratt, Ezekiel Lyon 1816, 244
Pratt, Fielden 1784/94, 7
Pratt, Florence E. 1852, 46, 101,
   102, 104, 111
Pratt, Florence Rosedale 1891, 45
Pratt, Floyd 1897, 259
Pratt, Floyd Theodore 1927, 18
Pratt, Floyd Thomas 1948, 8, 18
Pratt, Forrest 1895, 258
Pratt, Frances 1784, 241, 250
Pratt, Frances Adeline 1846, 260
Pratt, Frances Eufracia 1823, 244
Pratt, Frances Minerva 1867, 17, 18
Pratt, Francis C. 1894, 12
Pratt, Francis M. 1848, 244
Pratt, Francis Marion 1834, 262
Pratt, Frank, 230
Pratt, Frank 1899, 145, 151
Pratt, Fred 1904, 259
Pratt, Frederick Noel 1937, 161
Pratt, Frederick Noel, Jr. 1967, 161
Pratt, G. L., 262
Pratt, G. W., 199
Pratt, Garland, Jr. 1838, 262

Pratt, Genoa 1963, 90
Pratt, George 1774, 240, 241, 243
Pratt, George Morgan 1841, 263
Pratt, George Taylor 1813, 244
Pratt, George Thomas 1843, 77, 81, 88, 89, 91, 92, 263
Pratt, George W. 1840, 263
Pratt, George Washington 1827, 260
Pratt, George Washington 1842, 45
Pratt, George Washington 1903, 147
Pratt, Georgia 1882, 120
Pratt, Geraldine Josephine 1929, 155
Pratt, Gertrude Bertha 1876, 90, 92, 95
Pratt, Grace 1887, 71
Pratt, Gregory Allen 1965, 154
Pratt, H. B., Rev., 263
Pratt, Harriett E. 1848, 77, 82
Pratt, Harrison Campbell 1876, 120, 159
Pratt, Harrison Campbell 1943, 162
Pratt, Harry Edward 1928, 155
Pratt, Harry Johnson 1894, 237
Pratt, Harry Thompson 1893, 127, 130
Pratt, Helen Evelyn 1910, 137, 139
Pratt, Henrietta, 262
Pratt, Henry 1820, 26, 29, 69
Pratt, Henry 1893, 13
Pratt, Henry Absalom 1859, 12
Pratt, Henry Arthur 1902, 19
Pratt, Henry Carlton "Foots" 1939, 157
Pratt, Henry Lewis 1848, 42
Pratt, Henry Oliver 1905, 147, 155
Pratt, Henry pre/1765, 6, 7, 8, 20, 25, 28
Pratt, Henry Sidney 1873, 45
Pratt, Henry Thompson 1861, 120, 126, 127, 134, 136, 162, 199, 235, 254
Pratt, Henry Winslow 1868, 17, 18
Pratt, Henry, Jr. 1800, 6, 7, 8, 9, 10, 16, 17, 20, 21, 23
Pratt, Howell T., 263
Pratt, Hugh 1809, 236, 237

Pratt, Hugh 1900, 259
Pratt, Ida, 259
Pratt, Inez., 231
Pratt, Irene 1898, 11
Pratt, Irene Cumi 1863, 42
Pratt, Isaac 1802, 259
Pratt, Isaac Thompson 1827, 26, 27, 28, 29, 41, 68, 112, 115, 116, 117, 118, 120, 126, 134, 140, 143, 145, 147, 159, 164, 166, 169, 198, 199, 204, 206, 208, 209, 227
Pratt, Isaac, Jr. 1835, 260
Pratt, Isabel, 2
Pratt, Isabelle Julia, 253
Pratt, J. H., 264
Pratt, J. M., 101
Pratt, Jack Lafayette 1838, 260
Pratt, Jacob Henry 1848, 9, 10
Pratt, Jacqueline Ann 1965, 155
Pratt, James, 5, 27, 228, 235
Pratt, James 1742, 233, 234, 235, 236, 237
Pratt, James 1788, 257
Pratt, James 1807, 242
Pratt, James 1822, 9, 10, 12, 21
Pratt, James 1832, 230
Pratt, James A., 87
Pratt, James A. 1841, 77, 80, 81, 83, 85, 86, 264
Pratt, James A. 1865, 13
Pratt, James Alexander 1824, 260
Pratt, James Alton 1896, 46
Pratt, James Arthur 1848, 258
Pratt, James Carl, 231
Pratt, James Charles 1853, 69, 72
Pratt, James Dallas 1848, 45
Pratt, James Dallas 1937, 46
Pratt, James David 1969, 150
Pratt, James Douglas 1926, 205
Pratt, James Glen 1969, 46
Pratt, James H. 1874, 85, 86
Pratt, James Halbert 1876, 247
Pratt, James Madison 1862, 115, 120
Pratt, James Manley 1856, 255
Pratt, James Marion 1882, 53

Pratt, Mary Sue, 88
Pratt, Mary Susan 1844, 77, 81, 82
Pratt, Mary Virginia 1879, 49
Pratt, Mathise 1842, 242
Pratt, Matilda Ellen 1868, 13
Pratt, Matilda Jane 1842, 9, 16, 23, 24
Pratt, Melinda, 231
Pratt, Michael Allen 1958, 206
Pratt, Milley, 241
Pratt, Minnie 1876, 19
Pratt, Minnie A. 1898, 13
Pratt, Minnie Ann, 11
Pratt, Minnie J. 1872, 85, 86
Pratt, Molly, 69
Pratt, Nancy 1791, 261
Pratt, Nancy 1820, 257
Pratt, Nancy 1847, 230
Pratt, Nancy America 1868, 120, 140, 141
Pratt, Nancy Ann 1935, 161
Pratt, Nancy C. 1882, 12
Pratt, Nancy Elizabeth 1846, 258
Pratt, Nancy Ellen 1843, 42
Pratt, Nancy Fulks 1823, 26, 28, 29, 41, 46, 98, 99, 101
Pratt, Nancy Maria 1830, 9, 10, 11, 12, 21
Pratt, Nancy Mason 1954, 152
Pratt, Nancy Young 1856, 9, 11
Pratt, Nellie 1894, 231
Pratt, Nellie 1918, 261
Pratt, Nicholas H. 1811, 26, 27, 28, 29, 40, 41, 44, 49, 54, 69, 101, 115, 143, 264
Pratt, Nimrod 1841, 230
Pratt, Nora Esther 1893, 71
Pratt, Norma 1952, 148
Pratt, Oliver 1784, 7, 9, 25, 26, 27, 28, 29, 40, 41, 44, 65, 69, 77, 98, 99, 115, 116, 198
Pratt, Oliver 1853, 254
Pratt, Oliver 1865, 27, 120, 126, 127, 131, 134, 136, 139, 199, 254
Pratt, Oliver 1912, 162

Pratt, Oliver Marion 1862, 71
Pratt, Oliver pre/1765, 33, 34
Pratt, Oliver, Jr., 28, 29, 41, 69
Pratt, Oliver, Jr. 1908, 136, 137
Pratt, Orson, 3
Pratt, Orville Carac 1928, 19
Pratt, Orville Hayes 1911, 19
Pratt, Otway August 1887, 45
Pratt, Pamela Joan 1955, 147
Pratt, Parley, 3
Pratt, Patsey, 262
Pratt, Pattie Virginia, 51
Pratt, Paul Denny 1935, 154
Pratt, Paul F., 252
Pratt, Pauline, 131
Pratt, Pearl, 74
Pratt, Pearl 1899, 71
Pratt, Pearl A. 1892, 231
Pratt, Pearl M. 1891, 89
Pratt, Pearl V. 1877, 255
Pratt, Peggy Ruth 1936, 157
Pratt, Peter, 27
Pratt, Phebe 1797, 261
Pratt, Philip Alexander 1853, 40, 43
Pratt, Phoebe Jane 1859, 258
Pratt, Pleasant W. 1840, 265
Pratt, Polina 1865, 17, 18
Pratt, Polly, 236, 260
Pratt, Price Gilmer 1878, 85, 87
Pratt, Price Gilmer, Jr., 87
Pratt, R. H., 266
Pratt, Rainey, 259
Pratt, Ralph Alexander 1901, 17
Pratt, Rausie 1901, 71
Pratt, Raymond Leroy 1910, 261
Pratt, Rebecca Ann 1834, 245
Pratt, Rebecca Isabella 1811, 244
Pratt, Rebecca Isabella 1943, 91
Pratt, Rebecca m/1789, 3
Pratt, Rhinehart 1875, 19
Pratt, Richard, 2
Pratt, Richard 1617, 2
Pratt, Richard 1764, 3
Pratt, Richard 1840, 266
Pratt, Richard B., 87
Pratt, Rinard A. 1856, 9, 11

Pratt, Vivian 1913, 162
Pratt, Vivian Waller 1898, 46
Pratt, W. H., 199
Pratt, W. M., 232
Pratt, Walter Cable 1874, 90, 91
Pratt, Walter Elbert 1893, 199
Pratt, Walter Haven 1916, 92
Pratt, Walter James "Slick" 1924, 148
Pratt, Ward 1909, 259
Pratt, Wardie H. 1905, 71
Pratt, Wesley Oliver 1846, 42
Pratt, Weston Lee 1994, 75
Pratt, Wilburn 1880, 259
Pratt, Willard 1858, 43
Pratt, William, 3, 4, 5, 27
Pratt, William 1734, 255, 256
Pratt, William 1776, 240, 243, 244, 245
Pratt, William 1795, 261
Pratt, William 1798, 257, 258
Pratt, William 1811, 257
Pratt, William 1823, 266
Pratt, William 1830, 260
Pratt, William 1845, 230
Pratt, William 1850, 77, 82
Pratt, William 1897, 13
Pratt, William B. 1893, 254
Pratt, William Buchanan 1809, 244
Pratt, William Cody 1917, 261
Pratt, William F. 1838, 237
Pratt, William Frank 1928, 151
Pratt, William Franklin 1867, 247
Pratt, William Gary 1960, 75
Pratt, William H. 1840, 267
Pratt, William H. 1842, 266
Pratt, William H. 1871, 10
Pratt, William Halbert 1844, 247
Pratt, William Harrison 1840, 44
Pratt, William Henry 1815, 26, 28, 29, 41, 69
Pratt, William Henry 1903, 71
Pratt, William J. 1821, 267
Pratt, William James, 46
Pratt, William m/1817, 236
Pratt, William Mann 1909, 147

Pratt, William R. 1841, 267
Pratt, William Warfield 1853, 120
Pratt, William Zachariah 1858, 255
Pratt, William, Jr., 257
Pratt, Willie, 230
Pratt, Willis 1804, 242
Pratt, Willis Layton, 242
Pratt, Wilson 1906, 71
Pratt, Zebulon, 4
Pratt, Zephaniah, 4
Pratt, Zephaniah m/1790, 261
Pratt, Zephaniah, Jr., 299
Pratt, Zorobabel, 5
Price, Bessie Olivine, 105
Price, Harry H., 86
Price, Howard Orin, 106
Price, Mary Frances 1921, 99, 106
Pritchett, Alta Jane 1898, 184
Pritchett, Aneliza Florence 1874, 196
Pritchett, Archibald Alfred 1897, 194
Pritchett, Axie Sarah 1869, 193
Pritchett, Barbara 1830, 169
Pritchett, Barbara 1854, 167
Pritchett, Barbara Ellen 1890, 178
Pritchett, Beatrice Joyce 1903, 185
Pritchett, Catherine Annie 1919, 178
Pritchett, Catherine Letitia 1865, 194
Pritchett, Charles William 1934, 197
Pritchett, Clarence Linden 1870, 195
Pritchett, Clarice 1908, 194
Pritchett, Clyde Lee, 185
Pritchett, Cynthia 1864, 193
Pritchett, David 1800, 165
Pritchett, David Harold 1871, 193
Pritchett, Dee Kenneth, 186
Pritchett, Donald Keith 1918, 178
Pritchett, Douglas Jackson 1858, 197
Pritchett, Eddy Campbell 1792, 165
Pritchett, Edward Barret 1932, 197
Pritchett, Eliza Ann 1817, 166
Pritchett, Elizabeth, 164
Pritchett, Elizabeth Ann 1869, 194

Pritchett, Elizabeth Arminta 1868, 179
Pritchett, Elizabeth Electa 1900, 194
Pritchett, Ellis 1891, 196
Pritchett, Emily Elizabeth 1907, 184
Pritchett, Enid Marie, 185
Pritchett, Ernest Edwin 1892, 195
Pritchett, Eunice 1804, 165
Pritchett, Eunice 1854, 179
Pritchett, Fannie Elizabeth 1865, 169
Pritchett, Frances Gertrude, 178
Pritchett, Franklin Carl 1901, 195
Pritchett, Fred Herman 1940, 197
Pritchett, George 1879, 177
Pritchett, George Edwin 1914, 178
Pritchett, Gerald Darius 1900, 185
Pritchett, Gertrude Alice 1885, 178
Pritchett, Glenn Albert 1888, 178
Pritchett, Grace Martha 1880, 196
Pritchett, Grace Pearl 1887, 196
Pritchett, Grant 1874, 193
Pritchett, Hannah 1862, 193
Pritchett, Hazel Burdella 1893, 185
Pritchett, India Marie 1872, 196
Pritchett, Iva Pearl 1889, 195
Pritchett, James Coit 1939, 197
Pritchett, James DeCalb 1849, 197
Pritchett, James Lawrence 1912, 197
Pritchett, James Linden 1893, 196
Pritchett, James Mitchell 1817, 165, 166, 192
Pritchett, James Mitchell 1893, 196
Pritchett, James William 1740, 164
Pritchett, Jessie Adaline 1915, 178
Pritchett, John Albert, 178
Pritchett, John Anderson 1794, 118, 164, 165, 166, 179, 186
Pritchett, John Anderson 1840, 166, 195
Pritchett, John Colman 1896, 184
Pritchett, John David, 178
Pritchett, John Douglas 1853, 167, 177
Pritchett, John Edgar 1877, 196
Pritchett, John Edwin 1881, 169, 178

Pritchett, John Frank 1895, 185
Pritchett, John Jackson 1883, 196
Pritchett, John Lester 1883, 197
Pritchett, John William 1860, 179, 182
Pritchett, Joyce Ruby, 186
Pritchett, Judy Shirlene, 186
Pritchett, June Elmo 1913, 186
Pritchett, Katherine Emaline 1867, 169
Pritchett, Kenneth Ernest 1942, 197
Pritchett, Kittie Eveline 1882, 183
Pritchett, Kittie Evelyn 1851, 179
Pritchett, Kitty Emeline Alice 1860, 169
Pritchett, Leon Gay 1895, 195
Pritchett, Leonard 1895, 196
Pritchett, Leonidas Alfred 1838, 193
Pritchett, Leonidas Alfred, Jr. 1874, 194
Pritchett, Leora 1895, 184
Pritchett, Lester 1895, 196
Pritchett, Levi Franklin 1847, 197
Pritchett, Louisa 1860, 193
Pritchett, Lowell Robert 1924, 178
Pritchett, Lydia Margaret 1896, 195
Pritchett, Lynn Wiley 1945, 197
Pritchett, Maggie Ann 1890, 184
Pritchett, Margaret Adeline 1860, 168, 178
Pritchett, Margaret Christian 1878, 195
Pritchett, Margaret Elizabeth, 178
Pritchett, Marjorie Elinore, 178
Pritchett, Mark Harold 1948, 197
Pritchett, Martha Ellen 1888, 183
Pritchett, Mary Ann 1821, 167, 170, 171, 174
Pritchett, Mary Ann 1871, 194
Pritchett, Mary Elizabeth 1858, 193
Pritchett, Mary Elizabeth 1883, 178
Pritchett, Mary Elizabeth 1886, 183
Pritchett, Mary Loretta 1889, 185
Pritchett, Mary Virginia Desserete 1864, 169

Ratliff, Abigail Christina 1989, 143
Ratliff, Cary Allen 1954, 143
Ratliff, Joseph Jackson, 109
Ratliff, Kim 1962, 109
Ratliff, Spencer Neal 1987, 143
Ratliff, Taylor William 1985, 143
Rawlinson, Magdalene 1887, 248
Rawson, Charles, 131
Rawson, Hazelle Lillian 1895, 131
Rawson, Olive Ann 1862, 189
Rawson, Sarah Emily, 183
Raymond, Anna Lillian, 185
Redman, Christian, 233
Redman, John, 233
Redman, Katherine, 233
Redman, Mary, 233
Redman, Nathaniel, 2
Redmon, Nancy, 75
Redwine, Charles Henry, 108
Redwine, Imogene Ann 1924, 108
Reed, John Harvey, 22
Reed, Lucille, 12
Reed, Virginia Lee, 159
Rees, Byron, 181
Reeves, Daniel Munroe 1966, 104
Reeves, Robert, 104
Reeves, Sharon, 59
Reiter, Anna, 46
Remmick, Tillie, 196
Ressequie, Una Maybelle, 59
Rice, Deborah Louise 1950, 204
Rice, Gerald Lee 1943, 205
Rice, Gwendalyn Kay 1961, 204
Rice, Hugh Paschel, 204
Rice, Hugh Paschel 1919, 204
Rice, James Paschel, Jr., 204
Rice, James Paschel 1941, 204
Rice, Stacey Lynn 1976, 204
Rice, Susan Elizabeth 1961, 205
Richards, Joseph Morris, 182
Richardson, David, 52
Richardson, Eula Viola 1909, 19
Richter, George W. 1872, 19
Ricks, Edward, 245
Rigby, Charles Lyle 1913, 183
Rigby, Charles Martin 1870, 183

Rigby, Elmer Eckersley 1884, 188
Rigby, Emma Arzella, 183
Rigby, Leo Deloy, 183
Rigby, Lloyd Lamar 1911, 183
Rigby, Martha Fanny, 183
Rigby, Max E., 188
Rigby, Verla Mae, 183
Rigby, William Neldon, 183
Riser, Doris 1914, 45
Riser, Scott Randolph, 45
Robbins, Betsy 1885, 168
Robbins, Richard A., 143
Robbins, William Carter, 168
Roberts, Amy Renae 1977, 161
Roberts, Atha, 182
Roberts, Byron Dixon 1920, 182
Roberts, Carl Augustus 1878, 182
Roberts, Carl Dixon 1903, 182
Roberts, Fred Dixon 1906, 182
Roberts, Hannah, 235
Roberts, James, 161
Roberts, Kenneth Dixon, 182
Roberts, Melford Augustus 1901,
    182
Roberts, Thomas Dixon 1913, 182
Roberts, Wilford Dixon, 182
Roberts, Willa, 182
Robertson, Alexander, 174
Robertson, Alexander Nephi 1865,
    174
Robertson, Crystal, 174
Robertson, Dell, 174
Robertson, Dell Brooks, 174
Robertson, Eldridge, 174
Robertson, Ellen, 171
Robertson, Ellen 1894, 174
Robertson, George Isaac 1901, 174
Robertson, John, 174
Robertson, Louisa, 257
Robertson, Marion Thomas, 174
Robertson, Susan Elizabeth 1896,
    174
Robinson, Andrew Clay 1995, 107
Robinson, Barry Clay 1957, 107
Robinson, Dana Lynn 1986, 107
Robinson, Edna Adele 1883, 197

Robinson, Effie May, 57
Robinson, Eloise, 176
Robinson, Gatha Dale, 227
Robinson, George, 38
Robinson, Kelly Marie 1990, 107
Robinson, Sterling Rupert, 107
Rock, Ester, 187
Rockefeller, John D., 3
Rodgers, Helen Irene, 183
Rodriguez, Elizabeth 1973, 137
Rodriguez, Esther 1963, 137
Rodriguez, Olivia 1961, 137
Rodriguez, Oscar, 137
Rodriguez, Oscar, Jr. 1965, 137
Rodriguez, Rebecca 1970, 137
Rodriguez, Sammie 1967, 137
Rogers, Alfred Henry 1852, 132
Rogers, Clarence E. 1875, 132
Rogers, Emma Theresa, 59
Rogers, Harry Foster, 131, 132
Rogers, Rosanne Dawn 1962, 132
Rogers, Rosemary Faith 1963, 132
Rogers, Roshay Lavonne 1960, 132
Rose, Clay, 72
Rose, Doris Lucile, 189
Rose, Honey, 74
Rose, Mahala, 74
Rose, Mahalia, 72
Rose, Robert 1818, 72
Ross, Barry, 139
Ross, G. B., 123
Ross, Lillian, 103
Rouse, Sarah, 165
Rowland, Michael W., 204
Rule, Jane, 178
Rush, Harold, 64
Rutledge, Bruce 1958, 90
Rutledge, Jamie Caroline 1993, 91
Rutledge, Morgan Leah 1990, 91
Rynearson, Almira, 192
Rytting, August Wilhelm 1860, 246
Sandall, Roger Linn, 188
Sanders, Carol 1953, 105
Sanders, David Walker, 197
Sanders, Florence Dunn, 104
Sanders, John Frank, 184

Sanders, Olive Loretta 1870, 184
Sanders, Willis O'Neal, 141
Sanderson, Ruby Sanderson, 186
Sangid, Josie Anne 1936, 94
Sangid, Nasaib Berkat, 94
Sargent, Alice, 171
Sargent, Florence Alpha, 188
Satterlee, Rufus Burlus, 139
Sauer, Leonora Mae, 192
Sauers, Joanna D. 1861, 85
Savage, Bud, 37
Savard, Juliette, 61
Sayers, Annie E. 1853, 88
Sayers, Fannie P. 1854, 88
Sayers, Helen H. 1856, 88
Sayers, Joanna 1846, 88
Sayers, Joanna D. 1861, 83
Sayers, John Thompson, 88
Sayers, Maggie 1861, 88
Sayers, Mary Easter 1841, 88, 89,
    91, 92
Sayers, Mary W. 1863, 83, 85
Sayers, Rachel 1824, 88
Sayers, Susan J. 1848, 88
Scarr, Nancy, 165
Schaerrer, Ada, 168
Schindler, Albert August, 59
Schindler, Ruth Ressiquie 1906, 59
Schmidt, Gretchen, 161
School, Elizabeth 1775, 241, 242
Scott, Evelyn Kathleen 1964, 139
Scott, Gail 1948, 142
Scott, Henry Paul, 139
Scott, Julia, 11
Scyphers, Calvin Martin, Jr., 95
Scyphers, Fannie Vernon 1904, 95
Seaman, Amy Hope 1975, 106
Seaman, Ashley Elizabeth 1973, 106
Seaman, William, 106
Seaman, William Scott 1971, 106
Seaman, William, Jr. 1945, 106
Sechrist, Dorothy, 211
Seely, John Delbert 1917, 184
Selfe, Conner Allen 1992, 142
Selfe, Timothy Wayne 1966, 142
Severson, Alice Louise, 192

Sexton, Carrie, 57
Sexton, Charles M., 99
Sexton, Laura Maria, 45
Shaffer, Teresa, 90
Shannon, Andrew, 65
Shannon, John, 65
Shaw, Norma, 192
Shaw, Relia, 172
Sheffield, Edwin C., Jr., 103
Shelley, Isaac James 1836, 42
Shelley, John Abraham 1864, 42
Shelley, Mamie Malinda 1887, 42
Shelton, Frances Gordon, 94
Shepard, Mary, 18
Shepherd, Oscar Ivie 1910, 170
Sherfey, Linda, 63
Sherwood, Frank, 175
Shewbridge, Hope, 67
Shipe, James, 193
Short, Reuben Loran, 193
Shorter, Henry, 232
Shortt, Mary Elizabeth, 155
Shouse, Dorothea 1968, 108
Shouse, Robert Nelson, 108
Shuffelbarger, Emma Frances, 111
Shupe, James, 193
Siert, Rogene Mary 1946, 62
Sill, Eldon Emmett, 190
Simmerly, John Henry, 14
Simmerman, Betty Pratt, 88
Simmerman, George Bentley 1904, 88
Simmerman, George Bentley, Jr., 88
Simmerman, Thomas Edward, 88
Simmons, Carl H. 1895, 15
Simmons, Harvey J., 15
Simmons, Jemima E., 237
Simmons, Phoebe, 15
Simmons, William S. 1891, 15
Simpson, Myron John, 176
Skaggs, Nadine Mae 1905, 18
Skibba, Gail, 123
Skidmore, Zelda, 187
Slater, Arnold Ianthus, 189
Slater, Ivy Cassenda 1899, 192
Sloan, D. C., 87

Sloan, Ruth C. 1909, 87
Sloan, Sarah J. 1835, 83, 85
Sloan, Virginia S., 87
Smith, Almina, 257
Smith, Austin, 257
Smith, Briscoe, 235
Smith, David Rexford, 161
Smith, David Rexford, Jr., 161
Smith, Debra Ann, 161
Smith, Dicey, 256
Smith, Elizabeth, 234
Smith, Elizabeth Sue 1943, 90
Smith, Joseph, 3
Smith, Kelly Jorden, 161
Smith, Lucille Willie 1909, 90
Smith, M. A., 255
Smith, Mary, 260
Smith, Mary Ann, 235, 244
Smith, Maurice, 183
Smith, Nellie, 231
Smith, No given name, 83
Smith, Robert William, 161
Smith, Robert William, Jr., 161
Smith, Sara Lane, 51
Smith, Sarah V. 1840, 255
Smith, Thomas, 239
Smith, William Claude, 188
Smith, William Garfield, 224
Smitley, Louise, 46
Smyer, R. B., 252
Smyth, Belle A., 89
Snapp, Charles Gilbert, 108
Snapp, Doris Imogene 1927, 108
Snedden, Harold E., 211
Snedden, Rebecca Ann, 211
Snow, Clyde Ellison, 183
Snowden, Joe Rodney 1947, 62
Snowden, Meghan Brooke 1977, 62
Snowden, Roscoe, 62
Sorenson, Eva 1892, 187
Souders, John Nelson, 16
Southwick, Delbert, 43
Sparger, H. Merritt, Jr., 105
Sparger, Jennifer Ann 1972, 105
Speer, No given name, 253

Surton, Sarah Alice 1900, 173
Swanson, William, 239
Swasey, Charles A., 171
Synovec, Mary, 120
Syres, Pauline Ida, 96
Tabor, Joe, 111
Talbert, Andrew J. 1833, 66
Talbert, Basil 1806, 65, 66
Talbert, Charles, 65
Talbert, Cynthia Elizabeth 1902, 67
Talbert, Eleanor, 65, 67
Talbert, Elizabeth 1836, 68
Talbert, Emma Catherine, 68
Talbert, Findlay, 68
Talbert, Frank Lee 1885, 67
Talbert, Grace, 67
Talbert, Harry, 67
Talbert, Harry 1865, 67
Talbert, Harry, Jr., 68
Talbert, Isaac Henry, 68
Talbert, Isaac Henry "Tony" 1912, 148
Talbert, James 1845, 68
Talbert, James 1862, 67
Talbert, Joe, 68
Talbert, John, 68
Talbert, Mable, 68
Talbert, Marcus Aurelius 1900, 67
Talbert, Margaret 1870, 68
Talbert, Mary Ann 1838, 68
Talbert, Nancy C. 1842, 68
Talbert, Nyoka Vesoline, 141
Talbert, Oliver 1840, 68
Talbert, Pierce, 67
Talbert, Robert Luther 1860, 66
Talbert, Thomas Thompson 1848, 68
Talbert, Walter, 68
Talbert, Walter R., 148
Talbert, Zoe, 67
Talbot, John, 235
Tate, Dorcas, 99
Tate, William, General, 99
Tatum, Grace, 92
Taylor, Ada Caroline, 188
Taylor, Ada Vilate, 177
Taylor, Allen Ammon 1906, 189

Taylor, Amy 1891, 187
Taylor, Arthur Leland 1904, 188
Taylor, Betsy, 168
Taylor, Betty Tate 1932, 111, 143
Taylor, Blaine Cabble, 188
Taylor, Carolyn Warner 1936, 153
Taylor, Charles, 111, 143
Taylor, Charles Brittain, 141
Taylor, Colleen, 191
Taylor, Darwin Fredrick 1896, 191
Taylor, David Henry, 188
Taylor, David Riley 1869, 188
Taylor, Dee Jay 1913, 189
Taylor, Delbert Guy 1894, 191
Taylor, Delbert Ray, 191
Taylor, Deloris Elizabeth, 192
Taylor, Dorthulia, 191
Taylor, Eli Marshall, 188
Taylor, Elizabeth Jane 1865, 187
Taylor, Florence Emily 1896, 188
Taylor, Gerald Lynn, 191
Taylor, Geraldine, 192
Taylor, Golden Ray 1903, 188
Taylor, Grace Ethel 1892, 191
Taylor, Harold Pleasant 1905, 192
Taylor, Harvey George, 153
Taylor, Hutton, Judge, 96
Taylor, Ira Joseph 1889, 191
Taylor, James Edwin 1900, 188
Taylor, Joan Lee 1950, 96
Taylor, Joseph Lake 1864, 190
Taylor, Joseph Levi, 191
Taylor, Joyce, 204
Taylor, Karen, 188
Taylor, Lavaughn Leo, 192
Taylor, Lawrence Ivan 1898, 191
Taylor, Lois, 191
Taylor, Lola Evelyn 1917, 177
Taylor, Lorin Ray 1887, 190
Taylor, Loy Warren, 188
Taylor, Mac Byram, 192
Taylor, Marion Earl, 192
Taylor, Martha, 170
Taylor, Mary Christine, 141
Taylor, Mary Louise 1863, 17
Taylor, Megnild Gunda, 188

Washington, George, 228, 229
Watson, Lois, 186
Watters, Frank Pratt, 231
Watters, Hilda, 231
Watters, Jean Lee, 231
Watters, Keith, 231
Watters, Mike, 231
Watters, Pat, 231
Watters, Rodney, 231
Watters, Wanda Pratt, 231
Watters, Zelda, 231
Watts, Charles Daniel, 258
Weaver, Crissie Louise, 191
Weaver, Susan, 102
Webb, Francis Marion 1853, 145
Webb, Gale, 96
Webb, Gale Bradley 1961, 96
Webb, Jennie 1879, 145
Webb, Whitney Lee 1990, 96
Welker, Delbert Orville, 187
Wells, Elizabeth, 189
Wells, Liddie Renee, 227
Wells, Martha Laurrennia 1885, 181
Wember, Asa Frederick 1976, 52
Wember, David Gerald, 52
Wember, Summer Laurel 1978, 52
Wengert, No given name, 45
Wert, Christopher Thomas 1972, 106
Wert, Gregory Leon 1975, 106
Wert, Thomas Frederick, III, 106
West, Susan, 17
Westergard, Hans Christian, 193
Wheeler, Alonzo, 190
Wheeler, No given name, 28
Whillock, Daphine Lee 1923, 107
Whillock, Robert Lee, 107
Whitaker, Charles Robert, III 1955, 113
Whitaker, Charles Robert, Jr., 113
Whitaker, Jabez, 66
Whitaker, James, 66
Whitaker, Martha Elizabeth, 66
Whitaker, Randall Dean 1951, 113
Whitaker, Susan Merlene, 172
White, Hazel, 180
White, Jacob Adamson 1990, 143

White, Lillie, 204
White, Nathan Smith, IV 1955, 143
White, No given name, 15
White, Pat, 120
Whitehead, Branda, 97
Whitehead, Sidney Albert, 186
Whitesides, Ila 1917, 190
Whitinger, Ruth M., 14
Whitlow, Paula Kay 1959, 96
Whitlow, Willard Wanlas, 96
Whitman, Elizabeth, 87
Whitsett, Willie Rose, 74
Whitten, Frances Lodaska, 244
Wildey, Randy, 207
Wildey, Sean Wolfe 1990, 207
Wilhelm, Janice Marie, 112
Wilhite, Billy Junior, 185
Wilhite, Mary Lou, 185
Wilkins, Gary John, 59
Wilks, Jesse, 236
Williams, J. C., III, 123
Williams, Joe, 28
Williams, Joseph E., Dr., 65, 67
Williams, Margaret, 176
Williams, Martha Jane, 175
Williams, Price, 246
Williams, Samuel, 166, 195
Willis, Harold Dean, 59
Wilson, Nina Ann 1905, 91
Wilson, Sada, 14
Wilson, Wynema E., 237
Wimmer, Charles Stanley 1954, 143
Wintermyer, Adam Gangi 1983, 112
Wintermyer, Ashleigh Lynn 1988, 112
Wintermyer, Edward, 112
Wise, Shirley, 96
Wittek, No given name, 162
Witten, Maria Josephine 1861, 187
Wolfe, Chester Hardin 1898, 206
Wolfe, Chester Hardin, Jr. 1921, 206
Wolfe, George Hammond, 206
Wolfe, Jo Ann 1947, 207
Wolfe, Nancy Dale 1949, 207
Wolfe, Rose Allen 1948, 206
Wolfe, Roy Pratt 1924, 205, 207

Wood, Charles Alfred, 195
Wood, Ilene Verness, 180
Wood, Sarah Margaret 1883, 87
Wood, William James 1841, 87
Woodcock, Homer, 15
Woodfield, Rosene Maria 1887, 189
Woodford, James, 236
Woodford, Nancy, 236
Woodland, Alma 1908, 131
Woodland, George, 131
Woodmore, Charles Howard 1942, 142
Woodmore, Christine Ann 1971, 142
Woodmore, James Edward 1970, 142
Woodmore, Tracie Lynn 1967, 142
Woodrum, David, 142
Woodrum, David, Jr., 142
Woodward, Bessie Eva, 187
Woodward, Carma June, 186
Woodward, Donald Eugene, 186
Woodward, Milton Hales, 185
Woodward, Patricia Lillian, 186
Woodward, Thomas Milton, 186
Woodward, Wayne Russell 1946, 186
Woodward, Zola Maurine, 186
Woolford, Elizabeth, 52
Woolford, Jane, 52
Woolford, William, 52
Workman, Elizabeth Ann, 193, 196
Workman, Julia Rhoana 1880, 248
Worley, Bryne Lee 1969, 58
Worley, Captola, 56
Worley, Carl, 56
Worley, Carl, Jr., 56
Worley, Carol, 58
Worley, Cynthia Lynn 1971, 96
Worley, Dale 1902, 57
Worley, Edward Lee 1937, 58
Worley, Ethel, 57
Worley, Harold Eugene, 58
Worley, James Clinton, 58
Worley, Judy, 58
Worley, Kenneth, 57
Worley, Kristi Lee 1980, 96

Worley, Lee Roy, 58
Worley, Leona Ann 1903, 57
Worley, Mark Evan 1973, 58
Worley, Marva Lee, 58
Worley, Marvin Jackson, 58
Worley, Naomi, 57
Worley, Noah Estel, 96
Worley, Pamela Jill 1972, 58
Worley, Sarena, 56
Worley, Sharon, 58
Worley, Steven Ashley 1974, 58
Worley, Thelma, 58
Worley, Tony Wayne 1948, 96
Worley, Verdena, 56
Worley, Verna, 57
Worley, Wilburna, 56
Worley, William Patrick 1966, 58
Worley, William Tell ("Tell"), 56, 58
Worley, William Tell ("Will") 1884, 58
Worley, William Tell, Jr., 58
Wortham, Ann Lanier 1945, 51
Wortham, Charles Frederick, 51
Wortham, Charles Frederick, Jr. 1946, 52
Wortham, Ellen Randolph 1948, 52
Wortham, Margaret Thomas 1958, 52
Wortham, Marion Pratt 1954, 52
Wortham, Mary Douglas 1981, 52
Wortham, Virginia Pratt 1982, 52
Wortham, Ward Hawkins 1974, 52
Worthington, Alice Ann 1871, 246
Worthington, Angeline Martha 1858, 245
Worthington, Edward Joseph 1867, 246
Worthington, Franklin Richard 1869, 246
Worthington, James Henry 1860, 245
Worthington, James Mitchell 1831, 245
Worthington, Princetta 1874, 246